W9-CIC-231

600
ESSENTIAL
Words
for the
TOEIC* test

Test of English for International Communication

Lin Lougheed

BARRON'S

All inquiries should be addressed to:
Barron's Educational Series, Inc.
250 Wireless Boulevard
Hauppauge, New York 11788
http://www.barronseduc.com

Library of Congress Catalog Card No.: 98-51863
International Standard Book No. 0-7641-0879-4

Library of Congress Cataloging-in-Publication Data

Lougheed, Lin, 1946–
    600 essential words for the TOEIC test / Lin Lougheed.
        p.   cm.
    Includes index.
    ISBN 0-7641-0879-4
    1. Test of English for International Communication—Study guides.   2. English language—
Textbooks for foreign speakers.   3. English language—Examinations—Study guides.
4. Vocabulary—Examinations—Study guides. I. Title. II. Title: Six hundred essential words for
the TOEIC test.
PE1128.L643 1999
428.2'4—dc21   98-51863
                                                                                                              CIP

PRINTED IN THE UNITED STATES OF AMERICA
19 18 17 16 15 14 13 12 11 10

Table of Contents

What the Book Is About

The TOEIC (Test of English for International Communication) test measures the English proficiency of people working in international business or planning to use English to communicate with others. Although the test does not specifically test specialized vocabulary, the items on the exam are in specialized contexts.

This book will provide you with a basis to understand these specialized contexts that are often used on the TOEIC test. Each chapter covers a particular context that has appeared on the TOEIC test. The new words taught in each chapter are not specialized words. These words are more what is called general vocabulary. They can be used in many contexts.

However, these new words are used in a specialized context. Understanding these contexts and the words used in these contexts will help you improve your score on the TOEIC exam.

How to Use This Book

This book could also be titled *50 Days to a More Powerful Vocabulary*. There are 50 lessons. Every day, you can study one lesson. Every day you can learn 12 new words. In 50 days, you can learn 600 new words—words that will help you understand English better. And the better you understand English, the higher your TOEIC score will be.

You can sit down and in 30 minutes finish a lesson. But that is not the best way. To learn a new word, you must use it over and over. Try to spread your studying out over the whole day. Do a little bit whenever you have some free time. The 12 new words are used over and over and over in this lesson. Studying these words throughout the day will help you learn them and never forget them.

Start in the morning and look over the 12 new words and their definitions. Repeat them out loud. During the morning, read over the conversations. If you can, say the conversations out loud. The more ways you use a word (listening, speaking, reading, and writing), the better the chance you will remember it.

In the afternoon, do the exercises. In the evening, do the very last exercise. The last exercise is like a mini-test. It will tell you if you completely understood the meaning of the word and how to use it in a sentence.

Every day, do another lesson. At the end of the week, do the Word Review. I am sure you will answer every question correctly.

Most of the new words you learn in one lesson will be used again in another lesson. We recycle words just as we recycle paper. If you forget a meaning of a word, look up the word in the Word Index at the back of the book. That will tell you in which lesson you can find a definition and the pronunciation.

Strategies to Improve Your Vocabulary

The English language consists of more than 250,000 words, far more than most other languages—far more than we can include in this book. Here are some strategies that will help you remember words that you come across either in this book or in English books or magazines.

To learn a new word, of course, you first have to run across it. Therefore, you must read in English as much as you can. The best way to improve your vocabulary is to read routinely. The more you read, the more words you will encounter. The more words you run across, the more you will learn.

Once you have gotten into the habit of reading, you can systematically build your vocabulary by doing five things:

1. Analyze word parts.
2. Recognize grammatical forms.
3. Recognize word families.
4. Make your own personal dictionary.
5. Keep a daily reading log.

I. Analyze Word Parts

Many English words have Greek and Latin prefixes, roots, and suffixes. Memorizing a comprehensive list will increase your vocabulary exponentially. For example, a prefix is the part of a word that comes at the beginning of a word, like the prefix *pre-* at the beginning of the word *prefix*. The prefix *pre-* means *before*. Once you learn the meaning of this prefix, you will be able to use it to help you figure out the meaning of a new word that contains the same prefix, for example, *predetermine*, *predict*, *predecessor*.

Look at these other examples.

Prefix	re-	happens a second time
Root	circul	around
Suffix	-tion	the act of
Word	recirculation	repeating the act of motion in a circular path

Prefix	re-	happens a second time
Root	gener	bring to life
Suffix	-tion	the act of
Word	regeneration	the act of being brought to life again

Prefix	re-	happens a second time
Root	loc	place
Suffix	-tion	the act of
Word	relocation	the act of moving again to another place

By understanding that the prefix *re-* means *again*, you know that any word that begins with *re-* means something happens a second time. Students who become familiar with the most common prefixes, roots, and suffixes find that their vocabulary grows quickly. Examples of these prefixes, roots, and suffixes will be given throughout the book.

II. Recognize Grammatical Forms

Being familiar with all grammatical forms of a word helps you increase your vocabulary. Suffixes often give you a clue as to the meaning of a word and its grammatical position in a sentence. These suffixes can tell you whether the word may be a noun, verb, adjective, or adverb.

Common noun endings:
-tion	competition
-ance	deliverance
-ence	independence
-ment	government
-ism	Buddhism
-ship	friendship
-ity	community
-er	teacher
-or	doctor
-ee	attendee

Common verb endings:

-ize	memorize
-ate	refrigerate
-en	lengthen

Common adjective endings:

-y	happy
-ous	mountainous
-ious	serious
-able	capable
-al	musical
-ic	athletic
-ful	beautiful
-less	careless

Common adverb ending:

-ly	quickly

Learning about grammatical forms will help you identify the purpose of many words. As the endings become recognizable, they will help you figure out the meanings of new words.

Examples of these word forms will be given throughout the book.

III. Recognize Word Families

Like brothers and sisters in the same family, words can be related, too. These words have the same base but different grammatical forms. They are part of a word family. When you learn a new word, look in the dictionary for words in the same word family. Write them beside the word in your own dictionary. Make columns for nouns, verbs, adjectives, and adverbs and write down the words in the same family. For example:

verb	noun	adjective	adverb
to care	care	careful	carefully
to attend	attendance	attentive	attentively
to point	pointer	pointed	pointedly

Some members of a word family have all grammatical forms; others have just a few. Some words even have two grammatical forms of the same part of speech, but with different meanings like the nouns *attendance* and *attendee*. Examples of word families will be given throughout the book.

IV. Make Your Own Personal Dictionary

Create your own dictionary to keep track of all the new words you learn. Your own personal dictionary should look like a regular dictionary with different pages for words beginning with A, B, C, and so on.

You can photocopy the following sample dictionary page or you can use a sheet of paper to make one page for each letter of the alphabet. Put tabs on these pages and write the letter of the alphabet on the tab so you can find each letter more easily. You can add pages as necessary.

When you read or hear new words, you should write them in your own personal dictionary. You may even find other words in this book that you do not know. You can write these words in your personal dictionary, too. Try not to look up the meanings of these new words immediately. This will slow down your reading. Try to get the general meaning from the context. You can look up the specific meaning after you have formed a hypothesis.

My Personal Dictionary

New word

Original sentence

_____

Definition

_____

My sentence

_____

Word forms in sentences

_____

_____

_____

_____

Word families in sentences

_____

_____

_____

_____

Next to each word in your own personal dictionary, write a definition and make up a sentence including the word, using the dictionary as a guide. If possible, write the sentence where you originally discovered the word or a sentence whose context reminds you of the meaning.

While you are looking in the dictionary, search for words in the same word family. Write these words in your personal dictionary and make up sentences for these words, too. Notice which endings occur in each grammatical form.

Writing these sentences will help you remember the word later. It's easier to remember words when you put them in context. The more you use a word, the more likely you will remember it.

If you choose not to create your own personal dictionary, you can keep track of new words as you look them up in a regular dictionary. Take a yellow highlight pen and highlight the word you look up. At the end of the week or month, you can thumb through the dictionary and see at a glance how many words you have added to your vocabulary.

V. Keep a Daily Reading Log

It is important that you read something in English every day. You should set aside as much time as you can spare, but try to set aside at least 20 to 30 minutes every day just for reading and writing something in English. This time should not be used for reading text assigned from class or work. Select something that interests you and is appropriate for your level. It should not be too easy or too difficult. Here are samples of short passages you could read:

- the sports section of the newspaper
- an article from a popular magazine
- a chapter from a novel
- the label from an English/American product
- an advertisement in English

Try to vary the type of reading. Don't read only science journals or mystery novels. You want to build your vocabulary in a variety of areas. If you need special vocabulary for your job or course work, you could focus on these types of articles. But remember, the reading log should be material in addition to assigned readings.

Try to pick a time of day when your mind is alert. Don't try to study when you are tired.

Follow these steps to build a reading log.

1. Read WITHOUT stopping for about ten minutes.
   The first time you read a passage, do NOT stop to look up words. Native English readers often come across words they do not know in their reading. They get a general idea of the meaning of unknown words from the context. See if you can also get the gist of the idea without looking up the words in a dictionary.
2. Reread the passage and highlight unknown or unclear words.
   You can use a yellow highlight pen or underline the word. If you aren't permitted to write in the book, write the words down in your reading log.
3. Choose five key words.
   From all the words that you did not understand completely, select five of them for your dictionary. These should be words that kept you from understanding an entire sentence.
4. Summarize what you read.
   Write a summary about the passage you read and add it to your reading log. Summarize what you've read in approximately a three-sentence paragraph. If possible, make a copy of the passage or cut it out and paste it under the summary. If you're reading a book, write the title, pages read, and a summary of the story or argument of the book. Try to use your five new key words in your summary.

My Reading Log

Key words	Summary
	_____
	_____
	_____
	_____
	_____
	_____
	_____
	_____
	_____

Key words	(Article or photocopy of article)
1._____	
2._____	
3._____	
4._____	
5._____	

Key words	Summary
	_____
	_____
	_____
	_____
	_____
	_____
	_____
	_____
	_____

Key words	(Article or photocopy of article)
1._____	
2._____	
3._____	
4._____	
5._____	

Lesson 1

Contracts

Words to learn

abide by
agreement
assurance
cancel
determine
engage
establish
obligate
party
provision
resolve
specify

1. **abide by** v., to comply with; to conform
   a. The two parties agreed to abide by the judge's decision.
   b. For years he has abided by a commitment to annual employee raises.

2. **agreement** n., a mutual arrangement, a contract
   a. The landlord and tenant were in agreement that the rent should be prorated to the middle of the month.
   b. According to the agreement, the caterer will also supply the flowers for the event.

3. **assurance** n., a guarantee; confidence
   a. The sales associate gave his assurance that the missing keyboard would be replaced the next day.
   b. Her evident self-assurance made it easy to see why she was in charge of the negotiations.

4. **cancel** v., to annul; to call off
   a. The man canceled his magazine subscription and got his money back.
   b. When the concert was canceled, the singer sued to get her fee paid.

5. **determine** v., to find out; to influence
   a. After reading the contract, I was still unable to determine if our company was liable for back wages.
   b. The skill of the union bargainers will determine whether the automotive plant will open next week.

6. **engage** v., to hire; to involve someone or something
   a. We engaged a salsa band to play at the reception.
   b. Once we engaged Otto in the decision making for the project, he became much more supportive.

7. **establish** v., to institute permanently; to bring about
   a. Through her many books and interviews, Dr. Wan established herself as an authority on conflict resolution.
   b. The merger of the two companies established a powerful new corporation.

8. **obligate** v., to bind legally or morally
   a. The contractor was obligated by the contract to work 40 hours a week.
   b. I felt obligated to finish the project even though I could have exercised my option to quit.

9. **party** n., a person or group participating in an action or plan; the persons or sides concerned in a legal matter
   a. The parties agreed to a settlement in their contract dispute.
   b. The party of the first part generally has the advantage of preparing the contract or agreement.

10. **provision** n., a measure taken beforehand; a stipulation
    a. The father made provisions for his children through his will.
    b. The contract contains a provision to deal with how payments are made if John loses his job.

11. **resolve** v., to deal with successfully; to declare
    a. The mediator was able to resolve the problem to everyone's satisfaction.
    b. The businessman resolved to clean out all the files by the end of the week.

12. **specify** v., to mention explicitly
    a. Mary specified in the contract that her bill must be paid within 30 days.
    b. The letter does not specify which attorney is handling our case.

Short Conversations

Read the following conversations and see how the new words are used.

[M] Do you think we will ever **resolve** our difficulties with the computer company?
[W] I'm beginning to think that we should **cancel** our service and find another provider.
[M] Do we have any **obligation** to continue to pay them if we cancel our service?

[W] Now that the new contract has been negotiated, we will have to **abide by** it very closely.
[M] I'm not sure yet that this was a good **agreement** for us.
[W] Nevertheless, we gave our **assurance** we would fulfill the requirements.

[M] What does the new contract **establish** that the old one did not?
[W] Both **parties** agreed to the salary freeze for this year.
[M] Then, we should **specify** our expectations for a raise next year.

[W] We must **engage** a subcontractor to complete the work.
[M] Is there a **provision** for a subcontractor in the contract?
[W] We can **determine** that by reviewing the terms of the contract.

Word Families

verb	specify	The contract specifies the percentage of a raise the workers will see next year.
noun	specification	The work was done according to our specifications.
adjective	specific	We have not chosen a specific location for the reunion.

verb	agree	If both parties agree to the terms, we can finalize the contract.
noun	agreement	As soon as the labor agreement was signed, the factory resumed production of new cars and vans.
adjective	agreeable	The parties are agreeable to the terms.

verb	provide	Since the machine is very reliable, why don't we cancel the service contract they provided?
noun	provider	We must negotiate a new contract with our Internet service provider.
noun	provision	The provision for canceling the contract is in the last clause.

verb	obligate	The terms of the contracts obligate us to work for at least one more month.
noun	obligation	The factory managers have a legal and moral obligation to provide a safe work site.
adjective	obligatory	He finished his obligatory military service, and then joined his father on the orange farm.

Choose the word that best completes the sentence.

1. The contract calls for the union to _____ who their bargaining representative will be.
   (A) specific
   (B) specification
   (C) specifying
   (D) specify

2. The two sides were no closer to a final _____ at midnight than they were at noon.
   (A) agreement
   (B) agreeable
   (C) agree
   (D) agreed

3. I don't feel any _____ to give my boss more than two weeks notice when I leave.
   (A) oblige
   (B) obligatory
   (C) obliged
   (D) obligation

4. The _____ for terminating the contract were not discussed.
   (A) provide
   (B) provisions
   (C) provider
   (D) provisioning

Short Talk

Read the following passage and write the appropriate form of the new words in the blanks below.

abide by	cancel	establishment	provide
agreement	determine	obligates	resolve
assurance	engaging	parties	specifies

Contracts are an integral part of the workplace. In simple terms, contracts are an (5.) _____ between two or more (6.) _____ that (7.) _____ terms or something to be done and that (8.) _____ the parties to follow through. Contracts often include the amount that the client will pay the contractors and what services will be provided. For example, in your office, you may have a contract that provides (9.) _____ that your copier machine or phones will be repaired within a certain amount of time. This service can either be done off-site or at your (10.) _____. A contract often states ways to (11.) _____ if quality of work delivered is acceptable. Well-written contracts usually (12.) _____ ways to (13.) _____ problems like these when they happen. Before (14.) _____ in a contract, the parties should think carefully, as they will have to (15.) _____ the conditions specified in it. A contract usually specifies how the two parties can (16.) _____ it if either party fails to meet the terms.

Choose the underlined word or phrase that should be rewritten and rewrite it.

17. When attempts at <u>resolve</u> failed, both parties, <u>determined</u> to end the conflict, <u>agreed</u> to enter into a formal
    A   B   C
    contract and promised to <u>abide by</u> the terms.
    D

    _____

18. Both <u>parties</u> agreed that the contractor would <u>provide</u> technical assistance 24 hours a day, so it
    A   B
    was easy to <u>determination</u> that the two-day delay was not <u>acceptable</u>.
    C   D

    _____

19. We were <u>assured</u> by the cable company before we <u>engaged</u> in a contract that we could <u>cancellation</u> our
    A   B   C
    membership at any time with no further <u>obligations</u>.
    D

    _____

20. Luckily, our car insurance <u>establishments</u> the time period within which they provide assistance, <u>determines</u> the
    A   B
    repair shops we can use, sets a fee structure for <u>payment</u>, and provides a forum for <u>resolving</u> billing errors.
    C   C

    _____

Lesson 2

Marketing

Words to learn

attract
compare
compete
consume
convince
current
fad
inspire
market
persuade
productive
satisfy

1. **attract** v., to draw by appeal
   a. The display attracted a number of people at the convention.
   b. The new advertising attracts the wrong kind of customer into the store.

2. **compare** v., to examine similarities and differences
   a. Once the customer compared the two products, her choice was easy.
   b. The price for this brand is high compared to the other brands on the market.

3. **compete** v., to strive against a rival
   a. With only one store in the area, it is difficult for Hector's business to compete with large chains.
   b. We competed against three other agencies to get this contract.

4. **consume** v., to absorb; to use up
   a. The business plans consumed all of Fritz's attention this fall.
   b. Chen consumes more than his share of computer time.

5. **convince** v., to bring to believe by argument; to persuade
   a. The salesman convinced his customer to buy his entire inventory of pens.
   b. Before a business can convince customers that it provides a quality product, it must convince its marketing staff.

6. **current** adj., happening or existing at the present time; adv., to be on top of things
   a. It is important to read current magazines to see how competitors market their products.
   b. Good marketing requires keeping current with modern technology and best practices.

7. **fad** n., a practice followed enthusiastically for a short time; a craze
   a. The mini dress was a fad once thought to be finished, but now it is making a comeback.
   b. Classic tastes may seem boring but they have proven to resist fads.

8. **inspire** v., to spur on; to stimulate imagination or emotion
   a. The heart-wrenching video about world hunger inspired Kristen to get involved in food security issues.
   b. His painting style was inspired by the works of the Old Masters.

9. **market** v., the course of buying and selling a product; n., the demand for a product
   a. When Omar first began making his chutneys, he marketed them door-to-door to gourmet shops.
   b. The market for brightly colored clothing was brisk last year, but moving sluggishly this year.

10. **persuade** v., to move by argument or logic
    a. Juan, with his charming personality, eventually persuaded the pharmacist to stock samples of the new medicine.
    b. No amount of marketing could persuade Doris to give up her old, but reliable, laundry soap.

11. **productive** adj., constructive; high yield
    a. The unproductive sales meeting brought many staff complaints.
    b. Alonzo is excited about his productive sales territory.

12. **satisfy** v., to make happy
    a. Henri was perfectly satisfied with his new fishing rod and recommended the brand to many friends.
    b. If you don't know what kind of gift will satisfy your friend, think about giving a gift certificate instead.

Short Conversations

Read the following conversations and see how the new words are used.

[M]   We need to **attract** new customers to the business.
[W]   How can we **convince** them to buy our products?
[M]   Perhaps our ads could feature some of our **satisfied** customers.

[M]   With a new store opening across the street, we must work harder to **compete** in our market.
[W]   How can we be more **productive**?
[M]   Once customers **compare** us to the other stores, they will see that we offer a better deal.

[W]   There is a growing **market** for computer software.
[M]   Yes, **consumers** are looking for software for specific applications.
[W]   Accounting software is **currently** among the biggest sellers.

[M]   Our new line of dresses is **inspired** by the recent interest in 1960s fashion.
[W]   This look is just a **fad**.
[M]   Perhaps, but many customers will be **persuaded** by the new look.

Word Families

verb	attract	The store's poor location did not help it attract customers.
noun	attraction	Having a clown in the toy store was a foolproof attraction for getting kids to enter.
adjective	attractive	Lou ran his store on an old-fashioned premise: quality merchandise at attractive prices.

verb	compare	She compared the prices before she made a decision.
noun	comparison	There was no comparison in the quality of the two brands.
adjective	comparable	To get an average for home costs, the agent sought prices on comparable homes.

verb	consume	The analyst was able to consume new information quickly.
noun	consumer	The government tracks consumer spending closely.
adjective	consumable	He ran a study of the use of consumable goods.

verb	market	The sales department disagreed about how to market their newest product.
noun	marketing	A good director of marketing can find a way to sell even an unattractive product.
adjective	marketable	Once the sales manager decided to change the packaging, the product became much more marketable.

Choose the word that best completes the sentence.

1. Marketing specialists have conducted extensive studies of what _____ customers to buy a particular product.
   (A) attractive   (C) attracts
   (B) attraction   (D) attracting

2. Smart shoppers will _____ different but similar brands before making a decision.
   (A) compare   (C) comparative
   (B) comparison   (D) comparable

3. Manufacturers like to know what features _____ find useful.
   (A) consumers   (C) consumption
   (B) consume   (D) consumable

4. Without good _____, good products can go unsold.
   (A) market   (C) marketability
   (B) marketable   (D) marketing

Short Talk

Read the following passage and write the appropriate form of the new words in the blanks below.

attract	consumers	fad	persuaded
compared	convince	inspire	product
competes	current	market	satisfied

Yassir is getting ready to realize his dream: opening a business that sells plants on the Internet. After completing a business plan that helped him to determine that there was demand for his (5.) _____ in the (6.) _____, Yassir is ready to start promoting his business. Having (7.) _____ the bank that there was a market, that there were consumers willing to buy flowers on the Internet, he needed to find these (8.) _____.

Once he has an established base, Yassir, like other business owners will have to continually (9.) _____ new customers. At the same time, he must make sure current customers are (10.) _____. In order to be satisfied, (11.) _____ customers must be happy with the product they receive. Yassir's job is to (12.) _____ these customers to gain their repeat business. To do this, he will have to (13.) _____ consumers that he offers a good product at a good price, especially when (14.) _____ to the businesses with which he (15.) _____. And, of course, he will have to compete with other businesses on the price he charges and service he offers. He hopes that Internet businesses are here to stay and not a (16.) _____.

Choose the underlined word or phrase that should be rewritten and rewrite it.

17. George found it was <u>productive</u> and less expensive to <u>inspiration</u> loyalty in his <u>current</u> customers <u>compared</u> to
    the cost of advertising to attract new customers.
    (A)   (B)   (C)   (D)

    _____

18. Joelle cannot <u>compete</u> with the prices of jewelry found in stores, but she is able to <u>persuasion</u> <u>consumers</u> that
    (A)   (B)   (C)
    her handmade <u>products</u> are unique works of art.
    (D)

    _____

19. Adil's plan to market his soccer lessons meant <u>persuading</u> boys and girls that soccer was not a short-lived <u>fad</u>
    (A)   (B)
    and <u>convincing</u> parents that he offered a better service <u>comparison</u> to local soccer camps.
    (C)   (D)

    _____

20. The restaurant used an age-old <u>marketing</u> strategy of continually <u>attractive</u> new customers and <u>satisfying</u>
    (A)   (B)   (C)
    <u>current</u> customers with good food at good prices.
    (D)

    _____

Lesson 3

Warranties

Words to learn

characteristic
consequence
consider
cover
expire
frequently
imply
promise
protect
reputation
require
vary

1. **characteristic** adj., revealing of individual traits
   a. The cooking pot has features characteristic of the brand, such as "stay cool" handles.
   b. It is not characteristic of the store to be slow in mailing a refund check.
2. **consequence** n., that which follows necessarily
   a. The consequence of not following the service instructions for your car is that the warranty is invalidated.
   b. As a consequence of not having seen a dentist for several years, Lydia had several cavities.
3. **consider** v., to think about carefully
   a. The customer considered buying the VCR until he learned that the warranty coverage was very limited.
   b. After considering all the options, Della decided to buy a used car.
4. **cover** v., to provide protection against
   a. Will my medical insurance cover this surgery?
   b. Her car insurance provided for complete coverage against collision.
5. **expire** v., to come to an end
   a. The warranty protection on this product will expire one year after the date of purchase.
   b. I didn't have time to read another fitness magazine, so I let my subscription to the latest one expire.
6. **frequently** adv., occurring commonly; widespread
   a. Appliances frequently come with a one-year warranty.
   b. Warranties for this kind of appliance are frequently limited in their coverage.
7. **imply** v., to indicate by inference
   a. The guarantee on the Walkman implied that all damages were covered under warranty for one year.
   b. The travel agent implied that our hotel was not in the safest part of the city, but, when pressed for details, he said the location was fine.
8. **promise** v., n., to pledge to do, bring about, or provide
   a. A warranty is a promise the manufacturer makes to the consumer.
   b. The sales associate promised that our new mattress would arrive by noon on Saturday.
9. **protect** v., to guard
   a. Consumer laws are designed to protect the public against unscrupulous vendors.
   b. You can protect yourself from scams by getting detailed information on the seller.
10. **reputation** n., the overall quality of character
    a. Even though the salesperson showed me a product I had never heard of, I bought it because of the good reputation of the manufacturer.
    b. The company knew that the reputation of its products was the most important asset it had.
11. **require** v., to deem necessary or essential
    a. A car warranty may require the owner to have it serviced by a certified mechanic.
    b. The law requires that each item clearly display the warranty information.
12. **vary** v., to be different from another; to change
    a. The amount of protection offered by different policies will vary.
    b. Consumers' needs vary, so different kinds of warranties appeal to different types of consumers.

Short Conversations

Read the following conversations and see how the new words are used.

[M] What are the important **characteristics** of this warranty?
[W] The product is completely **covered** for one year.
[M] It seems that one-year warranties are the type most **frequently** provided for this kind of appliance.

[M] In order to have full **protection**, you must have the car serviced by an approved mechanic.
[W] What are the **consequences** if I choose not to use an approved mechanic?
[M] By not following the guidelines, you cause the warranty to **expire** immediately.

[W] This price on this toaster seems low. What's the **reputation** of the manufacturer?
[M] To be honest, I would have to say that the quality of this manufacturer's products **varies**.
[W] However, the manufacturer **promises** to replace the toaster if it breaks.

[M] I think the hotel **requires** that we stay for at least two nights to get the special rate.
[W] It's not completely clear, but I agree that the brochure **implies** a two-night stay.
[M] We'll need to **consider** changing our plans if we want the special rate.

Word Families

verb	consider	You should consider carefully whether a product will meet your needs.
noun	consideration	After long consideration, Heloise decided that the five-year warranty would be sufficient.
adjective	considerable	The fee for the extra year of protection was a considerable expense.

verb	protect	Juan protected the warranty by taking excellent care of his lawn mower.
noun	protection	For your own protection, you should have a warranty that provides for a replacement product.
adjective	protective	Alfredo is very protective of the condition of his car and gets all the preventive maintenance his warranty requires.

noun	reputation	The good reputation of the manufacturer inspired Maria Jose to try the new product.
adjective	reputable	Because the company had a reputable name, I did not spend sufficient time reading the details of the warranty.
adjective	reputed	The new store is reputed to carry items that are not of the highest quality.

verb	require	The warranty requires that you send the watch to an approved repair shop to have it fixed.
noun	requirement	The terms of the warranty divulge the legal requirement the manufacturer has to the consumer.
adjective	requisite	The warranty spelled out the requisite steps to take to request a replacement product.

Choose the word that best completes the sentence.

1. Jacques and Louisa will only _____ purchasing appliances that come with a money-back guarantee.
   (A) consideration (C) considering
   (B) consider (D) considerable

2. The level of _____ implied by the warranty was misleading.
   (A) protect (C) protection
   (B) protective (D) protector

3. It can be very helpful to consider the _____ of the manufacturer and the merchant when making a major purchase.
   (A) reputation (C) repute
   (B) reputable (D) reputed

4. If the appliance breaks down within two years of purchase, the manufacturer is _____ to send you a replacement at no charge.
   (A) requiring (C) requirement
   (B) requisite (D) required

Short Talk

Read the following passage and write the appropriate form of the new words in the blanks below.

characteristics	coverage	implies	reputations
consequences	expire	promise	required
consider	frequently	protect	vary

Warranties are a seller's (5.) _____ to stand behind its products. Most major purchases like computers or cars come with a warranty, as do smaller purchases, like stereos or other electronic housewares. Warranties are not (6.) _____ by law, but are (7.) _____ found on most products. If you are making a purchase, you should (8.) _____ the individual (9.) _____ of a warranty, as each can (10.) _____ in the amount of (11.) _____ it provides. At the minimum, warranties are required to provide what the product (12.) _____ that it will do; for example, that a blender will blend or a hair dryer will dry hair. Most warranties are good for a fixed time, then they (13.) _____. You can (14.) _____ yourself by buying products from companies with good (15.) _____ and taking good care of your new purchase. There are (16.) _____ to not taking care of a product as most warranties require that you use the product in a certain manner.

Choose the underlined word or phrase that should be rewritten and rewrite it.

17. Claude read the <u>required</u> warranty only to find that, while the manufacturer <u>promised</u> to repair or replace the
    A   B
    CD player, the <u>coverage</u> had <u>expiration</u>.
                   C   D
    _____

18. Before buying a new appliance, compare the <u>characteristics</u> of similar products and their warranties, which
                                                A
    <u>protect</u> your purchase and <u>frequently</u> <u>various</u> from product to product.
    B   C   D
    _____

19. Bassem discovered the <u>consequent</u> of not following instructions: because he had not had the <u>required</u> service
                          A   B
    performed on his car, his warranty <u>coverage</u> no longer <u>protected</u> him from mechanical failure.
                                       C   D
    _____

20. It is especially important to <u>consideration</u> the <u>reputation</u> of a manufacturer when buying a product <u>protected</u> by
                                  A   B   C
    an <u>implied</u>, and not directly stated, warranty.
       D
    _____

Business Planning

1. **address** v., to direct to the attention of
   a. Marco's business plan addresses the needs of small business owners.
   b. Be certain to pay attention to addressing the cost of infrastructure when you estimate your expenses.

2. **avoid** v., to stay clear of; to keep from happening
   a. To avoid going out of business, owners should prepare a proper business plan.
   b. Lloyd's errors in accounting could have been avoided by a business consultation with his banker.

3. **demonstrate** v., to show clearly and deliberately; to present by example
   a. Alban's business plan demonstrated that he had put a lot of thought into making his dream a reality.
   b. The professor demonstrated through a case study that a business plan can impress a lender.

4. **develop** v., to expand, progress, or improve
   a. Lily developed her ideas into a business plan by taking a class at the community college.
   b. The restaurant Wanda opened ten years ago has developed into a national chain.

5. **evaluate** v., to determine the value or impact of
   a. It's important to evaluate your competition when making a business plan.
   b. The lenders evaluated our creditability and decided to loan us money.

6. **gather** v., to accumulate; to conclude
   a. We gathered information for our plan from many sources.
   b. I gather that interest rates for small businesses will soon change.

7. **offer** v., to propose; to present in order to meet a need or satisfy a requirement
   a. We offered the job of writing the business plan to Devon.
   b. Jackie must offer her banker new statistics in order to encourage the bank to lend her money toward her start-up business.

8. **primary** adj., most important; first in a list, series, or sequence
   a. The primary reason for writing a business plan is to avoid common errors.
   b. Writing the business plan was the primary task, then seeking funding, followed by finding a suitable building.

9. **risk** n., the chance of loss or damage
   a. The primary risk for most start-up businesses is insufficient capital.
   b. Expanding into a new market is a big risk.

10. **strategy** n., a plan of action
    a. A business plan is a strategy for running a business and avoiding problems.
    b. Let's develop a strategy for promoting our ice cream parlor.

11. **strong** adj., powerful; economically or financially sound
    a. The professor made a strong argument for the value of a good business plan.
    b. Even in a strong economic climate many businesses fail, so do your planning carefully.

12. **substitute** v., to take the place of another
    a. Here's a model business plan; just substitute the specifics of your business.
    b. Don't try to substitute intuition for good planning.

Short Conversations

Read the following conversations and see how the new words are used.

[W] Alexa is **developing** a business plan. I told her you might be able to help with the market research.
[M] I'm proud of her. Going into business for yourself can be **risky**, but very rewarding.
[W] I know she is very serious about careful planning to **avoid** making obvious mistakes.

[M] The first problem Athos encountered was how to **evaluate** his competitor's share of the market.
[W] Can't he **gather** information from trade journals and the local trade association?
[M] I don't know if those sources **offered** him enough hard data to analyze the competition's share of the market.

[W] The data we've analyzed so far **demonstrate** that our potential customers want great service more than a great price.
[M] That surprises me. I had assumed that the price of the product was the **primary** motivation.
[W] I'm surprised, too. Let's make sure our business plan is **addressing** the need for extensive sales training.

[M] I can't believe McPhee's Sweet Shop went out of business. They once were such a **strong** competitor for everyone else in the candy market.
[W] When they started selling fruit juices and magazines, I wondered what their marketing **strategy** was.
[M] It certainly proves there's no **substitute** for a solid business plan.

Word Families

verb	demonstrate	Let me demonstrate how this computer program works.
noun	demonstration	After the lecture, there was a demonstration of new marketing techniques.
adjective	demonstrative	The densely encoded programming was demonstrative of the computer language of the era.

verb	develop	Our assignment is to develop a cogent business plan.
noun	development	The plan was under development and would not be ready for months.
noun	developer	The job developer was kept busy trying to place the recent college graduates.

verb	evaluate	Please review these articles and evaluate their usefulness for our plan.
noun	evaluation	Yoko feared the professor's evaluation of her business plan.
noun	evaluator	The independent evaluator reviewed our business plan and gave us good feedback.

verb	strategize	Instead of going into a panic, let's strategize the best way to meet the deadline.
noun	strategy	The business plan lays out a strategy for future growth.
adjective	strategic	The handout outlined the strategic points to cover in a business plan.

Choose the word that best completes the sentence.

1. I don't want to intrude, but would you like me to _____ how to use that machine?
   (A) demonstrate
   (B) demonstration
   (C) demonstrative
   (D) demonstrator

2. While you are _____ your business plan, it is a good idea to keep a resource library of valuable materials.
   (A) develop
   (B) development
   (C) developing
   (D) developer

3. After you turn in your business plan, you will receive a written _____ of your work within two weeks.
   (A) evaluator
   (B) evaluative
   (C) evaluate
   (D) evaluation

4. If we think _____, we can come up with a plan that promises success.
   (A) strategize
   (B) strategic
   (C) strategically
   (D) strategist

Short Talk

Read the following passage and write the appropriate form of the new words in the blanks below.

address	develop	offered	strategy
avoid	evaluation	primary	strength
demonstrate	gathering	risks	substitute

Every business must (5.) _____ a business plan. The business plan's (6.) _____ purpose is to improve the entrepreneur's control over the business and to (7.) _____ common mistakes. It is not an overstatement to say that a business will fail or succeed on the (8.) _____ of its business plan, so there is no (9.) _____ for a well-prepared plan. The business plan documents the (10.) _____ for growing the business. Think of the business plan as a road map that describes in which direction the company is going, what its goals are, where it wants to go, and how it is going to get there. The business plan helps the entrepreneur focus on setting the future course of the business.

In developing the plan, the entrepreneur will conduct research to determine a systematic and realistic (11.) _____ of the company's chances for success in the marketplace. In creating the plan, the entrepreneur must research the company's target market and define its potential. The entrepreneur must be able to prove through research that customers in the market need the good or service (12.) _____ and that a sufficient number of potential customers exists to support the business. Is the market growing or shrinking? Are customers' needs staying the same or changing?

A business plan also looks at the (13.) _____ the business faces. Chief among these is competitors. The business plan must analyze the company's competition by (14.) _____ information on competitors' market share, products, and strategies. The plan should (15.) _____ what distinguishes the entrepreneur's products or services from others already in the market. It is also common for businesses to fail because the owner fails to invest or seek sufficient capital to run the business. A good business plan should (16.) _____ this issue as well.

Choose the underlined word or phrase that should be rewritten and rewrite it.

17. By <u>addressing</u> potential problems upfront, Carlos was able to <u>demonstration</u> to his banker that he had <u>gathered</u> enough information to <u>avoid</u> business failure.
    A B C D
    _____

18. In a <u>risky</u> attempt to expand business, the company, whose <u>primary</u> focus was selling furniture, embarked on a <u>strategy</u> that involved <u>offers</u> interior design services.
    A B C D
    _____

19. Our business instructor <u>strongly</u> believes there is no <u>substitution</u> for a well-developed business plan, so all of his students were required to <u>develop</u> a plan that he would <u>evaluation</u> and give helpful criticism on.
    A B C D
    _____

20. Ms. Martinez developed her business plan by <u>addressing</u> the <u>risky</u> found in the market and <u>demonstrating</u> ways to <u>avoid</u> them.
    A B C D
    _____

Conferences

Words to learn

accommodate
arrangement
association
attend
get in touch
hold
location
overcrowded
register
select
session
take part in

1. **accommodate** v., to fit; to provide with something needed
   a. The meeting room was large enough to accommodate the various needs of the groups using it.
   b. Because the deadline for reserving rooms was past, the hotel manager could not accommodate our need for more rooms.

2. **arrangement** n., the plan or organization
   a. The travel arrangements were taken care of by Sara, Mr. Billings's capable assistant.
   b. The arrangement of speakers was alphabetical to avoid any hurt feelings.

3. **association** n., an organization of persons or groups having a common interest; a relationship or society
   a. Membership in a trade or professional association provides business contacts and mutual support.
   b. Local telephone companies formed an association to serve common goals, meet their common needs, and improve efficiency.

4. **attend** v., to go to; to pay attention to
   a. We expect more than 100 members to attend the annual meeting.
   b. The hotel manager attended to all our needs promptly.

5. **get in touch** v., to make contact with
   a. As soon as we arrive at the hotel, we will get in touch with the manager about the unexpected guests.
   b. The registration desk is a good central location for people to get in touch with each other.

6. **hold** v., to accommodate; to conduct
   a. This meeting room holds at least 80 people comfortably.
   b. She holds an annual seminar that is very popular.

7. **location** n., a position or site
   a. The location of the meeting was changed from the Red Room to the Green Room.
   b. Disney World was the perfect location for the annual meeting since many members could bring their families.

8. **overcrowded** adj., too crowded
   a. As soon as the guests entered the dining room for dinner, Sue Lin could see that the room would become overcrowded.
   b. To avoid being overcrowded, we limited the number of guests that members could bring.

9. **register** v., to record
   a. Hotels ask all guests to register and give a home address.
   b. More than 250 people registered to attend the afternoon seminar.

10. **select** v., to choose from a group
    a. The conference participant selected the marketing seminar from the various offerings.
    b. The winners were selected from the conference registrants.

11. **session** n., a meeting
    a. The morning sessions tend to fill up first, so sign up early.
    b. Due to the popularity of this course, we will offer two sessions.

12. **take part in** v., to join or participate
    a. The format for the session is very informal, which makes it easier for people to take part in the discussion.
    b. We could not get enough people to take part in the meeting, so we canceled it.

Short Conversations

Read the following conversations and see how the new words are used.

[M]   Has the committee **selected** a site for our conference next year?
[W]   Not yet. It's been difficult to find a site that can **accommodate** a group of our size.
[M]   With so many conference facilities available in this area, I would think we could find one that could **hold** the event.

[M]   We'll tour the hotel about a month before our **association** has its conference.
[W]   I'll want to see that all the **arrangements** for meeting rooms and audio equipment are taken care of.
[M]   While we are there, we'll **get in touch** with the manager to check on all the details.

[M]   This is the room where the morning **session** will take place.
[W]   It looks too small. Are you sure it can **hold** all the members who signed up?
[M]   It is the best room available. I hope it doesn't become **overcrowded**.

[M]   Since you decided to **attend** after the deadline passed, you will have to select from the workshops that are still available.
[W]   There are already too many participants **registered** for my first choice.
[M]   I'm sorry, but there are plenty of other **sessions** for you to **take part in**.

Word Families

verb	accommodate	The hotel staff was able to accommodate our many needs for the conference.
noun	accommodation	The accommodations at the hotel include swimming pool, gym, and restaurant.
adjective	accommodating	The conference center manager was extremely accommodating and tried to make our stay pleasant.

verb	attend	Gillian attended the reception for visiting ambassadors.
noun	attendee	More than 500 attendees packed the ballroom.
noun	attendance	Attendance was low for this year's annual meeting.

verb	select	Since there are overlapping workshops, participants will have to select which one most appeals to them.
noun	selection	His dinner selection of stuffed quail sounded better on the menu than it looked on the plate.
adjective	selective	The planning committee was very selective about who received invitations.

verb	register	He registered for his classes via the Internet.
noun	register	The hotel's register showed that only half the members had arrived.
noun	registration	Registration is a detail-oriented and crucial part of running any meeting.

Choose the word that best completes the sentence.

1. The banquet room could _____ up to 750 for dinner.
   (A) accommodated
   (B) accommodate
   (C) accommodation
   (D) accommodating

2. Helen made the final _____ for use of the conference room with the hotel's general manager.
   (A) arranging
   (B) arrange
   (C) arrangement
   (D) arranged

3. By adding more class _____, the staff was able to please more members.
   (A) select
   (B) selective
   (C) selecting
   (D) selections

4. The association's members were asked to _____ for the special session well in advance because space in the lecture hall was limited.
   (A) register
   (B) registration
   (C) registering
   (D) registrar

Short Talk

Read the following passage and write the appropriate form of the new words in the blanks below.

accommodate	attending	location	select
arrangements	get in touch	overcrowded	sessions
associations	hold	register	take part in

Many (5.) _____ and organizations hold annual conferences so that their members can (6.) _____ with each other and (7.) _____ educational programs. When planning a conference, event coordinators try to have a variety of (8.) _____ so people (9.) _____ can (10.) _____ a workshop or meeting that best suits their needs. When making (11.) _____ for a conference, they look for a site that will (12.) _____ all their needs. The site should be able to (13.) _____ the number of people expected to attend, without the meeting rooms being (14.) _____. Good event coordinators tour the site before making a final decision because brochures cannot show all the necessary details. Having meetings in a fun (15.) _____ can really encourage people to (16.) _____ for the meeting.

Choose the underlined word or phrase that should be rewritten and rewrite it.

17. The <u>location</u> could not hold the 50 people who <u>registration</u> for the <u>session</u>, so the room felt terribly <u>overcrowded</u>.
    A   B   C   D
    _____

18. Before <u>select</u> a site and making final <u>arrangements</u> for their annual convention, <u>associations</u> like to tour the
    A   B   C
    conference facility and <u>get in touch</u> with the site manager.
    D
    _____

19. Conference participants like to <u>take part in</u> as many <u>sessions</u> as possible, so <u>hold</u> the meetings sequentially in
    A   B   C
    adjacent <u>locations</u> can be helpful.
    D
    _____

20. When you <u>select</u> a conference site, make sure there are <u>places</u> for spouses accompanying the <u>attendance</u> to
    A   B   C
    <u>arrange</u> to visit.
    D
    _____

Word Review #1   Lessons 1–5 General Business

Choose the word that best completes the sentence.

1. Although negotiating a new contract was compli-
    cated, both parties came to an _____ that
    satisfied them.
    (A) agree
    (B) agreeable
    (C) agreement
    (D) agreeably

2. _____ conferences are a good way for
    employees to get in touch with people in similar
    organizations.
    (A) Associate
    (B) Associating
    (C) Associated
    (D) Association

3. When the family decided to open a restaurant,
    they had to find a _____ that would attract
    business.
    (A) locate
    (B) locator
    (C) locating
    (D) location

4. A _____ company will honor the terms set
    forth in its warranty.
    (A) repute
    (B) reputed
    (C) reputation
    (D) reputable

5. The goal of marketing is to _____ customers,
    to persuade them to buy a product or service.
    (A) attract
    (B) attractive
    (C) attraction
    (D) attractiveness

6. Once both parties have agreed to a contract, they
    have also agreed to abide by every _____
    provision.
    (A) specify
    (B) specific
    (C) specification
    (D) specificity

7. Good business planning includes developing an
    overall _____, addressing likely objections, and
    demonstrating why potential buyers need the
    product or service.
    (A) strategy
    (B) strategic
    (C) strategically
    (D) strategize

8. When you register for out-of-town conferences,
    make room _____ as soon as you decide to
    attend and always remember to ask whether the
    hotel will hold your reservation if you are late.
    (A) accommodate
    (B) accommodations
    (C) accommodating
    (D) accommodated

9. Marketers must avoid making promises they can't
    keep while they _____ the quality of their prod-
    uct or service.
    (A) demonstrate
    (B) demonstration
    (C) demonstrative
    (D) demonstrable

10. A consultant must adhere carefully to his contract
    if he wants to _____ a good business reputa-
    tion.
    (A) establish
    (B) establishment
    (C) established
    (D) establishing

Choose the underlined word or phrase that should be rewritten and rewrite it.

11. Any <u>association</u> should <u>inspiration</u> its members to build a <u>reputation</u> and <u>establish</u> a network of fellow workers.
      A   B   C   D

    _____

12. Never forget to <u>selecting</u> <u>accommodations</u> close to the <u>site</u> so you spend more time <u>taking part in</u> events and
            A   B   C   D
    take less time commuting.

    _____

13. Marketers know that they can <u>attract</u> more customers if they <u>compare</u> favorably with the competition and
                A   B
    <u>convince</u> customers that their product will <u>satisfaction</u> their needs.
     C   D

    _____

14. <u>Agreements</u> and <u>provisions</u> in a contract are <u>developed</u> to <u>resolution</u> issues before they arise.
      A   B   C   D

   _____

15. My favorite part of <u>registering</u> for conferences is <u>selection</u> which <u>sessions</u> I want to <u>attend</u>.
                        A   B   C   D

   _____

16. When planning your business, find a <u>location</u> that <u>attracts</u> customers and <u>implications</u> success even
                                  A   B   C

   while you <u>establish</u> your reputation.
             D

   _____

17. Warranty <u>coverage</u> offers customers <u>assure</u> and <u>protection</u> on the <u>products</u> they buy.
            A   B   C   D

   _____

18. The president of the company knew that he needed to <u>attractive</u> and <u>satisfy</u> <u>consumers</u> if he wanted
                                            A   B   C

   to avoid <u>failure</u>.
           D

   _____

19. Because I am more interested in the <u>sessions</u> for which I have <u>registration</u>, the <u>location</u> of the conference is
                                  A   B   C

   not of <u>primary</u> importance to me.
          D

   _____

20. Some of the best marketers are <u>inspired</u> by their belief in the <u>productive</u>, and an appreciation of its <u>strengths</u>
                              A   B   C

   and <u>characteristics</u>.
        D

   _____

Computers

1. **access** v., to obtain; to gain entry
   a. We accessed the information on the company's Web site.
   b. You need a password to access your account.

2. **allocate** v., to designate for a specific purpose
   a. The office manager did not allocate enough money to purchase software.
   b. The architects must allocate enough space for the word processing department.

3. **compatible** adj., able to function together
   a. This operating system is not compatible with this model computer.
   b. Users of software applications want new versions to be compatible with current versions.

4. **delete** v., to remove; to erase
   a. The technicians deleted all the data on the disk accidentally.
   b. This button on the keyboard deletes the characters from the screen.

5. **display** n., what is visible on a monitor; v., to show
   a. The light on the LCD display is too weak.
   b. The accounting program displays a current balance when opened.

6. **duplicate** v., to produce something equal; to make identical
   a. I think the new word processing program will duplicate the success of the one introduced last year.
   b. Before you leave, please duplicate that file by making a copy on a floppy disk.

7. **fail** v., not to succeed; not to work correctly
   a. The new printer failed to function properly.
   b. The power failed as we were downloading files.

8. **figure out** v., to understand; to solve
   a. By examining all of the errors, the technicians figured out how to fix the problem.
   b. We figured out that it would take us at least ten minutes to download the file.

9. **ignore** v., not to notice; to disregard
   a. When the director is working at the computer, she ignores everything around her.
   b. Don't ignore the technician's advice when connecting cables.

10. **search** v., to look for; n., investigation
    a. The computer searched for all names that began with *W*.
    b. Our search of the database produced very little information.

11. **shut down** v., to turn off; to cease operations
    a. Please shut down the computer before you leave.
    b. We always shut down the air conditioning system on the weekend.

12. **warn** v., to alert; to tell about a danger or problem
    a. The flashing light warns the computer user if the battery is low.
    b. There is an electrical hazard warning on the back of most electronic equipment.

Short Conversation

Read the following conversations and see how the new words are used.

[W] I did a computer **search** to see how much was spent on education last year.
[M] I'm sure you discovered that more money was **allocated** to the military than to education.
[W] Unfortunately, yes. I **fail** to see why we **ignore** this tragic fact.

[M] I can't **figure** this out. When I tried to **access** my E-mail program, the monitor went black.
[W] Sounds like there's a problem with the **display**.
[M] Let me **shut down** the computer and then try one more time.

[M] Have you **figured out** what the problem is?
[W] Yes, the new software program is not **compatible** with this operating system.
[M] I think we **warned** you about that before you purchased the program.

[W] I've made **duplicate** copies of my files and stored them on separate diskettes.
[M] That's a good idea. I accidentally **deleted** an important file and had no backup.
[W] You shouldn't **ignore** the **warnings** about always saving your data.

Word Families

verb	access	The best time to access the Internet is early in the morning.
noun	access	To gain access to the computer lab, all users must have a valid ID.
adjective	accessible	The staff assistant always keeps the door to her office open to show she is accessible.

verb	duplicate	If we work hard, we can duplicate last year's sales records for computers.
noun	duplicate	Don't worry, I have a duplicate on my hard drive.
noun	duplication	His success at our company was based on the duplication of management techniques he had used elsewhere in his career.

verb	fail	We failed to tell you that your records were deleted.
noun	failure	The power failure caused the system to shut down.
adjective	fallible	Everyone can make a mistake. Even a computer is fallible.

verb	warn	We were warned that our E-mail was not private.
noun	warning	The warning was written on the box.
adjective	warning	The warning signs were all there; we should have paid attention to them.

Choose the word that best completes the sentence.

1. In order to _____ your E-mail messages, you must type in your password.
   (A) access
   (B) accessible
   (C) accessed
   (D) accessibility

2. The computer staff is responsible for making sure all system files are _____.
   (A) duplication
   (B) duplicated
   (C) duplicator
   (D) duplicate

3. The computer will _____ you to save your work before quitting.
   (A) warning
   (B) warned
   (C) warn
   (D) warns

4. Our _____ to examine the capabilities of the computer carefully has cost us a lot of time and money.
   (A) fail
   (B) failure
   (C) failed
   (D) fallible

Short Talk

Read the following passage and write the appropriate form of the new words in the blanks below.

accessing	deleted	failure	search
allocated	display	figure out	shut down
compatible	duplicate	ignore	warning

We strongly urge you to read the manual before attempting to run this software program. Do not (5.) _____ this advice. We doubt that you can (6.) _____ the program on your own. This is especially important for owners of our competitor's products that are not (7.) _____ with this program. This incompatibility could cause your computer to crash or (8.) _____ without (9.) _____. This potential for system (10.) _____ is the reason we suggest you back up your files and (11.) _____ them on floppies.

If you need technical assistance, you can contact our technical support staff by (12.) _____ our company's Web page. The first (13.) _____ screen contains FAQ's, the most frequently-asked questions, about our software. There is also an index that will help you narrow your (14.) _____. This information is updated regularly and out-of-date material is (15.) _____. We have (16.) _____ a lot of space on our Web page for technical assistance. We urge you to take advantage of it.

Choose the underlined word or phrase that should be rewritten and rewrite it.

17. Our <u>competitors</u> learned our password and were able to <u>access</u> our computer records and <u>deletion</u> our <u>data</u>.
        A   B   C   D

    _____

18. The board <u>warned</u> us that they planned to <u>shut our department down</u>, but we <u>figured in</u> a way to <u>convince</u>
              A   B   C   D
    them that we were vital to the organization.

    _____

19. If the software is not <u>compatible</u> with the operating system, the computer may <u>fail</u> to function and <u>shut down</u>
                        A   B   C
    without <u>warn</u>.
           D

    _____

20. Our storeroom is full of <u>software</u> programs that are either <u>duplicates</u>, not <u>compatibility</u>, or those that no one
                            A   B   C
    can <u>figure out</u> how to use.
        D

    _____

Office Technology

1. **affordable** adj., able to be paid for; not too expensive
   a. The company's first priority was to find an affordable phone system.
   b. Obviously, the computer systems that are affordable for a Fortune 500 company will not be affordable for a small company.

2. **as needed** adv., as necessary
   a. The courier service did not come every day, only as needed.
   b. The service contract states that repairs will be made on an as-needed basis.

3. **be in charge of** v., to be in control or command of
   a. He appointed someone to be in charge of maintaining a supply of paper in the fax machine.
   b. Your computer should not be in charge of you, rather you should be in charge of your computer.

4. **capacity** n., the ability to contain or hold; the maximum that something can hold or do
   a. The new conference room is much larger and has a capacity of one hundred people.
   b. The memory requirements of this software application exceed the capacity of our computers.

5. **durable** adj., sturdy, strong, lasting
   a. This printer is so durable that, with a little care, it will last another five years.
   b. These chairs were more expensive, in the long run, but also more durable.

6. **initiative** n., the first step; an active role
   a. Employees are encouraged to take the initiative and share their ideas with management.
   b. Our technology initiative involves an exciting new database system and will help us revolutionize our customer service.

7. **physical** adj., perceived by the senses
   a. The physical presence of a computer expert is better than telephone support.
   b. The memory capacity of a computer doesn't correlate to its physical size.

8. **provider** n., a supplier
   a. The department was extremely pleased with the service they received from the phone provider.
   b. As your health service provider, we want to make sure you are happy and satisfied with the service you are receiving.

9. **recur** v., to occur again or repeatedly
   a. The subject of decreasing sales recurs in each meeting, sometimes several times.
   b. The managers did not want that particular error to recur.

10. **reduction** n., a lessening; a decrease
    a. The outlet store gave a 20 percent reduction in the price of the shelves and bookcases.
    b. The reduction in office staff has made it necessary to automate more job functions.

11. **stay on top of** v., to know what is going on; to know the latest information
    a. In order to stay on top of her employees' progress, she arranged weekly breakfast meetings.
    b. In this industry, you must stay on top of current developments.

12. **stock** n., a supply; v., to keep on hand
    a. The office's stock of toner for the fax machine was quickly running out.
    b. The employees stocked the shelves on a weekly basis.

Short Conversations

Read the following conversations and see how the new words are used.

[W]   The new office furniture store has some pretty good **reductions**.
[M]   But they don't have a very extensive **stock** of chairs and desks.
[W]   You could always buy on an **as-needed** basis and surely they could order more for you.

[M]   As part of the company's cost-saving **initiative**, we must have approval on all new purchases.
[W]   Who will **be in charge** of all the approvals?
[M]   Each of the department heads has been ordered to **stay on top of** the purchases.

[M]   With the tight budget, it's going to be difficult to find a larger **physical** plant.
[W]   I know, but at least we can reduce **recurring** supply orders so we have less to store.
[M]   That may not be possible; we are storing at **capacity** now.

[M]   It is time that we think about changing our office supplies **provider**.
[W]   He may not be perfect, but he is very **affordable**.
[M]   Maybe he is affordable, but his goods lacked **durability**.

Word Families

verb	initiate	The company will initiate its new products at the beginning of the year.
noun	initiative	The manager, knowing how concerned his employees were, took the initiative to provide training for them on the new equipment.
noun	initiation	As an initiation into the sales field, Mr. Jenkins was given the most problematic customer's account.

verb	recur	We don't want that problem to recur every month.
noun	recurrence	Every recurrence of the same problem costs us money.
adjective	recurring	Recurring problems waste time and money.

verb	provide	The company provides a five-year warranty on its products.
noun	provider	As your provider of network services, I promise to give you the best prices and service.
noun	provision	Our provisions of supplies should last to the end of the quarter.

verb	reduce	Buying in bulk can help to reduce costs.
noun	reduction	The introduction of the fax machine created a noticeable increase in phone bills.
adjective	reducible	Although our system is working at capacity, the amount of information being processed is not reducible.

Choose the word that best completes the sentence.

1. The employee preferred to have a _____ in salary than to have to continue working with her outdated computer.
   (A) reducing
   (B) reduction
   (C) reduce
   (D) reduces

2. When a problem _____ frequently, it is time to reexamine the process.
   (A) recur
   (B) recurrence
   (C) recurring
   (D) recurs

3. As promised in our last meeting, this contract _____ you with the best prices.
   (A) provide
   (B) provides
   (C) provision
   (D) provider

4. Hoping to repeat the success of the previous year's sales _____, the vice president held a meeting of all the managers.
   (A) initiated
   (B) initiating
   (C) initiative
   (D) initiation

Short Talk

Read the following passage and write the appropriate form of the new words in the blanks below.

affordable	durable	physical	reduce
as needed	is in charge of	provider	stays on top of
capacity	initiates	recurring	stock

Many companies have one person or a department that (5.) _____ running the office. If you have ever worked for a company that doesn't have an office manager, you very quickly learn to appreciate the importance of the job. Who is in charge of placing orders? Who services the fax machine or printer? Who makes sure that the office is presentable for customers? Are the new conference tables and shelves (6.) _____ as well as (7.) _____?

It is the office manager's responsibility to maintain an efficient and smooth-running office. He or she looks for ways to (8.) _____ costs and minimize interruptions in the day-to-day operations. Whereas functional managers know the (9.) _____ of their employees, the office manager knows the (10.) _____ capacity of the office and the supplies and machines that are in the office.

The office manager (11.) _____ the ordering of furniture and supplies, and (12.) _____ changing office technology. Over time, he or she may notice (13.) _____ problems that require changing a service (14.) _____. Furniture and large items are ordered on an (15.) _____ basis. Other frequently used materials, such as paper, folders, and mailing materials, are on an automatic ordering schedule and a (16.) _____ of those supplies is on hand at the office.

Choose the underlined word or phrase that should be rewritten and rewrite it.

17. The new account manager took the <u>initiative</u> of promising to <u>stay on top of</u> orders by <u>physical</u> inspecting the
                          A   B   C
    warehouse <u>stock</u>.
             D

    _____

18. Ordering <u>as need</u> was discouraged by the <u>provider</u> who was <u>in charge of</u> maintaining a high <u>capacity</u> turnover.
              A   B   C   D

    _____

19. A plan to <u>reduce</u> the <u>physical</u> space allotted to each employee is a <u>recurs</u> idea that is usually <u>initiated</u> by a
               A   B   C   D
    new manager.

    _____

20. The company <u>initiating</u> an <u>affordable</u> new program for the division that <u>reduced</u> wastes and increased <u>capacity</u>.
                      A   B   C   D

    _____

Office Procedures

1. **appreciate** v., to recognize, understand the importance of; to be thankful for
   a. He didn't appreciate the complexity of the operation until he had to do it by himself.
   b. The team members sent the director a card telling her how much they appreciated her time and dedication.

2. **be exposed to** v., to become aware of; to gain experience in
   a. Mergers require that employees be exposed to different business practices.
   b. New hires spend a week in each department so that they are exposed to the various functions in the company.

3. **bring in** v., to hire or recruit; to cause to appear
   a. The company president wanted to bring on an efficiency consultant.
   b. The company brought in a new team of project planners.

4. **casual** adj., informal
   a. Fridays are a casual dress day in the office.
   b. It was supposed to be a casual meeting, but everyone showed up in suits and ties.

5. **code** n., rules of behavior
   a. The new employees observed the unwritten code of conduct in their first week on the job.
   b. Even the most traditional companies are changing their dress code to something less formal.

6. **glimpse** n., a quick look
   a. The secretary caught a glimpse of her new boss as she was leaving the office.
   b. After one year with the company, he still felt as though he had only a glimpse of the overall operations.

7. **made of** v., to consist of
   a. This job will really test what you are made of.
   b. People say that the negotiator has nerves made of steel.

8. **out of** adj., no longer having, missing
   a. Orders should be placed before you run out of the supplies.
   b. The presenter ran out of time before he reached his conclusion.

9. **outdated** adj., obsolete; not currently in use
   a. The purpose of the seminar is to have employees identify outdated methods and procedures.
   b. Before you do a mailing, make sure that none of the addresses are outdated.

10. **practice** n., method of doing something
    a. Office practices may vary greatly from one company to another.
    b. The manager had started her practice of weekly breakfast meetings more than twenty years ago.

11. **reinforce** v., to strengthen, support
    a. The financial officer's unconventional method of analyzing data was reinforced by the business journal article.
    b. The employees were expected to reinforce what they had learned at the workshop by trying it out in the workplace.

12. **verbal** adj., oral
    a. Excellent verbal skills are expected in the marketing department.
    b. The employee was given a verbal warning after arriving late to work for the third time.

Short Conversations

Read the following conversations and see how the new words are used.

[M]   I **appreciate** the fact that you have taken time out of your schedule to come and talk with me.
[W]   I want to make sure that you understand the **practices** of the company.
[M]   It seems difficult for other employees to give me a **verbal** explanation of the practices, although they definitely are familiar with them.

[M]   Even though the new attorney is young, she **has been exposed to** many difficult situations.
[W]   Well, then we'll see what she is **made of** at the contract negotiations next week.
[M]   If she hasn't run **out of** energy, she'll be a definite asset.

[W]   I'd like to **reinforce** my knowledge of finance by taking a course at the college.
[M]   That's a great idea, but be careful because some of the courses are **outdated**.
[W]   I had a **glimpse** of that the other night when I sat in on a course that went over management techniques of the 70s.

[M]   I love our new dress **code**!
[W]   Yeah, **casual** Friday is terrific.
[M]   I'm glad they **brought in** the personnel manager who insisted on it.

Word Families

verb	appreciate	We appreciate the time that you have put into this project, but we need to see more positive results.
noun	appreciation	In appreciation for your hard work, we are giving you a top-priority project.
adjective	appreciated	The intern felt appreciated, like a member of the team.

verb	practice	All managers are expected to practice caution in their spending until the end of the year.
noun	practices	He was surprised at the difference in office practices from one local office to another.
adjective	practical	We need a practical solution to this common problem.

verb	reinforce	The practical training reinforced the theoretical studies.
noun	reinforcement	If reinforcement is needed, you have the support of the executive committee.
gerund	reinforcing	Reinforcing the preferred way of selling the product was one of their job requirements.

verb	verbalize	Well-established procedures are often difficult to verbalize.
adjective	verbal	The company operated on a practice of verbal and not written contracts.
adverb	verbally	No employees should be verbally reprimanded in front of their peers.

Choose the word that best completes the sentence.

1. Senior employees are often asked to
   _____ some office procedures.
   (A) verbally   (C) verbal
   (B) verbalize   (D) verbalizing

2. Ms. Handa was unable to express her
   _____ for all that her colleagues
   had done for her.
   (A) appreciation   (C) appreciating
   (B) appreciated   (D) appreciates

3. The new vacation policy will be strictly
   _____, and anyone who violates
   the policy will be reprimanded.
   (A) reinforce   (C) reinforced
   (B) reinforcing   (D) reinforcement

4. The _____ of answering each telephone call
   on the third ring requires a dedicated receptionist.
   (A) practices   (C) practiced
   (B) practicing   (D) practice

Short Talks

Read the following passage and write the appropriate form of the new words in the blanks below.

appreciation	casually	made of	practices
been exposed to	code	out of	reinforced
brought in	glimpse	outdated	verbalize

How many employees show any (5.) _____ for their corporate culture? How many executives appreciate what their corporate culture is and what it is (6.) _____? It is often (7.) _____ by the office procedures and routines that have been established over the years. A manager made her mark twenty years ago by dressing (8.) _____, thereby forever changing the dress (9.) _____. A director bought from the competition when he ran (10.) _____ stock and the practice soon became standard. These examples add to a company's culture.

Good employees know what the standard procedures are. This is an important element in recruiting new employees, as well as training workers. When training workers, it is often important to have them read the procedures, write their reactions, and (11.) _____ their opinions to these practices. This promotes a sense of cooperation between those who establish the (12.) _____ and those who must follow them.

Employees who have been with a company for many years may not be able to identify (13.) _____ practices because they haven't (14.) _____ anything else. What happens when a department needs an extra hand? Is a "temp" (15.) _____, or is someone borrowed from another department? The new recruits often ask the questions that allow more senior employees to get a (16.) _____ of the corporate culture.

Choose the underlined word or phrase that should be rewritten and rewrite it.

17. Although the dress <u>code</u> used to be very <u>formal</u>, it has become much more <u>casually</u> as the executives
             A   B   C
    <u>were exposed to</u> the local business atmosphere.
      D

    _____

18. In an effort to <u>expose</u> and improve some of our <u>outdated</u> operations, we have <u>brought in</u> a consultant to help
                 A   B   C
    us improve the <u>practical</u> of the R&D department.
          D

    _____

19. The manager tried to <u>reinforce</u> the idea that it was much easier to be given a <u>verbal</u> warning when they were
                  A   B
    running <u>out of</u> stock on an item than a written <u>warn</u>.
        C   D

    _____

20. The manager who was <u>brought in</u> to supervise the project <u>had been exposed with</u> a less <u>casual</u> style of man-
                    A   B   C
    agement that we felt was <u>outdated</u>.
                 D

    _____

Electronics

Words to learn

disk
facilitate
network
popularity
process
replace
revolution
sharp
skills
software
storage
technical

1. **disk** n., an object used to store digital information
   a. I lost the floppy disk on which I had saved my school assignment, so now I have to start all over again.
   b. It is important to make a backup disk of all documents on your computer.
2. **facilitate** v., to make easier
   a. The new computer program facilitated the scheduling of appointments.
   b. The director tried to facilitate the transition to the new policy by meeting with all staff who would be affected.
3. **network** n., an interconnected group or system; v., to connect; to broadcast over a radio or TV; to engage in informal communication
   a. There is a network of women professionals that meets once a month for drinks.
   b. We networked my assistant's computer to mine, so that we can easily share files.
4. **popularity** n., the state of being widely admired, sought, or accepted
   a. After the new commercials began running, the popularity of the batteries increased significantly.
   b. This brand of computers is extremely popular among college students.
5. **process** n., a series of operations or actions to bring about a result; v., to put through a series of actions or prescribed procedure
   a. There is a process for determining why your computer is malfunctioning.
   b. I've processed the data I collected and have gotten some interesting results.
6. **replace** v., to put back in a former place or position; to take the place of
   a. I've replaced the hard drive that was malfunctioning.
   b. We have been looking for three months and we've found no one who can replace our former administrator.
7. **revolution** n., a sudden or momentous change in a situation; a single complete cycle
   a. There has been a revolution in the workplace since computers became available for every employee.
   b. My CD player is broken; the disk cannot make a complete revolution around the magnet.
8. **sharp** adj., abrupt or acute; smart
   a. There was a sharp decline in calls to the help desk after we upgraded each employee's computer.
   b. The new employee is extremely sharp, being able to learn the new program in a few days.
9. **skills** n., a developed ability
   a. The software developer has excellent technical skills, and would be an asset to our software programming team.
   b. Salman's job as designer of electronic tools makes good use of his manual dexterity skills.
10. **software** n., the programs for a computer
    a. This new software allows me to integrate tables and spreadsheets into my reports.
    b. Many computers come pre-loaded with software.
11. **storage** n., the safekeeping of goods or information
    a. The double-sided disk has storage room for up to 500 megabytes of data.
    b. The sensitive electronic equipment must be kept in temperature-controlled storage.
12. **technical** adj., special skill or knowledge
    a. The newspaper article on the development of new fiber-optic cables was so full of technical language that only an electrical engineer could understand it.
    b. The computer can only be repaired by someone with technical knowledge.

Short Conversations

Read the following conversations and see how the new words are used.

[M] Having computers installed is nothing short of a **revolution** in this office.
[W] Yes, now we can **replace** all those typewriters that we hate to use.
[M] Good. Once the boss sees how computers **facilitate** our work, he'll wonder why we didn't start using them years ago.

[W] Unfortunately, I don't have the **skills** to retrieve this file.
[M] Are you looking on just your own computer, or have you looked on our office's **network** of computers.
[W] I'm afraid I don't know which directory the file might be **stored** in.

[W] This new **software** is **revolutionary**. It allows me to search all files for the names and addresses of clients and print them out.
[M] What is the **process** for doing that?
[W] It has a lot of **technicalities** only a programmer would understand, but simply stated, the disk can store an amazing amount of information.

[M] Do you stock floppy **disks** that I can use to store my data files?
[W] Their use has declined **sharply** as high-capacity disks have come onto the market, so I'm afraid we don't keep them in stock anymore.
[M] I didn't realize that they were no longer **popular**.

Word Families

verb	popularize	Films and television have popularized cell phones, and they are now widely used.
noun	popularity	The popularity of the product was extremely short-lived, and it soon disappeared from the store shelves.
adjective	popular	The new computer program was extremely popular, and people asked for it at all the stores.

verb	replace	I replaced the disks I borrowed from your office supply closet last week.
noun	replacement	A replacement for this damaged computer will cost you a lot of money.
adjective	replaceable	Don't worry about losing my disk as it is easily replaceable.

verb	revolutionized	Ms. Keller has revolutionized the computer industry during the last decade with her new programs and merchandising agreements.
noun	revolution	There has been a revolution in electronics technology that has allowed products like phones to get smaller and more portable.
adjective	revolutionary	The Internet is revolutionary in how it has changed the way we communicate with others around the world.

verb	store	He stored too much information on the shared drive, making it slow and cumbersome to search through.
noun	store	The store's inventory has to be entered manually into the database.
noun	storage	The storage closet is where you will find all our office supplies.

Choose the word that best completes the sentence.

1. The _____ of the new computer network was apparent among the employees after only a few months.
   (A) popular
   (B) popularize
   (C) popularity
   (D) population

2. We will _____ all of our outdated software with the newest versions.
   (A) replacement
   (B) replaced
   (C) replaceable
   (D) replace

3. There is a _____ approach to software integration that all the big software developers are trying out.
   (A) revolutionized
   (B) revolutionary
   (C) revolution
   (D) revolt

4. The hard disk can _____ up to 25 gigabytes of data.
   (A) stores
   (B) storage
   (C) store
   (D) storing

Short Talk

Read the following passage and write the appropriate form of the new words in the blanks below.

disks	popular	revolutionized	software
facilitates	processing	sharply	storage
networks	replacements	skills	technical

Almost all businesses today, no matter what their size, rely on computers for many of their needs. Prices of computers have declined (5.) _____ over the years, resulting in their increased use in the office. Most offices now have (6.) _____ of computers, which are all electronically linked together. This (7.) _____ sharing and processing of data. Indeed, data (8.) _____ would not be possible without the technical wizardry of hardware manufacturers. Data storage (9.) _____ are a technological miracle.

Because of (10.) _____ advancements, you never need to worry about where to store or back up your data. The (11.) _____ capacity of a small disk is incredible. Manufacturers of (12.) _____ provide frequent upgrades. Unfortunately, these upgrades are often not compatible with earlier versions or other software. This means that you may have to find (13.) _____ for your favorite programs.

Administrators today are trained in the most (14.) _____ software programs. Highly skilled computer programmers and engineers are also very much in demand, especially when a computer or network malfunctions and causes problems.

Computers have (15.) _____ the workplace, and everyone, no matter how accomplished he or she is in other (16.) _____, needs to know how to use a computer for basic tasks, such as using electronic mail, searching the Internet for information, and writing a letter.

Choose the underlined word or phrase that should be rewritten and rewrite it.

17. Because computers <u>facilitate</u> the <u>processing</u> of information, they are extremely <u>popular</u>, and competition
    _A _B _C
    between computer manufacturers has increased <u>sharper</u> in recent years.
    _D

    _____

18. Some companies require that you not only know how to use <u>popularized</u>, current <u>software</u>, but that you have
    _A _B
    <u>technical</u> skills that enable you to use <u>networks</u> most effectively.
    _C _D

    _____

19. Having a <u>network</u> of computers has <u>revolutionary</u> not only how information is <u>processed</u>, but also how it can
    _A _B _C
    be <u>stored</u>.
    _D

    _____

20. I don't need to <u>replace</u> these <u>disks</u>, since the new <u>technology</u> gives me several options for data <u>stores</u>.
    _A _B _C _D

    _____

Lesson 10

Correspondence

Words to learn

assemble
beforehand
complicated
courier
express
fold
layout
mention
petition
proof
registered
revise

1. **assemble** v., to put together; to bring together
   a. Her assistant copied and assembled the documents.
   b. The mail room clerk read the directions before assembling the parts to the new postage printer.

2. **beforehand** adv., early, in advance
   a. To speed up the mailing, we should prepare the labels beforehand.
   b. The goods could have been shipped today had they faxed the order beforehand.

3. **complicated** adj., not easy to understand
   a. This word processing program is too complicated for a beginner to use.
   b. This explanation is too complicated; try to make it simpler.

4. **courier** n., adj., a messenger, an official delivery person
   a. We hired a courier to deliver the package.
   b. The courier service will clear the goods through customs.

5. **express** adj., fast and direct
   a. It's important that this document be there tomorrow, so please send it express mail.
   b. Express mail costs more than regular mail service, but it is more efficient.

6. **fold** v., to bend paper
   a. Fold the letter into three parts before stuffing it into the envelope.
   b. Don't fold the document if it doesn't fit the envelope.

7. **layout** n., a format; the organization of material on a page
   a. We had to change the layout when we changed the size of the paper.
   b. The layout for the new brochure was submitted by the designer.

8. **mention** v., to refer to; n., something said or written
   a. You should mention in the letter that we can arrange for mailing the brochures as well as printing them.
   b. There was no mention of the cost in the proposal.

9. **petition** n., a formal, written request; v., to make a formal request
   a. The petition was photocopied for the workers who will take the copies to collect the necessary signatures.
   b. We petitioned the postal officials to start delivering mail twice a day in business areas.

10. **proof** v., to look for errors
    a. This letter was not proofed very carefully; it is full of typing mistakes.
    b. Very few people bother to proof their E-mails before they send them; consequently, E-mails often contain spelling errors.

11. **registered** adj., recorded and tracked
    a. Since the mail was registered, we know when it was received and who signed for it.
    b. Send this package by registered mail and insure it for $500.

12. **revise** v., to rewrite
    a. The brochure was revised several times before it was sent to the printer.
    b. We will need to revise the form letter since our address has changed.

Short Conversations

Read the following conversations and see how the new words are used.

[M] Here are the documents we need to **assemble** for the meeting.
[W] You should have asked me **beforehand**. I'm too busy now.
[M] I thought I had **mentioned** that I would need your help today.

[M] The **layout** of this pamphlet should be simpler. It's hard to read and it looks very unprofessional.
[W] It is too **complicated**, isn't it?
[M] And the size of the paper is wrong, too. We can't **fold** this sheet into three parts.

[M] Did you see the number of signed **petitions** we've received for more parking spaces?
[W] It's one of our big problems at this branch. I hope management will do something about it when they see these **petitions**.
[M] Many of them arrived by express mail and some were even **registered** for good measure.

[M] Did you **proof** the letter before you sent it?
[W] We **proofed** it, but we didn't send it. We decided to **revise** the opening paragraph.
[M] Well, now it's too late to send it by **courier**. You had better fax it.

Word Families

verb	complicate	Don't try to complicate things by making two-sided copies; single-sided will do.
noun	complication	There are a few complications with your layout, but they can be easily solved.
adjective	complicated	The revisions in the document made it more complicated, rather than simpler.

verb	register	Register this letter and bring back the receipt.
noun	registration	Registration for the seminar can be done by fax.
adjective	registered	Always get a receipt for registered mail.

verb	mention	As I mentioned in my note to you, you should try to be less wordy and more concise in your writing.
noun	mention	The mention of layoffs made us worry.
adjective	mentionable	No one considered the mediocre design a mentionable achievement.

verb	proof	It is everyone's responsibility to proof his or her own work before sending it out.
noun	proofreader	The errors were not found by the proofreader.
gerund	proofing	Proofing a document is best done by starting at the end and reading backward.

Choose the word that best completes the sentence.

1. I don't want to _____ matters, but have you considered using color to make your brochure stand out?
   (A) complicate
   (B) complication
   (C) complicated
   (D) complicating

2. It's worth _____ in the memo that we've finished the draft of the proposal.
   (A) mentionable
   (B) mentioning
   (C) mention
   (D) mentioned

3. The mail room is rarely asked to send letters by _____ mail.
   (A) registering
   (B) registered
   (C) register
   (D) registration

4. To send out business letters without _____ them is unprofessional.
   (A) proofing
   (B) proof
   (C) proofreader
   (D) proofread

Short Talk

Read the following passage and write the appropriate form of the new words in the blanks below.

assemble	courier	layout	proofed
beforehand	express	mention	registered
complicated	folding	petition	revision

In small offices, it is often the executive assistant who must manage all of the printed material that the firm produces. The job responsibilities include typing and printing out the correspondence. These letters and memos must all be carefully (5.) _____ to make sure they are error-free. If not, the errors should be corrected. If the meaning is not clear, the correspondence should be revised. This (6.) _____ should be done (7.) _____, not when the letter is ready to be sent.

Before putting correspondence into an envelope, the executive assistant must (8.) _____ all the various attachments and other documents to be enclosed with the letter. When (9.) _____ the correspondence, the assistant should make sure that when opening the envelope, the recipient sees the letterhead first.

Once prepared, the correspondence must be sent appropriately. Local, urgent mail could be hand-delivered by a (10.) _____ service. Long-distance, urgent mail could be sent overnight or by (11.) _____ mail. If a record is required, mail can be (12.) _____ and receipts are given.

In addition to transmitting and receiving faxes, the executive assistant must work closely with company officials. When the company executives have to make a presentation, the executive assistant often becomes a graphic designer charged with the (13.) _____, or the look of, the graphics and text for the printed materials used during the presentations. Did I (14.) _____ that these duties generally involve learning extremely (15.) _____ design software? It's a wonder that more executive assistants don't (16.) _____ their bosses for a raise.

Choose the underlined word or phrase that should be rewritten and rewrite it.

17. The manager sent the <u>letter</u> by <u>express</u> mail, but he neglected to have it <u>proof</u> <u>beforehand.</u>
                      A   B   C   D

    _____

18. The letter was <u>revision</u>, then <u>folded</u> with the <u>petition</u>, and sent by <u>express</u> mail.
                    A   B   C   D

    _____

19. You <u>mentioned</u> that the word processing program was <u>revised</u> but it is still extremely <u>complication</u> and
         A   B   C
    I couldn't run the program without reading the manual <u>beforehand</u>.
                                                              D

    _____

20. The <u>layout</u> of the <u>petition</u> must be <u>revised</u>, because it may be <u>fold</u> many times if we get a lot of signatures.
         A   B   C   D

    _____

Word Review #2   Lessons 6–10 Office Issues

Choose the word that best completes the sentence

1. Who is _____ hiring?
   (A) in charge by
   (B) in charge on
   (C) in charge of
   (D) in charge for

2. Most office furniture is bought more on the basis of _____ than comfort.
   (A) afford
   (B) affording
   (C) afforded
   (D) affordability

3. The office _____ samples of its products.
   (A) display
   (B) displayed
   (C) displaying
   (D) displayable

4. The staff expressed their _____ for the leadership of their boss.
   (A) appreciate
   (B) appreciated
   (C) appreciating
   (D) appreciation

5. Ms. Ming was pleased that the new employee showed such _____ .
   (A) initiate
   (B) initiative
   (C) initiated
   (D) initiating

6. Before you send the letter, you should _____ it to make sure there are no errors.
   (A) proof
   (B) fold
   (C) petition
   (D) assemble

7. The secretary sent a copy of the revised contract by _____ mail.
   (A) register
   (B) registered
   (C) registering
   (D) registration

8. Many office supply businesses specialize in furniture that is as _____ as it is affordable.
   (A) duration
   (B) durable
   (C) durability
   (D) durableness

9. The office manager finally _____ why the new software wasn't working properly.
   (A) figured in
   (B) figured for
   (C) figured out
   (D) figured about

10. The letter from our accountant _____ that our petty cash spending was almost equal to budgeted items.
    (A) mention
    (B) mentioned
    (C) mentioning
    (D) mentionable

Choose the underlined word or phrase that should be rewritten and rewrite it.

11. The <u>technology</u> expert in charge of the office computers must <u>stay on top of</u> recent <u>software</u> applications and
    A   **B**   **C**
    order them as <u>needy</u>.
    D

12. Although <u>affordable</u> is important, computer buyers need to be sure that the machines are <u>durable</u> and have
    A   **B**
    sufficient RAM <u>capacity</u> for file <u>storage</u>.
    C   **D**

13. Writing letters on a computer makes <u>layout</u> and revisions simple, allows the writer to <u>store</u> addresses
    A   **B**
    <u>beforehand</u>, and <u>displayable</u> previous correspondence to the same client.
    C   **D**

14. The company has just <u>brought on</u> a junior executive who seems to <u>appreciate</u> being exposed to <u>complicated</u>
                       A   **B**   **C**

    business <u>practical</u>.
            D

    _____

15. The <u>courier</u> insisted that I sign the document as <u>prove</u> that he had delivered the <u>software</u> from our <u>provider</u>.
         A   **B**   **C**   **D**

    _____

16. The office manager doesn't want anyone to <u>mention</u> things like a product that is <u>out of</u> stock, programs that
                                           A   **B**

    are <u>outdated</u>, or computers that have <u>shut up</u>.
       C   **D**

    _____

17. The office has a <u>recur</u> problem with an <u>outdated</u> <u>network</u> system that does not have the <u>capacity</u> to accommo-
                A   **B**   **C**   **D**

    date all of our new employees.

    _____

18. For most business presentations, computers have <u>complicated</u> tables that can be <u>assembling</u> <u>beforehand</u> and
                                                A   **B**   **C**

    inserted in the <u>layout</u> where needed.
                   D

    _____

19. The new <u>software</u> was the beginning of a <u>revolutionary</u> that would modernize <u>outdated</u> processes and
            A   **B**   **C**

    <u>practices</u>.
      D

    _____

20. Our new copier will <u>duplicate</u>, <u>assemble</u>, <u>reduction</u>, and <u>fold</u> documents for mailing.
                       A   **B**   **C**   **D**

    _____

Job Advertising and Recruiting

1. **abundant** adj., plentiful, in large quantities; n., a large number
   a. The computer analyst was glad to have chosen a field in which jobs were abundant.
   b. The recruiter was surprised at the abundance of qualified applicants.
2. **accomplishment** n., an achievement, a success
   a. The success of the company was based on its early accomplishments.
   b. In honor of her accomplishments, the manager was promoted.
3. **bring together** v., to join, to gather
   a. Every year, the firm brings together its top lawyers and its newest recruits for a training session.
   b. Our goal this year is to bring together the most creative group we can find.
4. **candidate** n., one being considered for a position, office, or award
   a. The recruiter will interview all candidates for the position.
   b. The president of our company is a candidate for the Outstanding Business Award.
5. **come up with** v., to plan, to invent, to think of
   a. In order for that small business to succeed, it needs to come up with a new strategy.
   b. How was the new employee able to come up with that cost-cutting idea after only one week on the job?
6. **commensurate** adj., in proportion to, corresponding, equal to
   a. Generally the first year's salary is commensurate with experience and education level.
   b. As mentioned in your packets, the number of new recruits will be commensurate with the number of vacancies at the company.
7. **match** n., a fit, a similarity
   a. It is difficult to make a decision when both candidates seem to be a perfect match.
   b. Finding a good match is never easy.
8. **profile** n., a group of characteristics or traits
   a. The recruiter told him that, unfortunately, he did not fit the job profile.
   b. As jobs change, so does the company's profile for the job candidate.
9. **qualifications** n., requirements, qualities, or abilities needed for something
   a. The job seeker had done extensive volunteer work and, therefore, was able to add this experience to his list of qualifications.
   b. The applicant had so many qualifications, the company created a new position for her.
10. **recruit** v., to attract people to join an organization or a cause
    a. The company's policy is to recruit new employees once a year.
    b. When the consulting firm recruited her, they offered to pay her relocation expenses.
11. **submit** v., to present for consideration
    a. Submit your résumé to the human resources department.
    b. The applicant submitted all her paperwork in a professional and timely manner.
12. **time-consuming** adj., taking up a lot of time, lengthy
    a. Even though it was time-consuming, all of the participants felt that the open house was very worthwhile.
    b. Five interviews later, Ms. Lopez had the job, but it was the most time-consuming process she had ever gone through.

Short Conversations

Read the following conversations and see how the new words are used.

[M]   Have you **come up with** any ideas for finishing your job search?
[W]   It has been very **time-consuming** and draining, but I think it's coming to an end.
[M]   Does that mean that you've found a job that's the perfect **match**?

[M]   I've been looking at our company **profile**, and I don't know how we can get people interested in working here.
[W]   Let's **bring together** some people and see if they can stand us.
[M]   That's one way to see if there's a good **match**.

[W]   As a **candidate**, maybe I'm asking for too much, but I do have a preference in job location.
[M]   Tell me about your preferences and I'll see what I can do. I'll **submit** your request to the human resources department, but I can't guarantee anything.
[W]   I would like to be on the West Coast and have a starting salary that is **commensurate** with my five years of work experience.

[W]   The job **recruiter** said that we should send in résumés highlighting our **accomplishments**.
[M]   Then the company can see if we **match** with their list of **qualifications**.
[W]   I'm confident that even if I don't **match**, marketing jobs are **abundant** and I'll find something soon.

Word Families

verb	qualify	In order to qualify, you must have two years of work experience.
noun	qualifications	The manager made a list of qualifications for the vacant job position.
adjective	qualified	He found himself overqualified for the entry-level position.

verb	recruit	Large accounting firms recruit on college campuses every spring.
noun	recruitment	The company's recruitment resulted in ten highly qualified new employees.
noun	recruiter	As a recruiter, he traveled around the country speaking to recent college graduates.

verb	accomplish	You can accomplish anything if you put your mind to it.
noun	accomplishment	The company is proud of our team's accomplishments.
adjective	accomplished	The accomplished artist had his paintings in all the major galleries.

verb	submit	Anyone who is interested in the position should submit a résumé and writing samples.
noun	submission	I'm very sorry, the submission date was last week. We can't take any more applications.
noun	submittal	The submittal of his resignation prompted his colleagues to apply for his job.

Choose the word that best completes the sentence.

1. Your résumé shows you have _____ a great deal in your last position.
    (A) accomplish
    (B) accomplishment
    (C) accomplished
    (D) accomplishing

2. After _____ all his materials, he had no option but to sit back and wait for some response.
    (A) submitting
    (B) submitted
    (C) submission
    (D) submit

3. The company hired a professional _____ to fill the vacant positions.
    (A) recruited
    (B) recruiting
    (C) recruitment
    (D) recruiter

4. The applicants who _____ will be flown to the corporate office and interviewed there.
    (A) qualification
    (B) qualify
    (C) qualifying
    (D) qualifies

Short Talks

Read the following passage and write the appropriate form of the new words in the blanks below.

abundant	candidates	match	recruit
accomplishments	coming up with	profile	submit
bring together	commensurate	qualifications	time-consuming

Recruiting employees is a (5.) _____ and costly process. Therefore, employers want to (6.) _____ the right person with the right job the first time around. There are many ways to (7.) _____ good employees: advertising in newspapers and professional journals, recruiting on college campuses or at conferences, or getting referrals from headhunters.

Recruiting is a time for a company to brag about its (8.) _____ and excite people about its future. Each company is trying to (9.) _____ the best and the brightest, but they are not alone. Their competition is trying to do the same thing. When jobs are (10.) _____ and there is low unemployment, employers may face higher demands from job seekers. Conversely, when the economy is slowing down and jobs are few, employers are in a better position for attracting the best (11.) _____.

Employers look for certain characteristics and (12.) _____ in their employees. (13.) _____ a very specific (14.) _____ that fits the company culture and the specific job requirements is a difficult job. Employers want to see a well-rounded candidate and someone who has related work experience. They are willing to offer a salary that is (15.) _____ with that experience. Employers will make hiring and salary determinations based on the information candidates (16.) _____ throughout the application and interview process.

Choose the underlined word or phrase that should be rewritten and rewrite it.

17. When jobs are <u>abundant</u>, <u>recruit</u> are more flexible and often try to <u>match</u> job seekers with minimal
           A   **B**   **C**

    <u>qualifications</u> with any job.
       D

    _____

18. Employers <u>recruit</u> <u>candidacies</u> whose academic <u>accomplishments</u> are <u>commensurate</u> with the nature and
             A   **B**   **C**   **D**

    demands of a job.

    _____

19. The human resources manager <u>came up with</u> such a specific <u>profile</u> for the entry-level job that it was
                         A   **B**

    impossible to find <u>qualify</u> <u>candidates</u>.
              c   **D**

    _____

20. If we could <u>bring together</u> the skills of these two <u>candidates</u>, we would have a perfect <u>matching</u> and this
            A   **B**   **C**

    <u>time-consuming</u> process would come to an end.
       D

    _____

Applying and Interviewing

1. **ability** n., a skill, a competence
   a. The designer's ability was obvious when she showed the interviewer her portfolio.
   b. The ability to work with others is a key requirement.
2. **apply** v., to look for; to submit an application
   a. The college graduate applied for three jobs and received three offers.
   b. Everyone who is interested should apply in person at any branch office.
3. **background** n., a person's experience, education, and family history
   a. Your background in the publishing industry is a definite asset for this job.
   b. The employer did a complete background check before offering him the job.
4. **be ready for** v., to be prepared
   a. The applicant had done all of her research and felt that she was ready for the interview with the director of the program.
   b. The employer wasn't ready for the applicant's questions.
5. **call in** v., to request
   a. The young woman was so excited when she was called in for an interview that she told everyone she knew.
   b. The human resources manager called in all the qualified applicants for a second interview.
6. **confidence** n., a belief in one's abilities, self-esteem
   a. Good applicants show confidence during an interview.
   b. He had too much confidence and thought that the job was his.
7. **constantly** adj., on a continual basis, happening all the time
   a. The company is constantly looking for highly trained employees.
   b. When my friend was looking for a job, he constantly checked his messages to see if anyone had called for an interview.
8. **expert** n., a specialist
   a. The department head is an expert in financing and is known around the world.
   b. The candidate demonstrated at the interview that he was an expert in marketing.
9. **follow up** v., to take additional steps, to continue; n., the continuation of a previous action
   a. Always follow up an interview with a thank-you note.
   b. As a follow up, the candidate sent the company a list of references and published works.
10. **hesitate** v., to pause; to be reluctant
    a. Don't hesitate to call if you have any questions concerning the job.
    b. We shouldn't hesitate to offer the job to the best-qualified applicant; otherwise she may not be available.
11. **present** v., to introduce; to show; to offer for consideration
    a. The human resources director presents each candidate's résumé to the department supervisor for review.
    b. The candidate presented her qualifications so well that the employer offered her a job on the spot.
12. **weakness** n., a fault; a quality lacking strength
    a. Interviewers often ask applicants about their strengths and weaknesses to get a sense of their characters.
    b. The candidate's only weakness seems to be her lack of experience in fund-raising.

Short Conversations

Read the following conversations and see how the new words are used.

[M] Do you remember the first time you **applied** for a job?
[W] I remember, I had absolutely no **confidence** in myself.
[M] And look where you are now: an **expert** in the field of computer networks.

[M] The two top candidates have very different **backgrounds**.
[W] Yes, but they both demonstrate a great **ability** to get the job done.
[M] Let's see how well they **present** themselves in front of the group of directors.

[M] I blew the interview—I **hesitated** after every question. I'm sure they saw a **weakness** my **inability** to respond quickly.
[W] You should still **follow up** in a couple of days and ask them if they have made a decision.
[M] No, I think I have to **be ready** for a rejection.

[M] My job is to **constantly** look for qualified candidates.
[W] Do you do a **background** check?
[M] My assistants do that and then all the qualified candidates **call in** for an interview.

Word Families

verb	apply	Your chances are better if you apply for a job in the spring.
noun	applicant	The manager selected him from all the applicants.
noun	application	The department can't process your application until all documents have been received.

verb	present	I'd like to present my résumé for your consideration.
noun	presentation	The applicant's presentation made a favorable impression.
adjective	presentable	The applicant was well dressed and presentable.

noun	expert	Don't portray yourself as an expert if you aren't.
noun	expertise	The worker gained expertise over the years and was promoted to a higher position.
adjective	expert	As an expert negotiator, she should have no problems getting what the company wants.

noun	confidence	It's refreshing to see a manager with so much confidence in her employees.
adjective	confident	Don't be too confident until you actually have an offer.
adverb	confidently	The applicant confidently walked into the interview, sat down, and began to talk about himself.

Choose the word that best completes the sentence.

1. As the interview continued, the applicant's _____ began to decline.
   (A) confidently
   (B) confident
   (C) confidence
   (D) confidential

2. So many well-qualified people _____ for the position that we won't be able to make a decision for several weeks.
   (A) apply
   (B) application
   (C) applicant
   (D) applied

3. During an interview, it is important to _____ your weaknesses in a way that shows you are working to improve them.
   (A) presentation
   (B) present
   (C) presentable
   (D) presenting

4. The applicant's unique _____ enabled her to have almost any job that she wanted.
   (A) expertise
   (B) experts
   (C) expertly
   (D) expert

Short Talks

Read the following passage and write the appropriate form of the new words in the blanks below.

abilities	backgrounds	constantly	hesitant
apply	called in	experts	present
are ready for	confidence	follow up	weaknesses

How many times in your life will you search for a new job? The (5.) _____ say probably more times than you think! Some people find the job search time-consuming and hard on their self- (6.) _____. The best job hunters are those who never stop looking and don't dwell on their (7.) _____. They network (8.) _____: at meetings, at social gatherings, and with people they meet on the street. They (9.) _____ periodically with contacts and acquaintances to keep up with new developments.

Good job hunters assess and update their (10.) _____ and their (11.) _____ all the time. Before they even (12.) _____ for a position, they have researched the field and the specific companies they are interested in. They know where they could fit into the company and they tailor their résumés for each position. Therefore, when they are (13.) _____ for an interview, they're prepared. They (14.) _____ anything!

At the interview, these job hunters know that they must (15.) _____ themselves in the best way possible. This is their opportunity to shine. It is also their opportunity to see if this is truly the job that they want. If either party is (16.) _____ at the interview, it may be a sign that it isn't a good fit.

Choose the underlined word or phrase that should be rewritten and rewrite it.

17. The <u>application's</u> <u>hesitation</u> at answering questions about her <u>ability</u> led the employer to believe that she
         A   B   C
    wasn't <u>ready</u> for the position.
         D

    _____

18. Even though the applicant is an <u>expertise</u> in the field, he didn't seem to <u>be ready</u> by the interview and wasn't
                              A   B
    very skilled at <u>presenting</u> his achievements or <u>background</u>.
                C   D

    _____

19. Because the job hunter had evaluated his <u>abilities</u>, he was <u>confidence</u> that he would be <u>called in</u> to <u>present</u> his
                                    A   B   C   D
    credentials.

    _____

20. My <u>expert</u> advice is, after you have submitted your <u>application</u>, <u>follow up</u> <u>constant</u> to see if there are
       A   B   C   D
    any openings.

    _____

Hiring and Training

1. **conduct** v., to hold, to take place, to behave; n., one's behavior
   a. Interviews were conducted over a period of three weeks.
   b. The trainees' conduct during training was unacceptable; something must be done.
2. **generate** v., to create, to produce
   a. The new training program generated a lot of interest among employees.
   b. The job fair at the college campus should generate interest in our company.
3. **hire** v., to employ, to offer a job or position; n., an employee
   a. She was hired after her third interview.
   b. The new hire has integrated well with his colleagues.
4. **keep up with** v., to stay equal with
   a. The workers were told that they must keep up with the changes or they would find themselves without jobs.
   b. Employees are encouraged to take courses in order to keep up with new developments.
5. **look up to** v., to admire, to think highly of
   a. Staff members looked up to the director because he had earned their respect over the years.
   b. There are few people in this world that I look up to as much as I look up to you.
6. **mentor** n., a person who guides and instructs, a resource
   a. The mentor helped her make some decisions about combining career and family.
   b. One problem with many programs is that the mentors don't feel invested in the progress of the employees with whom they are working.
7. **on track** adj., on schedule; focused
   a. If we stay on track, the meeting should be finished at 9:30.
   b. You have a lot of work; if you can't stay on track, let me know immediately.
8. **reject** v., to turn down; to say no, to not accept
   a. Even though Mr. Lukin rejected their offer, they remained in contact.
   b. Ms. Gauchet rejected the offer because they could not offer her the salary that she requested.
9. **set up** v., to establish, to arrange; adj., established, arranged
   a. Set up a time and place for the meeting and then inform everyone who is involved.
   b. Check with your supervisor to make sure that your office is all set up before you begin work.
10. **success** n., an accomplishment; reaching a goal
    a. The director's success came after years of hiring the right people at the right time.
    b. When the manager won an award, he attributed his success to his colleagues.
11. **training** n., the preparation or education for a specific job
    a. The new hire received such good training that, within a week, she was as productive as the other workers.
    b. The training is designed to prepare all workers, new and old, for the changes that the company will face.
12. **update** v., to make current; n., the latest information
    a. The personnel officer updated the employees on the latest personnel changes.
    b. Our latest update shows that business is down 15 percent.

Short Conversations

Read the following conversations and see how the new words are used.

[M]   How has the week of **training** gone so far?
[W]   We have a large group, but we've been able to stay **on track** and get a lot accomplished.
[M]   Everyone is commenting on the amount of excitement that your program has **generated**.

[M]   Finally, all the new employees have been **hired**.
[W]   It was difficult to **keep up with** their demands.
[M]   They asked for a lot, but I'm confident that they will be very **successful** and be an asset to the company.

[M]   I've been asked to be a **mentor** to a new **hire** for the first time. Do you have any advice?
[W]   It's an important responsibility. Make sure you **set up** some guidelines for you and the employee.
[M]   O.K. I don't want to disappoint him. I know he **looks up** to me.

[M]   Have you **updated** Ms. Lappat's files yet?
[W]   I'm doing that now. I have to make a note about her **conduct** yesterday.
[M]   It was disappointing and, of course, we'll have to **reject** her request for a raise.

Word Families

verb	hire	The personnel director needed to hire 15 people within a week.
noun	hire	The new hire quickly gained a reputation for excellent work.
gerund	hiring	The hiring took the company much longer than expected.

verb	reject	The candidate rejected the offer the first time, but the second time she accepted it.
noun	rejection	Rejections are difficult, but you can learn something from them.
gerund	rejecting	Rejecting a job offer before you have it is not a smart thing to do.

verb	succeed	In order to succeed in this business, you must be persistent.
noun	success	Don't let success go to your head!
adjective	successful	The trainers were very successful with this last group of new hires.

verb	train	Even though you were trained on a Macintosh, you'll have to learn how to use a PC.
noun	trainer	The trainer stayed after the meeting to answer any questions.
noun	trainee	Each new employee spends six weeks as a trainee.

Choose the word that best completes the sentence.

1. Unfortunately, not all candidates can be offered a job; some have to be _____.
   (A) rejected
   (B) rejecting
   (C) rejection
   (D) reject

2. The _____ of the program depends on the active participation of everyone.
   (A) successfully
   (B) succeed
   (C) successful
   (D) success

3. After he was _____, he continued to take classes to upgrade his skills.
   (A) hiring
   (B) hires
   (C) hired
   (D) hire

4. In all my years of _____, I have never seen such a motivated group of new hires.
   (A) trainee
   (B) training
   (C) trains
   (D) trainer

Short Talks

Read the following passage and write the appropriate form of the new words in the blanks below.

conducted	keep up with	on track	successfully
generate	look up to	rejected	training
hires	mentor	set up	update

After the ads have been placed, and the interviews have been (5.) _____, decisions have to be made. Who should the company bring onboard? Job offers are extended and they are either accepted or (6.) _____. For those who accept the offer, the job search has been completed (7.) _____. But for both the employer and the new hire, the job has just begun.

Companies want new employees to (8.) _____ new business and new ideas as soon as possible. Before they can do that, the new (9.) _____ need some (10.) _____. All companies have unique expectations and methods of operating. Company trainers conduct workshops and seminars for both experienced and new workers. All employees must prepare for the future and continuously (11.) _____ themselves in their field. Nowadays, workers are expected to (12.) _____ the latest trends and information. Otherwise, they fall behind.

Many companies (13.) _____ a mentoring program for new employees. The (14.) _____ is usually an experienced manager or employee and should be someone whom the new employee can (15.) _____. Mentors often review goals and objectives with their mentorees and help them to stay (16.) _____.

Choose the underlined word or phrase that should be rewritten and rewrite it.

17. The <u>training</u> session will be <u>conduct</u> by someone the participants can <u>look up to</u> and who will <u>generate</u>
       A   B   C   D
    interest.

    _____

18. The new <u>hired</u> felt <u>rejected</u> when his <u>mentor</u> didn't respond to his request for <u>training</u>.
           A   B   C   D

    _____

19. In order to stay <u>on track</u> and to <u>keep up with</u> the latest changes, he asked his newly <u>hired</u> secretary to send
               A   B   C
    him <u>updating</u> on the hour.
        D

    _____

20. They <u>set up</u> the program so that the employees could <u>conduct</u> research and <u>generate</u> materials and feel very
       A   B   C
    <u>succeeded</u> when they were finished.
      D

    _____

Salaries and Benefits

1. **basis** n., the main reason for something; a base or foundation
    a. The manager didn't have any basis for firing the employee.
    b. On the basis of my ten years of loyalty to this company, I feel that I deserve three weeks vacation.
2. **be aware of** v., to be conscious of; to be knowledgeable about
    a. The new staff member wasn't aware of the company's position on working a second job.
    b. Are you aware of the new employee's past work history?
3. **benefits** n., the advantages provided to an employee in addition to salary; v., to take advantage of
    a. Although the analyst earned a better salary at his new job, his benefits were better at his previous job.
    b. We all benefit from the company's policy of semiannual reviews.
4. **compensate** v., to pay; to make up for
    a. The company compensates employees for overtime by paying more for those extra hours worked.
    b. The company will compensate employees for any travel expenses.
5. **delicate** adj., sensitive; adv., with sensitivity
    a. Contract negotiations are very delicate and should be conducted by senior management.
    b. The manager delicately asked about the health of his client.
6. **eligible** adj., able to participate in something; qualified
    a. Some employees may be eligible for the tuition reimbursement plan.
    b. I don't understand why I'm not eligible if I have been with the company for over a year.
7. **flexible** adj., not rigid, able to change easily
    a. Sometimes the manager is too flexible and his workers take advantage of him.
    b. Younger workers tend to be more flexible with their work schedules.
8. **negotiate** v., to talk for the purpose of reaching an agreement, especially on prices or contracts
    a. You must know what you want and what you can accept when you negotiate a salary.
    b. The associate looked forward to the day that she would be able to negotiate her own contracts.
9. **raise** n., an increase in salary
    a. The supervisor expected a substantial raise and was disappointed with the 2 percent increase she received.
    b. With his raise, Mr. Drvoshanov was able to afford to buy a new car.
10. **retire** v., to stop working; to withdraw from a business or profession
    a. She retired at the age of 64 but continued to be very active with volunteer work.
    b. Many people would like to win the lottery and retire.
11. **vested** adj., absolute, authorized
    a. The day that Ms. Weng become fully vested in the retirement plan, she gave her two weeks' notice.
    b. The company has a vested interest in the happiness of its employees.
12. **wage** n., the money paid for work done, usually hourly
    a. Hourly wages have increased by 20 percent over the last two years.
    b. The intern spends more than half of her wages on rent.

Short Conversations

Read the following conversations and see how the new words are used.

[M]   I don't quite understand when I will be **eligible** for vacation.
[W]   The supervisor is pretty **flexible** about that. You should talk to her.
[M]   I thought it was a very strict policy. **I wasn't aware of** that **flexibility**!

[M]   We can't seem to make ends meet with my hourly **wage**.
[W]   Maybe you should ask for a **raise**.
[M]   But, I don't want to ask for too much **compensation**; the company just offered me health coverage.

[M]   After two years, am I partially **vested** in the 401(k) plan?
[W]   I believe so, but you should speak with the **benefits** manager in the Human Resources Department.
[M]   It's hard to imagine that I'll **retire** five years from now.

[M]   How was your workshop on salary **negotiation**?
[W]   It became very **delicate** because my boss and I didn't agree.
[M]   On the **basis** of that experience, you should attend workshops by yourself in the future.

Word Families

verb	compensate	The company compensates its full-time employees well.
noun	compensation	Compensation will be based on your work performance over the past six months.
adjective	compensatory	Compensatory time is given in lieu of overtime pay.

verb	benefit	In order to benefit from the plan, you must fill out the paperwork and submit it to the personnel office.
noun	benefits	The new employee's benefits went into effect three months after his start date.
adjective	beneficial	The service that the insurance has provided has been very beneficial.

verb	negotiate	The employee prepared a list of her accomplishments to share with her supervisor so that she could negotiate a higher salary.
noun	negotiation	The director was very pleased that the negotiations brought about the end of the strike.
noun	negotiator	I should take lessons from Mr. Tarsa; he is such a skilled negotiator.

verb	retire	Many people don't know what to do with all their time when they retire from work.
noun	retirement	The administrator added more money to the fund for her retirement.
adjective	retired	The retired worker came back to the office from time to time to see his friends.

Choose the word that best completes the sentence.

1. What is the company's policy on
   _____ for part-time workers?
   (A) benefited   (C) benefits
   (B) beneficial   (D) benefit

2. When the _____ continued into the
   evening, we decided to break for dinner.
   (A) negotiator   (C) negotiate
   (B) negotiations   (D) negotiated

3. No one is sure what will happen to the company
   when the president finally _____.
   (A) retires   (C) retired
   (B) retirement   (D) retiree

4. The tired employee hoped that she would be
   _____ for all the long hours she kept and weekends she worked.
   (A) compensation   (C) compensated
   (B) compensates   (D) compensate

Short Talks

Read the following passage and write the appropriate form of the new words in the blanks below.

basis	compensated	flexibility	retirement
be aware of	delicate	negotiated	vested
benefits	eligible	raise	wage

An important part of the job search often comes after an offer has been made. Papers should not be signed until you have successfully (5.) _____ your salary and (6.) _____. You want to make sure you will be adequately (7.) _____ for your skills, work, and time. This is a (8.) _____ and difficult area. You should (9.) _____ what the salary ranges are at the company and in the field.

Some workers are not on a salary; rather they work for an hourly (10.) _____. In some cases, workers who earn an hourly wage have more (11.) _____ with the hours they work. The trade-off is that the worker may not receive any benefits. For those workers on a salary, the base salary that is negotiated is critical, because most subsequent pay raises come in small incremental amounts. Most companies have a review process either on an annual or semiannual (12.) _____. As a result of the review, an employee may receive a (13.) _____.

Each employee has a unique situation. Health insurance coverage and (14.) _____ plans may be essential to some employees, whereas they are not important to others. Many companies will offer benefits in such a way that it is to the employee's advantage to stay with the company for a longer period of time. Employees may not be (15.) _____ to sign up for a retirement plan until they have been with the company for one year and employees are not fully (16.) _____ in these plans until they have five years of service under their belts. Some bonus plans are paid out over a period of years. Vacation time increases after more years of service.

Choose the underlined word or phrase that should be rewritten and rewrite it.

17. He was not <u>aware of</u> the changes to the <u>benefits</u> plan, which placed a limit on the contributions he could make
           A   **B**
    to his <u>retirement</u> account; they had previously been very <u>flexibility</u>.
        C   **D**

    _____

18. The employees waited until they were fully <u>vest</u> and then <u>delicately</u> made their boss <u>aware of</u> their plans for
                                      A   **B**   **C**
    <u>retirement</u>.
    D

    _____

19. Salary <u>negotiation</u> is a <u>delicately</u> matter, but necessary if you want to be <u>compensated</u> well and get the <u>raises</u>
            A   **B**   **C**   **D**
    you deserve.

    _____

20. Only employees who are paid on the <u>basis</u> of an hourly <u>wage</u> are <u>eligibility</u> for the <u>raise</u>.
                                        A   **B**   **C**   **D**

    _____

Promotions, Pensions, and Awards

1. **achieve** v., to succeed, to reach a goal
   a. I hope to achieve as much as you have in your short time with the company.
   b. The new Board of Directors has achieved all of its goals in the first six months.

2. **contribute** v., to add to; to donate, to give
   a. Make sure your boss is aware of the work you contributed to the project.
   b. All employees are asked to contribute a few minutes of their spare time to clean up the office.

3. **dedication** n., a commitment to something
   a. The director's dedication to a high-quality product has motivated many of his employees.
   b. We would never be where we are today if it weren't for many long hours and so much dedication.

4. **look forward to** v., to anticipate, to be eager for something to happen
   a. The regional director was looking forward to the new, larger offices.
   b. We look forward to seeing you at the next meeting.

5. **looked to** v., to depend on, to rely on
   a. The workers always looked to him to settle their disagreements.
   b. The staff is looking to their supervisor for guidance and direction.

6. **loyal** adj., faithful, believing in someone or something
   a. You have been such a loyal advisor for so many years, I'm not sure what I'll do without you.
   b. Even though your assistant is loyal, you have to question his job performance.

7. **merit** n., excellence, high quality
   a. Employees are evaluated on their merit and not on seniority.
   b. Your work has improved tremendously and is of great merit.

8. **obvious** adj., easy to see or understand
   a. The marketing coordinator is the obvious choice to replace Ms. Nance.
   b. In many companies, it is very obvious who will be promoted.

9. **productive** adj., useful, getting a lot done
   a. The researcher wasn't as productive when he first started working here.
   b. The managers had a very productive meeting and were able to solve many of the problems.

10. **promote** v, to give someone a better job; to support, to make known
    a. Even though the sales associate had a good year, it wasn't possible to promote him.
    b. The Assistant Director promoted the idea that the Director was incompetent.

11. **recognition** n., credit, praise for doing something well
    a. The president's personal assistant was finally given the recognition that she has deserved for many years.
    b. Recognition of excellent work should be routine for every manager.

12. **value** n., worth
    a. It is difficult to put a value on the work that an employee does.
    b. Employees value their colleagues' opinions.

Short Conversations

Read the following conversations and see how the new words are used.

[M]   I'm **looking forward** to the awards ceremony tonight!
[W]   So am I. I hope Darrell finally gets some **recognition** for all the work that he has done.
[M]   He certainly has been very **productive** in the last few months.

[M]   Sometimes your assistant doesn't feel as though you **value** her work.
[W]   I judge work by **merit**, not by the quantity of paper produced.
[M]   But it's **obvious** that she's just trying to please you.

[M]   Who will they **promote** next?
[W]   That new manager has a lot of **dedication** and ambition.
[M]   No, they won't **promote** him. He hasn't been with the company long enough and hasn't contributed enough.

[M]   Have you **achieved** the goals you set for yourself last year?
[W]   I was **looking to** you to help me prioritize my goals.
[M]   I may be a **loyal** friend, but I can't help you do everything!

Word Families

verb	achieve	Making a list of your objectives will help you achieve them.
noun	achievement	His achievements were noticed by the vice president and he was sent to the London office.
noun	achiever	Mr. Vadji always considered himself a high achiever.

verb	contribute	All employees were urged to contribute something useful at the staff meetings.
noun	contribution	Each of you has made a significant contribution to our team's success.
noun	contributor	As contributors to the company's outstanding year, all employees will receive an additional holiday bonus.

verb	dedicate	The manager dedicates too much time to reports and not enough time to the customer.
noun	dedication	Margo's dedication to the company was rewarded with a two-week trip to Hawaii.
adjective	dedicated	Before the change in management, he used to be a more dedicated worker.

verb	promote	In order to move ahead in the company, you must promote yourself.
noun	promotion	Promotions are given to those who prove their worth.
noun	promoter	As the main promoter of the product, Ms. Ross was responsible for the marketing campaign.

Choose the word that best completes the sentence.

1. Hard work and _____ will help you move up the corporate ladder.
   (A) dedicated   (C) dedication
   (B) dedicates   (D) dedicated

2. Because you are a valued and dedicated employee, we are _____ you to director of the department.
   (A) promoting   (C) promotion
   (B) promote   (D) promoter

3. When he thought about his long career, he realized that his biggest _____ was in developing the new leaders of the company.
   (A) achiever   (C) achievement
   (B) achieved   (D) achieves

4. She has _____ so much time and energy to the project that her name should appear on the award.
   (A) contributes   (C) contributed
   (B) contribution   (D) contributor

Short Talks

Read the following passage and write the appropriate form of the new words in the blanks below.

achievers	look forward to	merit	promoted
contributions	looked to	obvious	recognition
dedicated	loyalty	productive	value

Everyone enjoys receiving (5.) _____ for the work that they do. Today, we will honor several employees who have been with the company since we opened our doors. Their (6.) _____ to the company is an honor for us. No (7.) _____ can be placed on these employees; they are priceless to us. Since 1965, these individuals have been (8.) _____ to higher paying positions not for their connections or their degrees, but for what they have done for the company. In other words they have been promoted on their (9.) _____. These high (10.) _____ are a credit to our community.

All of us, over the years, have (11.) _____ these fine employees for advice and guidance. These (12.) _____ individuals have acted as valued mentors and leaders. They have made (13.) _____ in developing more (14.) _____ ways to serve our customers and opening new markets. They have taken risks. Sometimes, they made mistakes. But they learned along the way and shared that knowledge with others.

It should be (15.) _____ who I am talking about. I (16.) _____ working more closely with them in their new positions as Vice Presidents of Marketing and of Operations. Please, join me in congratulating these two fine individuals on their promotion and receipt of the Henry Award for Excellence.

Choose the underlined word or phrase that should be rewritten and rewrite it.

17. The assistant <u>looked forward to</u> the time when she would finally be <u>recognized</u> for her hard work and
    　　　　　　A　　　　　　　　　　　　　　　　　　　　　B
    <u>dedicated</u> and be <u>promoted</u> to director.
    　C　　　　　　　D
    _____

18. The worker made <u>value</u> <u>contributions</u> to the project and he <u>looked forward to</u> receiving a <u>promotion</u>.
    　　　　　　　　　A　　　B　　　　　　　　　　　　　　C　　　　　　　　　　　　　　D
    _____

19. The <u>merit</u> of his work was never <u>recognized</u> by all but the <u>obviously</u> lack of <u>loyalty</u> led to his dismissal.
    　　　A　　　　　　　　　　　　B　　　　　　　　　　　　C　　　　　　　D
    _____

20. It is <u>obvious</u> that we must <u>look to</u> our customers for ideas in order for us to become more <u>production</u> and
    　　　A　　　　　　　　　　B　　　　　　　　　　　　　　　　　　　　　　　　　　C
    <u>achieve</u> greater results.
    　D
    _____

Word Review #3   Lessons 11–15 Personnel

Choose the word that best completes the sentence.

1. _____ with a good ad is time-consuming.
   (A) Coming up
   (B) Coming to
   (C) Coming by
   (D) Coming on

2. To _____ the best and the brightest, companies have to be willing to pay well.
   (A) recruit
   (B) recruits
   (C) recruiting
   (D) recruitment

3. A qualified candidate usually exudes _____.
   (A) confident
   (B) confidence
   (C) confidential
   (D) confidentially

4. Any applicant is wise to _____ an interview with a note or a phone call.
   (A) follow after
   (B) follow behind
   (C) follow up
   (D) follow with

5. Workers are promoted on their _____ and merits.
   (A) achieve
   (B) achieved
   (C) achiever
   (D) achievements

6. The benefits package is an important aspect of contract _____.
   (A) negotiate
   (B) negotiable
   (C) negotiations
   (D) negotiated

7. Some employees have to wait years before they are fully _____ in the company pension plan.
   (A) vest
   (B) vested
   (C) vesting
   (D) vests

8. Health _____ are very important for an employee who develops a serious medical problem.
   (A) benefit
   (B) benefits
   (C) beneficial
   (D) beneficiary

9. A _____ and hard-working employee can look forward to rapid promotions
   (A) dedicate
   (B) dedication
   (C) dedicating
   (D) dedicated

10. A company that recognizes _____ merit will receive employee loyalty in return.
    (A) obvious
    (B) obviously
    (C) oblivious
    (D) obliviously

Choose the underlined word or phrase that should be rewritten and rewrite it.

11. <u>Candidates</u> with <u>backgrounds</u> that match the company's <u>profile</u> should be <u>success</u> in getting a job.
       A   B   C   D

    _____

12. The manager <u>conducts</u> <u>train</u> sessions to help employees to <u>keep up with</u> changes in health <u>benefits</u>.
                    A   B   C   D

    _____

13. The employees had <u>achieved</u> <u>recognizing</u> for their <u>valued</u> <u>contributions</u> to the project.
              A   B   C   D

    _____

14. The manager immediately <u>recruitment</u> the young woman who demonstrated the kind of <u>confidence</u>,
                       A   B
    <u>background</u>, and <u>ability</u> he had been looking for.
       C   D

    _____

15. The new employee <u>looked forward to</u> rapid <u>promoted</u> through <u>dedication</u> and high <u>productivity</u>.
               A   B   C   D

    _____

16. You should <u>be aware that</u> employers don't always <u>compensation</u> their employees with wages <u>commensurate</u>
                     A   **B**   **C**
    with their <u>merit</u>.
            D

    _____

17. <u>Negotiate</u> for a <u>raise</u> in <u>wages</u> can be a <u>delicate</u> process.
   A   **B**   **C**   **D**

    _____

18. <u>Loyal</u> workers should <u>be ready</u> to work overtime without <u>compensation</u> in exchange for <u>flexibility</u> schedules.
   A   **B**   **C**   **D**

    _____

19. If you are lucky, you can find an <u>expert</u> in your field who will be your <u>mentor</u>, keeping you <u>on tracks</u>
                                      A   **B**   **C**
    and helping you to overcome your <u>weaknesses</u>.
                                     D

    _____

20. Consultants were <u>called in</u> to <u>set by</u> new procedures for doing <u>background</u> checks and processing job
                      A   **B**   **C**
    <u>applications</u>.
       D

    _____

Shopping

1. **bargain** n., something offered or acquired at a price advantageous to the buyer
   a. We were thrilled with the bargains we found at the clothing sale.
   b. Lois compared the sweaters carefully to determine which was a better bargain.

2. **bear** v., to have a tolerance for; to endure
   a. Moya doesn't like crowds so she cannot bear to shop during the holiday rush.
   b. If you can bear with me, I'd like to stop in one more store.

3. **behavior** n., the manner of one's actions
   a. Annu is conducting a survey on whether consumer behavior differs between men and women.
   b. Suspicious behavior in a department store will draw the attention of the security guards.

4. **checkout** n., the act, time, or place of checking out, as at a hotel, library, or supermarket
   a. The line at this checkout is too long, so let's look for another.
   b. Get in the checkout line now and I'll join you with the last items.

5. **comfort** n., a condition or feeling of pleasurable ease, well-being, and contentment
   a. I like to dress for comfort if I'm spending the day shopping.
   b. Arlo likes to go to the mall where he can shop in comfort, regardless of the weather.

6. **expand** v., to increase the size, volume, quantity, or scope of; to enlarge
   a. The new manager has significantly expanded the store's inventory.
   b. The shoe store is out of room and is thinking about expanding into the adjacent vacant building.

7. **explore** v., to investigate systematically
   a. The collector likes to explore antique shops looking for bargains.
   b. While his mother shopped for clothes, Michael wandered off to explore the toy section.

8. **item** n., a single article or unit
   a. The grocery store has a special checkout line for people who are purchasing less than ten items.
   b. Do you think I can get all these items into one bag?

9. **mandatory** adj., required or commanded; obligatory
   a. The jewelry store has a mandatory policy of showing customers only one item at a time.
   b. There is a mandatory limit of nine items for use of this checkout line.

10. **merchandise** n., items available in stores
    a. I am very impressed with the selection of merchandise at this store.
    b. Helen wanted to make sure that the store had a wide variety of merchandise before she committed to buying a gift certificate.

11. **strict** adj., precise; exact
    a. The store's policy states that returns must be made within 30 days of purchase, but the staff is not strict in enforcing it.
    b. There is a strict limit of four items per person that can be taken into the changing room.

12. **trend** n., the current style; vogue
    a. The clothing store tries to stay on top of all the new trends.
    b. Mioshi followed market trends closely before she bought a clothing franchise.

Short Conversations

Read the following conversations and see how the new words are used.

[M]   If we hurry, we can get into the **checkout** aisle before the clerk takes his break.
[W]   There is a **mandatory** limit of nine items. Do we meet that criterion?
[M]   Oh dear, I didn't count. Do you think they are **strict** about enforcing that rule?

[M]   For my class in consumer **behavior**, we are secretly watching what people buy.
[W]   I'm sure you'll find that people hunt for **bargains** to save money.
[M]   Actually, shoppers told us they bought brands they knew best and felt most **comfortable** with, regardless of price.

[M]   The selection of **merchandise** in this store is really wonderful.
[W]   They have really **expanded** the menswear section since the last time we shopped here.
[M]   I think they are capitalizing on the "casual Friday" **trend** at most offices.

[M]   I need a new winter coat, but I can't **bear** the thought of spending the weekend in the mall.
[W]   I'm just the opposite. My hobby is **exploring** new stores around the city.
[M]   You must know every new **item** of merchandise at every store.

Word Families

noun	comfort	This car is designed with plush seats for your comfort and air bags for your safety.
adjective	comfortable	I prefer this sweater because it's more comfortable.
adverb	comfortably	I'd suggest buying the larger table, which comfortably seats six.

verb	expand	The music store expanded its selection by offering more classical music on compact discs.
noun	expansion	The expansion of our sales territory into a new region will mean more stock will have to be ordered.
adjective	expanded	The expanded inventory is great, but it's hard to find room to store it.

verb	explore	Ms. Marce explored the bins of hardware, looking for the right size nails.
noun	exploration	The store designer's exploration of the art of different cultures gave the store an exotic look.
adjective	exploratory	The oil company's exploratory drill led to a new supply of petroleum.

noun	strictness	Ms. Judd was appalled at the strictness of the store's policy not to renew her gift certificate after it had expired.
adjective	strict	Our store has a strict policy of no returns.
adverb	strictly	The no-food-or-drinks rule is strictly enforced in the bookstore.

Choose the word that best completes the sentence.

1. It's hard to tell if these shoes will be _____ because the leather is so stiff.
   (A) comfort
   (B) comfortably
   (C) comfortable
   (D) comforting

2. Due to the store's success, the owners began to plan an _____ into a larger location.
   (A) expansion
   (B) expand
   (C) expanse
   (D) expanded

3. I'd like to _____ this issue with you, but I don't have time today.
   (A) exploratory
   (B) exploration
   (C) explorer
   (D) explore

4. We _____ adhere to the store's policy of only specially ordering products that have been paid for in advance.
   (A) strictness
   (B) strict
   (C) strictly
   (D) strictest

Short Talk

Read the following passage and write the appropriate form of the new words in the blanks below.

bargains	checkout	exploring	merchandise
bear	comforting	items	strictly
behavior	expand	mandatory	trend

Some people love to shop. Others can't (5.) _____ shopping and only go when their clothes are completely worn-out. No one can get away from shopping—unless you can do without eating! Consumption and consumer (6.) _____ affects everything we do.

Some purchases are absolutely (7.) _____. Everyone needs to eat, wear clothing, and sit on furniture. Other purchases are (8.) _____ for luxury (9.) _____. The vast majority of what most of us buy is somewhere in between essential items and frivolous items.

Most people shop by visiting stores on the weekend. It's fun to (10.) _____ the number of places you shop in by (11.) _____ new stores—even if you don't make a purchase. It's also (12.) _____ to return to stores you know well, where you know what the (13.) _____ selection is likely to be.

Most shoppers are looking for (14.) _____. Some people even check out all the aisles looking to see if the items they normally use have been marked down. Everyone loves finding that their favorite items are discounted to a lower price. A sale makes going to the (15.) _____ counter a happier event.

A recent (16.) _____ is shopping from the comfort of home. Many people like to shop by catalogs and over the Internet. You can get almost everything, from books to apparel, by mail, without having to leave your home.

Choose the underlined word or phrase that should be rewritten and rewrite it.

17. The growing trend toward shopping by mail is based in part on changing patterns of behave, such as the
    A   B
    perceived lack of time, expanded activity schedules, and increased desire for comfort.
                            C   D

    _____

18. Radica couldn't bearable the thought of wasting money, so she strictly adhered to a budget that allowed her to
                      A   B
    look only for merchandise available at a bargain.
                  C   D

    _____

19. By exploring secondhand shops along the canal, Jorge found a number of trendy fashions that allowed him to
        A   B
    expansion his wardrobe at a bargain rate.
    C   D

    _____

20. The sign above the supermarket checkout made it clear that the line was for customers with 15 itemize or
                                    A   B
    fewer; Ivy quickly counted her merchandise to determine if she complied with the mandatory limit.
                                    C   D

    _____

Lesson 17

Ordering Supplies

1. **diverse** adj., different; made up of distinct qualities.
   a. The Office Supply Warehouse offers a diverse range of office supplies.
   b. The diversity of staff in this office is amazing.

2. **enterprise** n., a business; a large project
   a. The new enterprise quickly established an account with the office supply store.
   b. This enterprise has become unmanageable and is beginning to lose money.

3. **essential** adj., indispensable, necessary
   a. Having Ann on this team is essential if we are to win the contract.
   b. A good record-keeping system is an essential component of inventory control.

4. **everyday** adj., routine, common, ordinary
   a. Though they are more expensive, these folders will withstand everyday wear and tear.
   b. This everyday routine of having to check inventory is boring.

5. **function** v., to perform tasks
   a. The daily functioning of this office has been compromised.
   b. She functioned as the director while Mr. Gibbs was away.

6. **maintain** v., to continue; to support, to sustain
   a. I've been maintaining a list of office supplies that are in greatest demand.
   b. Trying to maintain two different stockrooms is too much work.

7. **obtain** v., to acquire
   a. I've been trying to obtain a list of supplies from the administrator for three weeks now.
   b. The employee obtained the report from her supervisor.

8. **prerequisite** n., something that is required or necessary as a prior condition
   a. One of the prerequisites for this job is competence in bookkeeping.
   b. Here are the prerequisites that you need to purchase before coming to class.

9. **quality** n., a distinguishing characteristic; a degree of excellence
   a. The most important qualities we look for in a supplier are reliability and quick response.
   b. The quality of their clothes has fallen ever since they started using cheaper fabrics to make them.

10. **smooth** adj., without difficulties; deliberately polite and agreeable in order to win favor
    a. The transition to the new supplier went smoothly and there was no interruption in shipments.
    b. Her smooth manner won her the appreciation of the manager but not her colleagues.

11. **source** n., the origin
    a. I can't tell you the source of this information.
    b. The source of this rare pottery that we are selling in our shop is a small village in India.

12. **stationery** n., writing paper and envelopes
    a. We do not have enough stationery, so please order some more.
    b. The new stationery featured the company's logo in blue ink at the top of the page.

Short Conversations

Read the following conversations and see how the new words are used.

[M]   Do you know of a wholesale **source** for glassware?
[W]   As a matter of fact, I know of a supplier who sells top-**quality** wine glasses.
[M]   Well, I'm looking for a **diverse** range of glassware, but I can call to find out more information about how many different types of products they carry.

[W]   What is the **everyday** dress code for your office?
[M]   Since you're going to be **maintaining** inventory, casual slacks will be fine.
[W]   I'm happy to hear that because one of my **prerequisites** for taking this job is being able to wear casual clothing.

[W]   Where do we usually **obtain** our **stationery**? I need to place a special order immediately.
[M]   There's a small start-up **enterprise** across the street that we use and they're pretty quick.
[W]   That's good; a quick turnaround is **essential** in this case.

[M]   To ensure that the **everyday** routine for filling orders is followed, we're going to switch to a computerized system.
[W]   If that goes **smoothly**, this department should start functioning more efficiently.
[M]   That's what we're hoping for; it's part of our efforts to improve the **quality** of our services.

Word Families

verb	diversify	We are going to diversify our product line and start selling software as well as computers.
noun	diversity	The diversity of services that your company offers amazes me.
adjective	diverse	The wholesaler offered a more diverse range of computer accessories than I expected.

verb	function	He is still functioning as administrator until they find a replacement.
noun	function	The function was attended by all the leading scientists.
adjective	functional	This machine is not functional; we need to purchase a new one.

verb	maintain	Don't worry, I'll maintain the good relationships that you've established with our clients.
noun	maintainability	The maintainability of our second office is called into question by next year's budget cutbacks.
adjective	maintainable	This level of performance will not be maintainable without increasing salaries.

verb	smooth out	In order to smooth out the process of ordering supplies, we're going to use this new software to keep track of purchases and deliveries.
adverb	smoothly	The meeting went smoothly, and the contract was signed without any disagreements.
adjective	smooth	The vendor was so smooth on the phone that he had no difficulty in obtaining an appointment with the busy executive.

Choose the word that best completes the sentence.

1. The _____ of companies that now take orders over their Web sites is remarkable.
    - (A) diversify
    - (B) diverse
    - (C) diversity
    - (D) diversion

2. We need to have a spare copier since the only one that is _____ is on its last leg.
    - (A) functioned
    - (B) functions
    - (C) functional
    - (D) function

3. In order to _____ our lead in the market, we'll have to find a cheaper source of industrial supplies.
    - (A) maintainable
    - (B) maintain
    - (C) maintaining
    - (D) maintainability

4. She _____ changed the topic of conversation, thus preventing a disagreement between her colleagues from turning into an argument.
    - (A) smoothly
    - (B) smooth out
    - (C) smooth
    - (D) smoothed

Short Talk

Read the following passage and write the appropriate form of the new words in the blanks below.

diverse	everyday	obtained	smooth
enterprise	functioning	prerequisites	source
essential	maintaining	quality	stationery

All businesses, large and small, must maintain an inventory of supplies. In most business offices, the types of essential, but common, (5.) _____ items needed, including (6.) _____, pens, staples, and folders, are easily (7.) _____ from office supply stores that provide the most commonly used items under one roof. Some of these stores will even take orders by telephone with free delivery.

However, some businesses require a more (8.) _____ range of supplies. For example, businesses that ship their products usually need cartons, styrofoam peanuts, mailing tape, and shipping labels on hand at all times. Though these items may be available from general office supply stores, there are other specialty stores that only sell packing and shipping supplies.

No matter what the type of business, the office administrator is in charge of ordering supplies and (9.) _____ an inventory. Having the (10.) _____ supplies on hand at all times is a (11.) _____ for the (12.) _____ and efficient (13.) _____ of the (14.) _____. The administrator should try to locate the cheapest (15.) _____ of the supplies required, but also pay attention to the (16.) _____ of the goods.

Choose the underlined word or phrase that should be rewritten and rewrite it.

17. <u>Maintain</u> excellent relationships with clients is an <u>essential</u> component of the <u>quality</u> of service for which this

   A   B   C
    <u>enterprise</u> has become renowned.

   D

    _____

18. Our <u>everyday</u> supplier of <u>stationery</u> has gone out of business, so finding another <u>source</u> to replace him is

      A   B   C
    <u>essentially</u>.

   D

    _____

19. A <u>prerequisite</u> for the <u>everyday</u> functioning of this international <u>enterprise</u> is a tolerance for <u>diverse</u>.

   A   B   C   D

    _____

20. In order to ensure that operations continue to run <u>smooth</u> and without interruption while the office administra-

                                                        A
    tor is on leave, you will need to <u>obtain</u> a list of suppliers who can provide us with <u>essential</u> items, such as

                                    B   C
    <u>stationery</u>, on short notice.

   D

    _____

Shipping

1. **accurate** adj., exact; errorless
   a. He counted the boxes three times to ensure his that figure was accurate.
   b. The bar code reader not only saved the carrier time but also gave more accurate information than did handwritten documents.

2. **carrier** n., a person or business that transports passengers or goods
   a. Lou, our favorite carrier, takes extra care of our boxes marked fragile.
   b. Mr. Lau switched carriers in order to get a price savings on deliveries out of state.

3. **catalog** n., a list or itemized display; v., to make an itemized list of
   a. The upcoming fall catalog shows a number of items from Laos that Mr. Lau has never before been able to offer.
   b. Ellen cataloged the complaints according to severity.

4. **fulfill** v., to finish completely
   a. The engineers fulfilled a client's request for larger display screens.
   b. Her expectations were so high, we knew they would be hard to fulfill.

5. **integral** adj., necessary for completion
   a. Good customer relations is an integral component of any business.
   b. A dependable stream of inventory is integral to reliable shipping of orders.

6. **inventory** n., goods in stock; an itemized record of these goods
   a. The store closes one day a year so that the staff can take inventory of the stockroom.
   b. Their inventory had not changed much over the years, which made the customers feel bored.

7. **minimize** v., to reduce; to give less importance to
   a. The shipping staff minimized customer complaints by working overtime to deliver the packages quickly.
   b. To keep the customers happy and to minimize the effect of the carrier strike, we shipped orders directly to them.

8. **on hand** adj., available
   a. We had too much stock on hand, so we had a summer sale.
   b. The new employee will be on hand if we need more help with shipping orders.

9. **remember** v., to think of again; to retain in the memory
   a. I remembered the delivery clerk's name as soon as I got off the phone.
   b. I will remember the combination to the safe without writing it down.

10. **ship** v., to transport; to send
    a. Eva shipped the package carefully, since she knew the contents were made of glass.
    b. Very few customers think about how their packages will be shipped, and are seldom home when the packages arrive.

11. **sufficient** adj., as much as is needed
    a. The postage on that box is not sufficient to get it to its destination.
    b. Harriett did not order sufficient packing materials, so there was a delay in getting the boxes in the mail.

12. **supply** v., to make available for use; to provide; n., stock
    a. Gerald supplied the shipping staff with enough labels to last a year.
    b. By making better use of our supplies, we can avoid ordering until next month.

Short Conversations

Read the following conversations and see how the new words are used.

[M] Is the price quoted here **accurate**?
[W] Yes, it is. The price printed in the **catalog** is incorrect.
[M] I hope the salesperson **remembered** to alert the customer about the discrepancy.

[M] We are completely out of packing **supplies** and cannot prepare any more boxes today.
[W] It's your job to make certain that you have **sufficient** packing materials.
[M] I thought we had enough boxes **on hand**, but I was wrong.

[M] Why did we change **carriers**? I thought the previous company was fine.
[W] Mr. Sato is trying to **minimize** his costs, and the new company delivers for less money.
[M] I hope it was a good decision, since a dependable carrier is so **integral** to our customer satisfaction.

[M] How will you **fulfill** this request for immediate delivery since the delivery men are still on strike?
[W] I'll have to find another way to **ship** it. Maybe I'll just get in the car and drive the package to its destination.
[M] We can't afford to move all of our **inventory** that way.

Word Families

noun	accuracy	His firm was well known for its accuracy in predicting how long shipping would take.
adjective	accurate	Don't forget to keep accurate records; you will need them when you have your annual inventory.
adverb	accurately	The in-depth shipping records made it possible for Max to accurately estimate when the mixing bowls would arrive in the store.

verb	fulfill	We take pride in fulfilling customers' unusual requests,
gerund	fulfilling	Fulfilling the requirement of the contract will necessitate hiring extra staff.
noun	fulfillment	Fulfillment of duties can be tedious, but job satisfaction demands attention to detail.

verb	minimize	To minimize any potential risk of injury, all workers must wear closed-toed shoes in the stockroom.
adjective	minimal	Luckily, the leak from the roof did only minimal damage to the inventory in the stockroom.
noun	minimum	The minimum is $50; orders of less will be assessed a shipping charge.

verb	ship	We ship all orders within 24 hours of your phone call.
noun	shipper	We can rely on our shipper to pack large, fragile items carefully.
noun	shipment	The shipment from the supplier was short a number of items, so we complained.

Choose the word that best completes the sentence.

1. To assure that your order is _____ filled, it will be checked by a two-person team.
    (A) accurately
    (B) accurateness
    (C) accurate
    (D) accuracy

2. The suppliers _____ the terms of our agreement and are now our supplier of choice.
    (A) fulfilling
    (B) fulfillment
    (C) fulfilled
    (D) fulfill

3. Keeping customer complaints to a _____ is the job of everyone who works in the store.
    (A) minimum
    (B) minimal
    (C) minimize
    (D) minimally

4. To keep distribution costs low, we have selected only two _____ firms for the region.
    (A) ship
    (B) shipment
    (C) shipping
    (D) shipper

Short Talk

Read the following passage and write the appropriate form of the new words in the blanks below.

accurate	fulfill	minimize	shipping
carrier	integral	on hand	sufficient
catalog	inventory	remember	supplies

For Mr. Park's Asian housewares store, shipping is an (5.) _____ part of the business. Many customers need to send their purchases to friends or relatives who live far away. Other customers, who do not live near one of his stores, shop through a (6.) _____ and need their orders sent by mail.

(7.) _____ is, of course, the process of getting goods delivered to a customer, but it is more than just getting a box in the mail. Goods must be packaged carefully to (8.) _____ breakage and ensure that they arrive safely. Staff members must keep (9.) _____ records of the inventory shipped, so Mr. Park knows at all times the answers to these questions: When did a box leave the store? Who was the (10.) _____ who delivered it? When did it arrive at its destination? Customers will have confidence in Mr. Park's business when he can give quick and accurate answers.

The shipping process must be tied to the store's (11.) _____. When orders are taken, the shipping staff must know that there is (12.) _____ inventory of the product on hand to (13.) _____ the request. If a product is on order, the sales staff should advise the customer to expect a delay. When orders are shipped out, they must be deleted from the inventory records so Mr. Park knows exactly how many items are (14.) _____ in his warehouse. It takes a good computer program to keep track of the additions and deletions to the inventory.

Sales staff must (15.) _____ to charge for shipping and appropriate taxes. Mr. Park must keep good records on the cost of the shipping and packing materials and other (16.) _____, the cost of the carriers, and staff time to assess whether he is billing enough to cover his shipping expenses.

Choose the underlined word or phrase that should be rewritten and rewrite it.

17. Keeping an <u>accurately</u> record of <u>inventory</u> and the names of <u>carriers</u> used for <u>shipping</u> is crucial in business.
               A   **B**   **C**   **D**

     _____

18. The ability to <u>fulfillment</u> customer requests <u>accurately</u> and quickly is <u>integral</u> in running a <u>catalog</u> business.
                   A   **B**   **C**   **D**

     _____

19. Keeping a <u>sufficient</u> <u>supply</u> of packing materials <u>on hand</u> can <u>minimal</u> problems in getting products in the mail.
                A   **B**   **C**   **D**

     _____

20. Edwin did not <u>remembrance</u> to include a <u>catalog</u> in the package until after the request was <u>fulfilled</u> and the
                    A   **B**   **C**
     <u>carrier</u> had arrived.
     D

     _____

Lesson 19

Invoices

Words to learn

charge
compile
customer
discount
efficient
estimate
impose
mistake
order
prompt
rectify
terms

1. **charge** n., an expense or a cost; v., to demand payment
   a. The extra charge for gift wrapping your purchase will appear on your invoice.
   b. The customer service representative was responsible for telling all existing customers that higher prices would be charged next month.

2. **compile** v., to gather together from several sources
   a. I have compiled a list of the most popular items in our sales catalog
   b. The clerk is responsible for compiling the orders at the end of the day.

3. **customer** n., one who purchases a commodity or service
   a. Let's make sure all invoices sent to customers are kept in alphabetical order.
   b. As part of our customer satisfaction plan, let's offer a discount to customers who pay their invoices within a week.

4. **discount** n., a reduction in price; v., to reduce in price
   a. We are offering a 10 percent discount to all new customers.
   b. They discounted the price on the merchandise damaged in shipment.

5. **efficient** adj., acting or producing effectively with a minimum of waste or unnecessary effort
   a. The accountant was so efficient in processing the customer receipts that she had the job done before lunch.
   b. Electronic invoicing has helped us to be efficient.

6. **estimate** v., to approximate the amount or value of something; to form an opinion about something; n., an approximation
   a. We estimated our losses this year at about five thousand dollars.
   b. In the owner's estimation, the high level of customer satisfaction was an adequate measure of how well the company was doing.

7. **impose** v., to establish or apply as compulsory; to force upon others
   a. The company will impose a surcharge for any items returned.
   b. We should not impose upon our staff by requiring them to work on weekends.

8. **mistake** n., an error or a fault
   a. I made a mistake in adding up your bill and we overcharged you twenty dollars.
   b. It was a mistake thinking that my boss would be reasonable when I explained my situation to him.

9. **order** n., a request made to purchase something; v., to command or direct
   a. The customer placed an order for ten new chairs.
   b. We were ordered to take inventory immediately, so we could account for the missing items.

10. **prompt** adj., being on time or punctual, carried out without delay; n., a reminder or a cue
    a. I want a prompt reply to my letter of complaint.
    b. The supervisor gave the new sales agent a prompt when she forgot to mention the company's money-back guarantee.

11. **rectify** v., to set right or correct
    a. He rectified the problem by giving the customer credit for the unused items that she returned.
    b. Embarrassed at his behavior, he rectified the situation by writing a letter of apology.

12. **terms** n., conditions
    a. The terms of payment were clearly listed at the bottom of the invoice.
    b. The terms of the agreement required that items be fully paid for before they would be shipped.

Short Conversations

Read the following conversations and see how the new words are used.

[M]   I have compiled a list of office supplies we need to order immediately.
[W]   Don't worry, I'll deal with it **promptly**.
[M]   Please also check the supply room before you send out the **order**, just to be sure I didn't make any **mistakes**.

[W]   I had a computer expert **estimate** the cost of installing new order processing software on our office computers.
[M]   What will they **charge** for doing that?
[W]   It's going to cost us about five hundred dollars, but according to the **terms** of payment, there'll be a fifty dollar discount if we pay the full amount up front.

[W]   My invoice indicates that you **imposed** an extra charge for shipping the merchandise I ordered. I thought shipping was free.
[M]   It must be a **mistake**. I don't know how that happened but I'll credit the cost of shipping to your account.
[W]   Thanks for **rectifying** this matter so **promptly**.

[M]   Why has this **customer** incurred extra finance charges on her phone bill?
[W]   She made a mistake and thought the price had been **discounted**.
[W]   If you had been more **efficient**, and reviewed the checks upon receiving them, this would not have happened.

Word Families

verb	estimate	We need to estimate the number of work hours spent on this project.
noun	estimation	Clients prefer itemization to estimation on their invoices.
gerund	estimating	Estimating an order for office supplies is difficult because of the increased size of the staff.

verb	impose	The state intends to impose an additional tax on certain office equipment.
noun	imposition	Clients complained when they discovered the contractor's imposition of charges that should have been included under the terms of the contract.
adjective	imposing	The new clients found the company's reputation imposing.

verb	mistaken	The receptionist dialed the wrong number because she had mistaken a "7" for a "4" in the phone number she wrote down.
noun	mistake	The manager called the supplier as soon as he saw the mistake on his invoice.
adjective	mistaken	The director admitted that he was mistaken about the amount of the discount for payment received in 30 days.

verb	prompt	The computer cursor prompted the temporary employee about where to insert information on the billing form.
noun	promptness	Employers appreciate promptness in their employees.
adjective	prompt	I am happy to receive statements that thank me for prompt payment.

Choose the word that best completes the sentence.

1. Although _____ expenses works well when applying for a contract, clients appreciate itemization on their invoices.
   (A) estimate
   (B) estimator
   (C) estimated
   (D) estimation

2. The customers usually pay their invoices promptly in order to avoid the _____ of late charges.
   (A) imposed
   (B) imposingly
   (C) impose
   (D) imposition

3. The customer was angry at the _____ on her invoice.
   (A) mistakes
   (B) mistaken
   (C) mistakable
   (D) mistaking

4. The client would appreciate it if the invoice could be sent _____ so he can pay it before the end of the fiscal year.
   (A) promptly
   (B) promptness
   (C) prompted
   (D) prompt

Short Talk

Read the following passage and write the appropriate form of the new words in the blanks below.

charges	discount	imposed	promptly
compiled	efficient	mistake	rectified
customer	estimated	order	terms

Mail-order companies need to have an (5.) _____ process for invoicing and billing customers. When a customer places an (6.) _____, a list of items must be (7.) _____ and an invoice generated. The invoice will list the items purchased, along with the cost of each item, and the quantity desired. (8.) _____ that will be incurred in shipping the items to the (9.) _____ are also added to the invoice. Sometimes shipping charges are simply (10.) _____ based on the weight or value of the items ordered.

The invoice also shows the (11.) _____ of payment. Payment is usually due within 30 days. Extra charges are often (12.) _____ on overdue accounts. Many companies also offer a small (13.) _____ if invoices are paid promptly.

Sometimes items get damaged or lost in transit, or customers discover that the wrong items have been shipped by (14.) _____. They will usually call the company to have the problem (15.) _____. Such complaints should be dealt with (16.) _____. If an item is missing, a replacement will be sent, usually at no additional charge to the customer.

Choose the underlined word or phrase that should be rewritten and rewrite it.

17. I found a mistake in the estimated shipping costs that will have to be rectify before we process this order.
    A B   C   D

    _____

18. We have imposing additional charges on the customer because she did not pay her bill promptly upon receiving her order.
    A B   C   D

    _____

19. The terms of the agreement we imposed on them gave us a discounting if we paid all charges within 15 days.
    A B C D

    _____

20. The customer service representative was very efficiently; she promptly dealt with any mistakes so as not to upset the company's customers.
    A B C D

    _____

Lesson 20

Inventory

Words to learn

adjust
automatic
crucial
discrepancy
disturb
liability
reflect
run
scan
subtract
tedious
verify

1. **adjust** v., to change in order to match or fit; to cause to correspond
    a. Adil adjusted the quantity of products listed in the computer to match the quantity found in the stockroom.
    b. The stockroom clerk adjusted the cooking pots on the shelf so they would be easier to count during inventory.

2. **automatic** adj., operating independently
    a. The automatic foot massager was so popular, we couldn't keep it in stock.
    b. The lights in the store are on an automatic timer, so they turn off one hour after the store closes.

3. **crucial** adj., extremely significant or important
    a. Knowing how many products we have in stock is crucial to our shipping procedures.
    b. Inventory is a crucial process and must be taken seriously by all staff.

4. **discrepancy** n., a divergence or disagreement
    a. The discrepancy between the two counts was easily explained.
    b. Unless you catch the error immediately, the discrepancy gets entered into the computer and becomes very difficult to correct.

5. **disturb** v., to interfere with; to interrupt
    a. Let's see how many products we can count in advance of inventory so we disturb fewer customers.
    b. I hope I'm not disturbing you, but I need to ask you to move so I can record the products behind you.

6. **liability** n., an obligation; a responsibility
    a. The store's insured liability protects against theft and damaged inventory.
    b. The slippery steps were a terrible liability for the store.

7. **reflect** v., to give back a likeness
    a. It's very important that the quantity on the printout reflects the number of items on the shelf.
    b. An inaccurate inventory count reflects poorly on the store.

8. **run** v., to operate
    a. As long as the computer is running, you can keep adding new data.
    b. We'll be running inventory next weekend, so don't make any other plans.

9. **scan** v., to look over quickly
    a. The computer's optical disk scanned in the price and ordering information.
    b. Jasmine quickly scanned the list to see if any information was missing.

10. **subtract** v., to take away; to deduct
    a. Once you ring up an item, the computer automatically subtracts it from the inventory log.
    b. Whoever did the inventory forgot to subtract the items that arrived damaged and were never put into the stockroom.

11. **tedious** adj., tiresome by reason of length, slowness, or dullness; boring
    a. This may be tedious work but you will be glad the inventory is accurate when you hit the busy holiday sales season.
    b. Counting merchandise all weekend is the most tedious job I can imagine.

12. **verify** v., to prove the truth of
    a. I can't verify the accuracy of these numbers, since I was not present for inventory weekend.
    b. The inventory process verifies that you have accounted for all the items that are supposed to be in the store.

Short Conversations

Read the following conversations and see how the new words are used.

[M] This platter is missing its price tag and bar code. I'll just **scan** in the price tag of something else that's the same price.
[W] Don't do that. Then the inventory won't **reflect** this sale accurately and the counts will be off.
[W] I didn't realize that such accuracy was so **crucial**.

[M] The computer says we have three of these bedspreads left. Can you go to the stockroom and **verify** that, please?
[W] If the computer says we have three, why would there be any **discrepancy**?
[M] Sometimes there are **adjustments** to the inventory and I don't want to tell this lady we have a bedspread if we are out of stock.

[M] Counting everything in the stockroom by hand is so **tedious**. I can't believe we are doing this.
[W] It's dull and dirty, but very important. The store is **liable** for every product in here, so the count must be accurate.
[M] Isn't the computer's **running** total accurate enough?

[M] Every time you make a sale, the computer **subtracts** the product from the inventory.
[W] I'm glad that's an **automatic** process.
[M] Twice a year, we close the store to do a physical count. We try not to **disturb** our customers any more often than that.

Word Families

verb	adjust	After you've verified the quantities in the stockroom, I'll adjust the numbers in the computer.
noun	adjustment	While the adjustments are being made to the computer inventory, the computer will be off-line and unavailable for use.
adjective	adjustable	The height of the shelves is adjustable, which makes it easier to reach and count the merchandise.

noun	automation	Computers have brought a heightened level of automation into the retail industry.
adjective	automatic	The automatic updating of the inventory is convenient, but always a day behind.
adverb	automatically	After every cash register transaction, the computer automatically updates the inventory record.

verb	disturb	Count as many of the items on the salesroom floor as you can without disturbing the customers.
noun	disturbance	After considering all the options, Ellen decided that closing the store a day to do the annual inventory would cause the least amount of disturbance for customers.
adverb	disturbingly	The computer count and the physical count were disturbingly incongruous, which distressed the store manager.

verb	reflect	The numbers in the computer log should accurately reflect the actual numbers available on the shelf or in the warehouse.
noun	reflection	Upon reflection, the supply clerk decided that there was an error in the inventory.
noun	reflector	Reflectors were attached to the corners of the shelves to alert the clerks that the shelf edges were sharp.

Choose the word that best completes the sentence.

1. The computer's inventory figures will be considered inaccurate until the store manager enters the data from the physical count and _____ the figures.
   (A) adjustment
   (B) adjusts
   (C) adjustable
   (D) adjusted

2. Although computers are essential, some of the inventory control cannot be performed _____, but must be done by physically counting the merchandise.
   (A) automatically
   (B) automatic
   (C) automation
   (D) automated

3. Do not _____ the staff when they are counting the items; they need to concentrate.
   (A) disturb
   (B) disturbance
   (C) disturbing
   (D) disturbingly

4. Having an accurate inventory count is a good _____ on a competent store manager.
   (A) reflectively
   (B) reflective
   (C) reflect
   (D) reflection

Short Talk

Read the following passage and write the appropriate form of the new words in the blanks below.

adjusted	discrepancies	reflect	subtracts
automatically	disturbances	running	tedious
crucial	liability	scanning	verifies

In a retail business, inventory has multiple meanings. Inventory means all the goods that a company has on hand or available to it in a warehouse. Inventory also means the process by which the business (5.) _____ the number of goods. An accurate account of the inventory available is (6.) _____. The amount of stock is a (7.) _____ because it is already owned by the business.

Taking an inventory is a physical count of the inventory holdings. Today, almost every business keeps a (8.) _____ inventory count by having its sales records tied by computer to its inventory. When a customer makes a purchase, the computer system tied to the register (9.) _____ the purchase from the inventory records. If a customer makes a return or an exchange, the inventory numbers will be (10.) _____ by the computer (11.) _____. That's often why (12.) _____ the barcode is so important in stores. If merchandise is broken or damaged in the stockroom or on the sales floor, the manager will ask the sales and stock help to change the stock holdings to (13.) _____ the loss.

As good as the computer records may be, they are just an estimate. At least once a year, most businesses do an actual physical count of the inventory. This process can be (14.) _____ but it is necessary as there are always (15.) _____ between what the computer says you own and what your physical count says. Often stores close for a day, or at least close early, so that staff can perform the inventory without (16.) _____.

Choose the underlined word or phrase that should be rewritten and rewrite it.

17. In order to <u>verification</u> our inventory records without <u>disturbing</u> our customers, we will attempt to resolve any
              A   B
    known <u>discrepancies</u> in the records and make <u>adjustments</u> while the store is still open.
           C   D

    _____

18. It is <u>crucial</u> to keep an accurate <u>run</u> total of items sold or damaged to avoid <u>adjusting</u> for any <u>discrepancies</u>
        A   B   C   D
    during a physical count.

    _____

19. Once you <u>scan</u> the bar code, the computer <u>automatically</u> <u>subtraction</u> the sold product from the inventory,
            A   B   C
    unless, of course, it is a return, in which case the <u>adjustment</u> is an addition.
                                               D

    _____

20. Doing a physical count of the inventory is a <u>tedious</u> job, but it is <u>crucial</u> to make sure the computer records
                                            A   B
    accurately <u>reflection</u> our holdings; this prevents any <u>discrepancies</u> from popping up later.
         C   D

    _____

Word Review #4   Lessons 16–20 Purchasing

Choose the word that best completes the sentence.

1. Most merchants are happy to find any way to
   _____ their customer base.
   (A) expand
   (B) expanding
   (C) expansion
   (D) expanded

2. All fashion _____ have a limited life span.
   (A) trend
   (B) trends
   (C) trendy
   (D) trending

3. It is a poorly run office that does not
   _____ adequate office supplies.
   (A) maintain
   (B) maintained
   (C) maintaining
   (D) maintenance

4. Sometimes office policy doesn't allow the company
   to _____ less expensive supplies when they
   are available from someone other than a preferred
   provider.
   (A) obtain
   (B) obtained
   (C) obtaining
   (D) obtainable

5. A supplier who has chronic trouble _____ his
   obligations to a customer will quickly lose
   customers.
   (A) fulfill
   (B) fulfills
   (C) fulfilling
   (D) fulfillment

6. To _____ disruption, buyers should order
   well ahead of need.
   (A) minimum
   (B) minimal
   (C) minimize
   (D) minimally

7. It is wise to begin by _____ an inventory
   of equipment on hand.
   (A) compile
   (B) compiling
   (C) compiler
   (D) compilation

8. If the provider does not meet his client's demand,
   he should _____ the problem as soon as
   possible.
   (A) rectify
   (B) rectifier
   (C) rectifiable
   (D) rectification

9. If some supplies show a steady rise in consump-
   tion, the office manager should make an appropri-
   ate _____ in his standard order.
   (A) adjust
   (B) adjuster
   (C) adjusting
   (D) adjustment

10. The office manager should also ascertain
    whether the inventory of supplies properly
    _____ the volume of use in the office
    (A) reflect
    (B) reflects
    (C) reflecting
    (D) reflection

Choose the underlined word or phrase that should be rewritten and rewrite it.

11. A wise <u>customer</u> will <u>efficiency</u> <u>catalog</u> all ordered <u>items</u> as they are received.
         A   B   C   D

    _____

12. Some <u>bargaining</u> hunters demonstrate unusual <u>behavior</u> as they <u>explore</u> the range of <u>merchandise</u>.
          A   B   C   D

    _____

13. The first priority should be to find a <u>source</u> for <u>essentially</u> <u>everyday</u> supplies such as <u>stationery</u>.
                             A   B   C   D

    _____

14. <u>Remember</u> to check the <u>accurate</u> of the invoice of <u>supplies</u> provided with each <u>shipment</u>.
      A   B   C   D

    _____

15. An <u>efficient</u> office will have someone check each invoice for such <u>mistakes</u> as whether the appropriate
         A   B
    <u>discounting</u> has been applied to the <u>charges</u>.
       C   D

    _____

16. However <u>tediously</u>, a <u>crucial</u> factor in maintaining inventory is to keep a <u>running</u> total of supplies used and to
            A   B   C
    <u>verify</u> that they are being used in the office.
     D

    _____

17. One should also <u>scan</u> the invoices for <u>discrepancies</u>, and be sure that overcharges are <u>prompt</u> <u>subtracted</u>.
                 A   B   C   D

    _____

18. The <u>diversity</u> of supplies ordered demands an <u>efficient</u> and <u>functioning</u> system of <u>qualities</u> control.
        A   B   C   D

    _____

19. A <u>mandatory</u> checking system, <u>strict</u> enforced, will ensure that the <u>inventory</u> <u>on hand</u> is adequate for efficiently
      A   B   C   D
    running the office.

    _____

20. Other aspects of ordering supplies include <u>estimating</u> whether the use of specific items should increase or
                                                       A
    decrease, or whether furniture is <u>comfortable</u> enough not to be a <u>liability</u> by <u>disturb</u> smooth operation of the
                                      B   C   D
    office.

    _____

Lesson 21

Banking

Words to learn

accept
balance
borrow
cautious
deduct
dividend
down payment
mortgage
restriction
signature
take out
transaction

1. **accept** v., to receive; to respond favorably
   a. The receptionist accepted the package from the courier.
   b. Without hesitating, she accepted the job of teller.

2. **balance** n., the remainder; v. to compute the difference between credits and debits of an account
   a. His healthy bank balance showed a long habit of savings.
   b. It took him over an hour to balance his checkbook.

3. **borrow** v., to use temporarily
   a. Do you want to borrow a pen?
   b. The couple borrowed money from the bank to buy a home.

4. **cautious** adj., careful, wary
   a. Chen's credit history was not favorable, so the bank was cautious about lending him more money.
   b. The bank manager was cautious when giving out information to people she did not know.

5. **deduct** v., to take away from a total; to subtract
   a. Before computing his taxes, Christophe remembered to deduct allowable home improvement expenses.
   b. By deducting the monthly fee from her checking account, Yi was able to make her account balance.

6. **dividend** n., a share in a distribution
   a. The stockholders were outraged when their quarterly dividends were so small.
   b. The dividend was calculated and distributed to the group.

7. **down payment** n., an initial partial payment
   a. By making a large down payment, the couple saved a great deal in mortgage interest.
   b. Karl was disappointed when the real estate agent told him he needed a larger down payment on the house.

8. **mortgage** n., the amount due on a property; v., to borrow money with your house as collateral
   a. Due to low interest rates, Sheila moved quickly to find a good deal on a mortgage.
   b. Hiram mortgaged his home to get extra money to invest in his business.

9. **restriction** n., a limitation
   a. There is a strict restriction on the number of free withdrawals a customer can make on his account each month.
   b. All these restrictions are limiting.

10. **signature** n., the name of a person written by the person
    a. Once we have your signature, the contract will be complete.
    b. The customer's signature was kept on file for identification purposes.

11. **take out** v., withdraw; remove
    a. My checking account allows me to take out money at any bank branch without a fee.
    b. They took out the chairs in the bank lobby so now there is no place to sit.

12. **transaction** n., a business deal
    a. Banking transactions will appear on your monthly statement.
    b. The most common transactions can be made from your personal computer.

Short Conversations

Read the following conversations and see how the new words are used.

[M] I need to cash a check. What kinds of identification do you **accept**?

[W] If you have an account with this bank, a photo ID, like a driver's license, is enough.

[M] I've lost my driver's license, but my **signature** is on file. Is that enough?

[M] Here's the contract for your loan. It's several pages long.

[W] It says here that the bank can automatically **deduct** the monthly payment from my checking account.

[M] That's right; all you'll need to do is to make certain that you always have enough in your **balance** to cover the automatic **deduction**.

[M] Let's look for a brochure that describes in detail the **mortgage** application process.

[W] If we save more money toward a **down payment**, we'll reduce the amount we need to borrow.

[M] It's good to be **cautious** when **borrowing** money. Often you can **borrow** money at a better rate when you have a larger **down payment**.

[M] I'm going to **take out** some money from my account and put it into a certificate of deposit (CD).

[W] That's a good idea. The **dividend** paid by a CD is better than that paid by a savings account.

[M] Yes, but that's why there are more **restrictions** on withdrawals and other **transactions** you can make with a CD.

Word Families

verb	accept	The bank will not accept a student ID as a valid form of identification.
noun	acceptance	The bank's acceptance of checks allows extra time for out-of-state checks to clear before they are credited to your account.
adjective	acceptable	Shorter banking hours would not be acceptable to many customers, who might close their accounts as a result.

verb	deduct	Remember to deduct the monthly bank fee from your statement.
noun	deductible	Taxes and health insurance payments are what we call deductibles because they are deducted from your paycheck.
noun	deduction	Deductions are made electronically every month and will appear on your statement.

verb	sign	Once you have signed the mortgage contract, the bank will make a check payable to you.
noun	sign	The sign in the bank's lobby announces their rates for savings accounts and for loans.
noun	signature	Your signature can be electronically recorded to be verified later.

verb	restrict	The bank's policies restrict the number of deductions you can make from your account without a penalty.
noun	restriction	The restrictions on who was eligible for a mortgage made it impossible for many low-income families to borrow money.
adjective	restricted	Information about your account is confidential and its use without your permission is restricted.

Choose the word that best completes the sentence.

1. I'm going to call the bank manager ahead of time to make certain that she will _____ a personal check to start a new account.
   (A) accept
   (B) accepted
   (C) acceptance
   (D) acceptable

2. Every month my automatic car loan payment shows up as a _____ on my monthly statement.
   (A) deduct
   (B) deduction
   (C) deducting
   (D) deducted

3. There is a counter in the bank lobby where customers can _____ their documents.
   (A) signing
   (B) signed
   (C) sign
   (D) signature

4. The number of withdrawals at no charge from your savings account is _____ to three.
   (A) restricting
   (B) restricted
   (C) restrict
   (D) restriction

Short Talk

Read the following passage and write the appropriate form of the new words in the blanks below.

accept	cautious	down payment	signature
balance	deductions	mortgages	take out
borrow	dividend	restrict	transact

Banks are not only places in which to save money or to (5.) _____ your financial business, but also institutions from which people can (6.) _____ money. Every day, people look to banks for loans, such as (7.) _____ for new homes. A loan is essentially a contract that binds the lender to a schedule of payments, so both parties should be (8.) _____ and not enter into the arrangement without thinking. Banks will look at such factors as how much people have saved towards (9.) _____ in determining whether to make a loan.

Banks have different kinds of accounts. Some pay high quarterly (10.) _____. Some accounts even severely (11.) _____ the number of times, if any, that you can access your account, or the amount of cash you can (12.) _____.

Today, electronic banking can be used to check the (13.) _____ on an account, or to see if automatic (14.) _____ have been made. This can all be done from your home or office computer. When you go to the bank, be sure to bring identification. Usually a bank will only (15.) _____ a photo ID; a (16.) _____ is not a valid ID.

Choose the underlined word or phrase that should be rewritten and rewrite it.

17. The <u>cautious</u> bank teller reluctantly <u>accepting</u> Charles's company ID card as valid identification, and he was
    _A   _B
    able to <u>take out</u> half of the <u>balance</u> of his savings account.
    _C   _D

    _____

18. Certain investment accounts are now earning higher <u>dividends</u> than before with fewer <u>restrictive</u> on the length
    _A   _B
    of deposit, number of <u>transactions</u>, or amount of <u>balance</u> in the account.
    _C   _D

    _____

19. The <u>mortgage</u> application clearly states that monthly <u>payments</u> will be directly <u>deduction</u> from the <u>balance</u> of
    _A   _B   _C   _D
    your in-house checking account.

    _____

20. The <u>restrictions</u> on <u>mortgages</u> available at low interest rates made Chen more <u>caution</u> about taking out his
    _A   _B   _C
    savings before they grew into a sizable <u>down payment</u>.
    _D

    _____

Lesson 22

Accounting

1. **accounting** n., the recording and gathering of financial information for a company
   a. Good accounting is needed in all businesses.
   b. Accounting for expenses is time-consuming.

2. **accumulate** v., to gather; to collect
   a. They have accumulated more than enough information.
   b. The bills started to accumulate after the secretary quit.

3. **asset** n., something of value
   a. The company's assets are worth millions of dollars.
   b. A sophisticated accounting system is an asset to a company.

4. **audit** n., a formal examination of financial records; v., to examine the financial records of a company
   a. No one looks forward to an audit by the government.
   b. The independent accountants audited the company's books.

5. **budget** n., a list of probable expenses and income for a given period
   a. The department head was pleased that she received a 10 percent increase in her budget.
   b. If the development group doesn't cut back expenses, they'll be over the budget.

6. **build up** v., to increase over time
   a. The firm has built up a solid reputation for itself.
   b. Be careful, your inventory of parts is building up.

7. **client** n., a customer
   a. We must provide excellent services for our clients, otherwise we will lose them to our competition.
   b. Maintaining close contact with clients keeps the account managers aware of changing needs.

8. **debt** n., something owed, as in money or goods
   a. The company has been very careful and is slowly digging itself out of debt.
   b. The banks are worried about your increasing debt.

9. **outstanding** adj., still due; not paid or settled
   a. That client still has several outstanding bills.
   b. Clients with outstanding bills will not receive further service until the bills are paid.

10. **profitable** adj., advantageous; beneficial
    a. Our accounting department has helped us to become more profitable.
    b. The new manager was unable to make the company profitable.

11. **reconcile** v., to make consistent
    a. The client uses his bank statements to reconcile his accounts.
    b. The accountant found the error when she reconciled the account.

12. **turnover** n., the number of times a product is sold and replaced or an employee leaves and another employee is hired
    a. We have to add another production shift to keep up with the high turnover rate.
    b. The overseas branch has much lower employee turnover than does domestic operations.

Short Conversations

Read the following conversations and see how the new words are used.

[M] Have you seen our **budget** for next year?
[W] How do they expect us to stay on track and meet our goals with such a small **budget**?
[M] We'll have to come up with something to increase our **assets**, or else we'll be out of a job!

[M] I'm going to see my **client** today. I'll be back at 4:30.
[W] Is this the **client** that you are trying to save from all of his **debt**?
[M] That's the one! How he **accumulated** so much **debt** in such a short period of time, I'll never understand.

[M] The **auditor** needs a list of all the **outstanding** accounts in order to **reconcile** the figures.
[W] Those **accounts** wouldn't be **outstanding** if we had had the personnel to follow up and collect the monies due.
[M] The **turnover** in that department is amazing; why don't workers stay longer?

[M] **Accounting** firms have undergone significant changes in the last decade.
[W] That's true, many have **built** up substantial consulting practices.
[M] Big salaries, big bonuses: they are more **profitable** than ever!

Word Families

noun	accountant	The accountant was precise and hardworking.
noun	accounting	Accounting is a popular field of study.
noun	account	The client closed his bank account and withdrew all of his money.

verb	accumulate	The owner's goal was to accumulate as much wealth as possible.
noun	accumulation	The accumulation of goods may lead to an inventory problem.
adjective	accumulated	The sum of all the accumulated resources equals your total assets.

verb	budget	There was no travel expense budgeted for the editorial department.
noun	budget	The boss asked for input on next year's budget.
adjective	budgetary	Due to budgetary constraints, we cannot hire additional staff at this time.

verb	profit	The engineer will profit from the successful introduction of the new product.
noun	profit	The profits exceeded all expectations.
adjective	profitable	Marketing is the most profitable department this year.

Choose the word that best completes the sentence.

1. All the employees will benefit if the company's _____ continue to increase.
   (A) profited
   (B) profitable
   (C) profits
   (D) profiting

2. The account manager has _____ a tremendous amount of wealth in a very short time.
   (A) accumulated
   (B) accumulation
   (C) accumulating
   (D) accumulates

3. At the end of next week, all the division heads will meet to present one consolidated _____.
   (A) budgeting
   (B) budget
   (C) budgeted
   (D) budgets

4. The firm's _____ studied finance and business administration.
   (A) account
   (B) accounting
   (C) accounted
   (D) accountant

Short Talks

Read the following passage and write the appropriate form of the new words in the blanks below.

accounting	audited	clients	profitable
accumulated	budget	debt	reconcile
assets	building up	outstanding	turnover

Accounting information is pulled together or (5.) _____ to help someone make decisions. A manager must come up with a (6.) _____ to help control expenses. A retail store owner realizes that her (7.) _____ have (8.) _____ bills. A restaurant owner wants to know if it is (9.) _____ to serve lunch. A nonprofit organization is being (10.) _____ by the government. All of these people and organizations could use the services of an accountant.

Accountants and (11.) _____ systems help a company stay on track. They raise flags when expenses are (12.) _____ and keep an eye on the (13.) _____ of inventory. They (14.) _____ their clients' accounts to ensure that their clients' records are correct. Good accounting systems allow managers to come up with ways to improve their business.

The accountant prepares information for both for internal and external use. Financial statements provide a quick look into the life of a business. They show how much (15.) _____ the company is carrying and how much its (16.) _____ are worth. The outside world uses this information to judge the health of the company.

Choose the underlined word or phrase that should be rewritten and rewrite it.

17. <u>Accountants</u> audit and <u>reconciliation</u> their <u>clients'</u> <u>accounts</u> at the end of each quarter.
        A   B   C   D

    _____

18. The <u>accumulated</u> of <u>debt</u> may be the result of a <u>build up</u> of <u>outstanding</u> payments.
              A   B   C   D

    _____

19. The <u>auditors</u> have analyzed the company's <u>budget</u> and have come up with a list of questions concerning the
        A   B
    <u>assets</u>, revenue, and <u>profitable</u>.
      C   D

    _____

20. Because of slow <u>turnover</u> and <u>outstanding</u> payments, the projected <u>budgetary</u> was inaccurate and the <u>profit</u>
                 A   B   C   D
    margin less than expected.

    _____

Lesson 23

Investments

1. **aggressive** adj., competitive; assertive
   a. The director's aggressive position on investing was frowned upon by the Board of Directors.
   b. Wall Street is a very aggressive atmosphere where only the strong survive.

2. **attitude** n., a feeling about something or someone
   a. The new fund manager's attitude changed quickly after the first big downturn in the market.
   b. Each investor should assess his or her own attitude toward investment.

3. **commitment** n., a promise
   a. The stockbroker's commitment to his clients is remarkable.
   b. The president made a commitment to his employees that they would be given shares of stock if the company was successful.

4. **conservative** adj., cautious, restrained
   a. Her conservative strategy paid off over the years.
   b. Generally, older people should be more conservative in their investing than younger people.

5. **fund** n., an amount of money for something specific; v., to provide money for
   a. He will have access to his trust fund when he is 21 years old.
   b. The company will fund the trip to the conference.

6. **invest** v., to put money into a business or activity with the hope of making more money; to put effort into something
   a. The chief financial officer invested in the stock at a very good time.
   b. Don't invest all of your time in just one project.

7. **long-term** adj., involving or extending over a long period
   a. The CEO's long-term goal was to increase the return on investment.
   b. Over the long term, unemployment is expected to remain steady.

8. **portfolio** n., a list of investments
   a. Investors are advised to have diverse portfolios.
   b. The investor's portfolio consisted of blue chip company stocks and government bonds.

9. **pull out** v., to withdraw, to stop participating; n., a withdrawal, removal
   a. His advisor suggested that she pull out her investments in the troubled country.
   b. The pull out of the bank has left the company without financing.

10. **resource** n., assets; valuable things
    a. If you don't invest in petroleum resources now, you will find that the stock prices will get away from you.
    b. The company's most valuable resource was its staff.

11. **return** n., the amount of money gained as profit
    a. The 44 percent return on the new stock was far more than the stockbroker had anticipated.
    b. Some investors are satisfied with a 15 percent return, while others want to see a much larger return.

12. **wise** adj., knowledgeable; able to offer advice based on experience
    a. Are you sure it was a wise decision to pull out all of your investments?
    b. The president, after 45 years on the job, was known as a wise investor.

Short Conversations

Read the following conversations and see how the new words are used.

[M] In order to minimize risks, investors should maintain a diverse **portfolio** by putting their money into various industry investments.
[W] You mean, we should invest in natural **resources**, like oil, and manufacturing industries, like pharmaceuticals, for example?
[M] Perhaps. Unless you are very **aggressive**, you don't want to have all your eggs in one basket.

[M] How did you make such **wise** and profitable investments?
[W] I never **invested** because I needed the money, so there was always less pressure.
[M] I hope my **returns** will be as good as yours some day.

[M] The experts seem to be changing their **attitude** about the stock market every day.
[W] You're right, one day I think I should **pull** my money **out** of foreign markets and the next day I'm not so sure.
[M] You know what they say: over the **long term,** things tend to equal out and become more balanced.

[M] I'm going to call human **resources** to change my level of contribution to my pension plan. I **committed** 5 percent of my salary but want to increase it.
[W] Are you happy with the **fund** that you are contributing to?
[M] It's a rather **conservative** fund, but it's exceeding all of my expectations!

Word Families

verb	commit	I'm committed to keeping the money in my pension fund until I retire.
noun	commitment	The employee's commitment to working hard and saving her money was commendable.
adjective	noncommittal	I had hoped that the discussion would yield a definite answer from them, but they were noncommittal.

verb	invest	The company has been successful because it has invested wisely in its resources.
noun	investment	The CFO is responsible for corporate investment.
noun	investor	The fall in the stock market shook up the investors.

verb	return	I wish I could return to the days where investing was simple.
noun	returns	Our returns on our investments exceeded expectations.
adjective	returnable	The merchandise is returnable as long as you have your receipt.

noun	wisdom	Common wisdom is to place your money in a variety of investments.
adjective	wise	The wise investor does her homework before parting with her money.
adverb	wisely	She planned her retirement wisely and was able to retire to her summer house.

Choose the word that best completes the sentence.

1. A good financial analyst will advise investors on strategies that will generate higher _____.
   (A) returned
   (B) returning
   (C) returns
   (D) returnable

2. After months of study and research, the _____ decided to put his money into new facilities and materials.
   (A) investor
   (B) investment
   (C) investing
   (D) invested

3. All employees are encouraged to _____ a percentage of their earnings to the retirement fund.
   (A) committed
   (B) commit
   (C) commitment
   (D) committing

4. Is it _____ to consider funding a new project when we haven't even seen the returns from the last one?
   (A) wisdom
   (B) wisest
   (C) wisely
   (D) wise

Short Talks

Read the following passage and write the appropriate form of the new words in the blanks below.

aggressive	committed	long-term	resources
attitude	fund	portfolio	return
conservative	invest	pull out	wise

Investment is a common, everyday occurrence. Companies (5.) _____ time and money in finding and training their employees. Employees invest in their own training and education. Financial investment takes place at a corporate level and at an individual level. Whether an individual or a company, a decision must be made on the percentage of (6.) _____ to have invested and the percentage to have in cash.

To avoid making stupid decisions, many people use financial advisors. Financial advisors help individuals and corporations make (7.) _____ investment decisions. What kind of portfolio should be maintained? What should be in this (8.) _____. At what point should an investor pull back or (9.) _____ of the market? What kind of (10.) _____ should the investor realistically expect? How much risk can an investor take (both emotionally and financially)? Investors who are (11.) _____ for the (12.) _____ can more easily weather the ups and downs of a market. As one analyst commented, "If you're staying awake at night thinking about the stock market, you probably have too much invested."

Many employees have retirement plans at work. They decide what level of contribution to make to a certain (13.) _____. These decisions and large company decisions depend to a large degree on (14.) _____. Is the decision maker (15.) _____ or (16.) _____? That attitude often depends on the age of the investor or on the stage and the needs of the business.

Choose the underlined word or phrase that should be rewritten and rewrite it.

17. The business woman decided to <u>invest</u> in <u>markets</u> that had a history of excellent <u>returning</u> in the <u>long term</u>.
                                  A   B   C   D

    _____

18. The investor credited her stockbroker for changing her <u>attitude</u> and renewing her <u>committed</u> to her less than
                                                    A   B
    <u>conservative</u> <u>portfolio</u>.
       C   D

    _____

19. The computer company, known for its <u>aggression</u> behavior, took a rather <u>conservative</u> position toward
                                            A   B
    <u>investing</u> in new <u>resources</u>.
       C   D

    _____

20. The <u>wise</u> <u>investor</u> knows when to <u>pulling</u> out and when to increase contributions to a <u>fund</u>.
        A   B   C   D

    _____

Lesson 24

Taxes

1. **calculate** v., to figure out; to compute
   a. You should calculate how much the party will cost.
   b. Mr. Mead calculated that leasing a car was cheaper than buying one.

2. **deadline** n., a time by which something must be finished
   a. The deadline was too tight and they couldn't finish the project.
   b. My best work is done with strict deadlines.

3. **file** v., to enter into public record; n., a group of documents or information about a person or an event
   a. After years of unhappiness, she filed for divorce.
   b. The police have a large file on the suspected thief.

4. **fill out** v., to complete
   a. Fill out the form and turn it in at the front desk.
   b. The company had over two hundred people fill out applications for the job.

5. **give up** v., to quit; to stop
   a. I gave up smoking last year.
   b. Ms. Gomez is so optimistic that she never gives up.

6. **joint** adj., together; shared
   a. We opened a joint bank account five years ago.
   b. The couple no longer files joint tax returns.

7. **owe** v., to have a debt; to be obligated to pay
   a. I'm sorry. I owe you an explanation.
   b. As the business grew, the owner paid back loans and owed less money.

8. **penalty** n., a punishment; a consequence
   a. Anyone who pays less than they should in taxes will face a penalty.
   b. Penalties are imposed to discourage underpayment of taxes by adding a percentage to the taxes you already owe.

9. **prepare** v., to make ready
   a. It takes hours to prepare my taxes.
   b. Are you prepared for the challenges of this new job?

10. **refund** n., the amount paid back; v., to give back
    a. With the tax refund, we bought two plane tickets.
    b. The government will refund any money that you overpaid.

11. **spouse** n., a husband or wife
    a. You may invite your spouse to the company party.
    b. His spouse was a classmate of mine in high school.

12. **withhold** v., to keep from; to refrain from
    a. My employer withholds money from each paycheck to apply toward my income taxes.
    b. The promotion was withheld until the allegations could be investigated.

Short Conversations

Read the following conversations and see how the new words are used.

[M]   Who **files** the taxes in your family?
[W]   Oh, my **spouse** always does them, although I would prefer to.
[M]   Well don't **give up**. Maybe one year he will let you do them.

[M]   Thanks for the information on the project. When is the **deadline**?
[W]   We need to **file** the forms by the beginning of next week.
[M]   I'll have Jack start to **prepare** them right away.

[M]   Welcome to the company! You need to **fill out** these tax forms.
[W]   How much money should I **withhold** from my paychecks?
[M]   If you want a tax **refund** at the end of the year, **withhold** as much as you can!

[M]   I'm working on my accuracy this tax season. I want to do my taxes quickly but also want to avoid **penalties**.
[W]   That's smart. Will you file a **joint** return?
[M]   Probably. I'll **owe** less money if I file **jointly**.

Word Families

verb	penalize	The government will penalize taxpayers who try to evade paying their fair share of taxes.
noun	penalty	For every dollar you owe in overdue taxes, a 10 percent penalty is imposed.
adjective	penal	Tax evasion is a penal offense.

verb	calculate	The young man tries to calculate his expenses every month.
noun	calculation	The calculation is no more difficult than high school math.
noun	calculator	In order to avoid making addition and subtraction errors, I suggest you use a calculator.

verb	owe	I owe you $100. Don't let me forget to pay you back!
noun	owner	The owner of the firm is also my neighbor.
gerund	owing	Owing to his financial situation, we do not want to do business with him.

verb	prepare	Most people wait until the last minute to prepare their tax returns.
noun	preparation	If you are organized, income tax preparation takes only a few hours.
adjective	preparatory	The preparatory work for doing my taxes is more time-consuming than filling out the forms.

Choose the word that best completes the sentence.

1. We didn't know we had to claim the interest from our savings account and were _____ for the error.
   (A) penalize
   (B) penalizing
   (C) penalty
   (D) penalized

2. The _____ of the forms took much less time than we expected.
   (A) preparatory
   (B) preparation
   (C) prepared
   (D) prepares

3. Many Americans find themselves in debt and _____ more money than they could imagine.
   (A) owe
   (B) owes
   (C) owner
   (D) owed

4. According to my _____, we owe a lot of money in taxes this year.
   (A) calculations
   (B) calculated
   (C) calculators
   (D) calculate

Short Talks

Read the following passage and write the appropriate form of the new words in the blanks below.

calculated	fill out	owe	refund
deadline	gave up	penalized	spouse
filed	joint	prepares	withhold

Every year, my wife gathers all of our pay stubs and expense reports and (5.) _____ to fill out our tax forms. She tries to finish them in March, well before the April 15th (6.) _____. It's a time-consuming process. There are receipts to find, records to organize, and forms to (7.) _____. When we first got married, we (8.) _____ separate returns. But now she marks me as her (9.) _____ and files the (10.) _____ return. It saves us money and saves me time!

My wife is very proud of her accuracy. The government has never sent the forms back with corrections. For several years now, we have received a (11.) _____. But this year, she (12.) _____ the numbers over and over again and found we had not paid enough taxes throughout the year. She didn't want to (13.) _____ any money. Finally, she (14.) _____ and sent in our check. Actually, it was my fault. I had changed jobs and didn't ask my employer to (15.) _____ enough money from my paychecks. I'm just glad we found and corrected the mistake before we got (16.) _____.

Choose the underlined word or phrase that should be rewritten and rewrite it.

17. The woman who <u>prepares</u> our taxes took such a long time to <u>fill out</u> our forms that we had to <u>filing</u> for an
    A · B · C
    extension of the <u>deadline</u>.
    D

    _____

18. Monies <u>withheld</u> before the <u>deadline</u> to <u>filing</u> taxes may be <u>refunded</u>.
    A · · · · · · · · · · · · B · · · · · · · · · C · · · · · · · · · · · · D

    _____

19. You can be <u>penalized</u> if you do not have enough of your earnings <u>withholding</u> from your salary, or if you leave
    A · B
    your <u>spouse's</u> income out of a joint <u>return</u>.
    C · · · · · · · · · · · · · · · · · · · D

    _____

20. Millions of Americans never <u>give up</u> the hope that, years after <u>filing</u> their tax forms, an error in <u>calculation</u> will
    A · B · · · · · · · · · · · · · · · C
    be found that results in a large <u>refunding</u> from the government.
    D

    _____

Lesson 25

Financial Statements

Words to learn

desired
detail
forecast
level
overall
perspective
projected
realistic
target
translation
typical
yield

1. **desired** adj., wished or longed for
   a. The desired outcome of a projected budget is increased control over the business.
   b. Lee needs his start-up business to match his current salary; a business plan will tell him how much income he needs to generate to meet the desired goal.

2. **detail** v., to report or relate minutely or in particulars
   a. The office manager detailed each step of the inventory process at the staff meeting.
   b. Fabio created a financial statement that detailed every expected expenditure for the next quarter.

3. **forecast** n., a prediction of a future event; v., to estimate or calculate in advance
   a. The financial forecast indicates a deficit in the next quarter.
   b. Analysts forecast a strong economic outlook.

4. **level** n., a relative position or rank on a scale
   a. We have never had an accountant work at such a sophisticated level before.
   b. The meeting was only open to staff at the assistant director level or higher.

5. **overall** adj., regarded as a whole; general
   a. The company's overall expectations were out of proportion.
   b. Overall, our costs are running true to prediction.

6. **perspective** n., a mental view or outlook
   a. The budget statement will give the manager some perspective on where the costs of running the business are to be found.
   b. Joseph's accountant gave him some perspective as well as some data on how much he could expect to earn in his first year in business.

7. **projected** adj., estimated, or predicted based on present data
   a. Based on the data at hand, I think our projected earnings for the next quarter are unrealistic.
   b. The manager was distressed at the projected number of staff hours to be paid on the next payroll cycle.

8. **realistic** adj., tending to or expressing an awareness of things as they really are
   a. Stefano found that an accurate accounting gave him a realistic idea of his business's financial direction.
   b. Realistic expectations are important when you review your financial statements.

9. **target** v., to establish as a goal; n., a goal
   a. We targeted March as the deadline for completing the financial statement.
   b. Most managers target desired income as the primary criterion for success.

10. **translation** n., the act or process of translating
    a. The translation of the statement from Japanese into English was very helpful.
    b. The accountant was able to provide a translation of the economic terms used in the meeting.

11. **typical** adj., conforming to a type
    a. A projected financial statement takes into account a business's typical expenses and a margin for unanticipated expenses.
    b. Part of a category summary is defining the expenses that are typical to the business in question.

12. **yield** n., an amount produced; v., to produce a profit
    a. Henry's budget gave him the desired yield: a better indication of his expected profit.
    b. The company's investment yielded high returns.

Short Conversations

Read the following conversations and see how the new words are used.

[M] I can't believe our sales **targets** for this month. I don't think I can make that many sales.

[W] I'm surprised at the **level** of sales activity our manager expects from us over the next quarter.

[M] Especially since we're a new company, and it requires more sales calls to **translate** into a sale.

[M] I'm developing a **projected** financial statement for my business.

[W] That's great. It will help you **forecast** periods where you might have financial problems.

[M] I'll also use it to see what kind of profits we can expect to **yield** this quarter.

[M] The financial statement will give you a good picture of your **overall** business health.

[W] I'll need a **perspective** on where my financial challenges will be.

[M] The income statement will show you in **detail** how much money you need to make each day and where your expenses are.

[M] If my **desired** yearly income for running the business is $50,000, can you show me how much money the business will have to bring in to cover costs?

[W] Certainly. I'll need to see some data on **typical** expenses and profits associated with your kind of business.

[M] My business is unique. I don't know how **realistic** the chances are of getting good data.

Word Families

verb	desire	Our manager is trying to predict how many customers will desire our product over the next quarter.
noun	desire	Her desire for greater control of the business led her to discuss her need for more information with her accountant.
adjective	desirable	The category summary, while desirable, was time-consuming to prepare.

verb	project	The budget summary helped us project our expenditures for the year.
noun	project	The financial project was time-consuming and challenging.
noun	projection	Maurice's projections for the upcoming fiscal year were not as helpful as we had hoped.

verb	realize	The plan helps her realize her dream of having the business turn a profit.
noun	reality	The financial statement reinforced the reality that our business is in deep trouble.
adjective	realistic	The accountant needs realistic numbers on which to base his plan.

verb	translate	The computer was able to translate data from the created spreadsheet into the spreadsheet program I prefer.
noun	translation	The translation of the document was provided at no charge.
adjective	translatable	The data was not translatable between programs and had to be entered by hand, which took hours.

Choose the word that best completes the sentence.

1. Before we begin, I think we should all focus on the _____ outcome of this effort.
   (A) desirableness
   (B) desire
   (C) desired
   (D) desirability

2. The _____ figures for the next quarter will not be available until a week from tomorrow.
   (A) project
   (B) projected
   (C) projection
   (D) projects

3. The projected financial statement demonstrated to Susan that her business had a _____ chance of increasing its profit over the next two quarters.
   (A) realistic
   (B) realist
   (C) realistically
   (D) reality

4. To create our financial strategy, our consultant took the experiences of similar businesses and _____ relevant outcomes to our situation.
   (A) translatable
   (B) translation
   (C) translator
   (D) translated

Short Talk

Read the following passage and write the appropriate form of the new words in the blanks below.

desired	level	projected	translate
detailed	overall	realistic	typical
forecasts	perspective	target	yield

A business budget focuses on future profits and future capital requirements. A budget can help the business owner determine the amount of profit the business is expected to make, the amount of sales it will take to reach a goal, and what (5.) _____ of expenses are attached to those sales. A business establishes a (6.) _____, a goal to work toward. A business (7.) _____ the sales that will be needed to reach this target.

Projecting or planning ahead is part of (8.) _____ business planning. When creating a (9.) _____ income statement, a business owner tries to determine how to reach the (10.) _____ target. The annual profit must be sufficient to (11.) _____ the owner a return for his or her time spent operating the business, plus a return on the investment. The owner's target income is the sum of a reasonable salary for the time spent running the business and a normal return on the amount invested in the firm.

After projecting the income needed, the business owner has to (12.) _____ the target profit into a net sales figure for the forecasted period. The owner has to determine whether this sales volume is (13.) _____. One useful technique is to break down the required annual sales into a daily sales figure to get a better (14.) _____ of the sales required to yield the annual profit.

At this stage in the financial plan, the owner should create a (15.) _____ picture of the firm's expected operating expenses. Many books and business organizations give (16.) _____ operating statistics data, based on a percentage of net sales. The business's accountant can help you assign dollar values to anticipated expenses.

Developing a projected income statement is an important part of any financial plan, as the process forces the business owner to examine the firm's future profitability.

Choose the underlined word or phrase that should be rewritten and rewrite it.

17. When the business did not <u>yield</u> the <u>desiring</u> profit <u>level</u>, the owner raised the daily sales <u>targets</u>.
                               A   B   C   D

    _____

18. The <u>projection</u> income statement <u>forecast</u> a <u>detailed</u> pathway for attaining the <u>desired</u> growth.
       A   B   C   D

    _____

19. A financial statement offers managers a <u>detailed</u> "snapshot" of what a <u>typical</u> day's sales must be in order to set a <u>reality</u> income <u>target</u>.
              A   B
       C   D

    _____

20. By posting the financial statement, the director gave the staff some <u>perspective</u> on how sales <u>targets</u> <u>translation</u> into <u>desired</u> financial goals.
            A   B
       C   D

    _____

Word Review #5   Lessons 21–25 Financing and Budgeting

Choose the word that best completes the sentence.

1. The Small Business Administration will help you to arrange to _____ money to start a business.
(A) borrow
(B) borrowed
(C) borrowing
(D) borrower

2. When we _____ a loan, we found very good terms.
(A) take out
(B) took out
(C) taken out
(D) taking out

3. Most people get nervous when someone is _____ their books.
(A) audit
(B) audits
(C) audited
(D) auditing

4. Sometimes it is difficult to _____ of bad investments.
(A) pull up
(B) pull out
(C) pull at
(D) pull to

5. I prefer _____ in social-conscience funds.
(A) invest
(B) investment
(C) investing
(D) investor

6. When the Dow is dropping, investors need to be _____.
(A) resource
(B) resources
(C) resourceful
(D) resourcefulness

7. Sometimes it is difficult to understand how the government _____ tax liability.
(A) calculating
(B) calculations
(C) calculators
(D) calculates

8. One decision with tax returns is whether to _____ itemizing in favor of the standard deduction.
(A) give up
(B) giving up
(C) gave up
(D) given up

9. The company's _____ earnings over the next six months were exciting.
(A) project
(B) projects
(C) projection
(D) projected

10. Some parts of the tax code are so confusing that they need _____.
(A) translate
(B) translates
(C) translated
(D) translation

Choose the underlined word or phrase that should be rewritten and rewrite it.

11. Banks are getting more demanding about minimum <u>down payments</u> they <u>accepting</u>, comparing <u>signatures</u> on
                                            A   B   C
checks, and imposing <u>restrictions</u> on withdrawals.
                         D

_____

12. When you are <u>aggressively</u> <u>building up</u> a <u>client</u> list, you need to <u>budgeted</u> extra funds for entertaining.
                     A   B   C   D

_____

13. A <u>long-term</u> investment <u>portfolio</u> should include some <u>conservatively</u> funds with reinvested <u>dividends</u>.
   A   B   C   D

_____

14. Financial statements should include <u>realistic</u> <u>targets</u> and a <u>detailing</u> <u>forecast</u>.
                                  A   B   C   D

_____

15.   Bank customers should use <u>cautious</u> about maintaining a <u>balance</u> so low that the bank <u>deducts</u> additional
                              A   **B**   **C**

      <u>penalties</u>.
        D

      _____

16.   Investing in a <u>conservative</u> fund requires a patient <u>attitude</u> and a <u>commitment</u> to not <u>pulled out</u> your
                             A   **B**   **C**   **D**

      investment.

      _____

17.   <u>Filing</u> your tax <u>returning</u> after the <u>deadline</u> can cost you more in <u>penalties</u>.
        A   **B**   **C**   **D**

      _____

18.   To reach your <u>desired</u> goal, check the <u>overall</u> <u>yielding</u> of the <u>fund</u> you are considering.
                        A   **B** **C**   **D**

      _____

19.   Filing a <u>joint</u> <u>return</u> with your <u>spouse</u> could leave you <u>owe</u> more than filing individually.
               A   **B**   **C**   **D**

      _____

20.   <u>Filling up</u> a <u>withholding</u> form <u>wisely</u> can cost you less in tax payments or increase the size of your <u>refund</u>.
        A   **B**   **C**   **D**

      _____

Property and Departments

1. **adjacent** adj., next to
    a. Take the elevator to the third floor and my office is adjacent to the receptionist area.
    b. The office manager found it very efficient to have the copier adjacent to the mail room.

2. **collaboration** n., the act of working with someone
    a. The manager had never seen such effective collaboration between two groups.
    b. We believe that it was our collaboration that enabled us to achieve such favorable results.

3. **concentrate** v., to focus; to think about
    a. In his quiet, corner office, the manager could finally concentrate and finish his work.
    b. We should concentrate our efforts on the last quarter of the year.

4. **conducive** adj., contributing to; leading to
    a. The new office arrangement is much more conducive to work than the dark, depressing space the company had before.
    b. Arranging chairs so that participants can see each other easily is conducive to open communication.

5. **disrupt** v., to interrupt; to disturb
    a. The conference was disrupted by a power outage.
    b. The strike disrupted the factory's production.

6. **hamper** v., to impede or interfere
    a. When the weight of the freezing rain broke the telephone lines, the telemarketers' jobs were seriously hampered.
    b. The lack of supplies hampered our ability to finish on schedule.

7. **inconsiderate** adj., rude, impolite
    a. Playing loud music in the office is inconsiderate and will not be tolerated.
    b. The directors concluded that the new employee wasn't inconsiderate, but he did exhibit some cultural differences.

8. **lobby** n., an anteroom, foyer, or waiting room
    a. The salesperson waited in the busy lobby for the buyer to see him.
    b. The reception area was moved from the lobby of the building to the third floor.

9. **move up** v., to advance, improve position
    a. As the employee moved up the corporate ladder, she never forgot where she started.
    b. In order to move up in the company, employees had to demonstrate their loyalty.

10. **open to** adj., receptive to; vulnerable
    a. What I valued most in my previous supervisor was that she was always open to ideas and suggestions.
    b. Since the junior executive was still on probation, he was open to much scrutiny and criticism.

11. **opt** v., to choose, to decide on
    a. The operations manager opted for the less expensive office design.
    b. If Mary opts to join that department, you will be working together.

12. **scrutinize** v., to look at carefully and closely
    a. After three months of scrutinizing the employee's work, the managers decided that he had, in fact, improved quite considerably.
    b. Because they were very competitive, the marketing staff scrutinized every presentation made by their colleagues in the sales department.

Short Conversations

Read the following conversations and see how the new words are used.

[M] What do you think about the plans for the new office **lobby**?
[W] I've spent a lot of time **scrutinizing** them and I'm quite pleased.
[M] I hope they're more **conducive** to conversation than is our current lobby.

[M] It was so **inconsiderate** of the marketing department to have a party in the middle of the afternoon.
[W] Unfortunately, your meeting was the one most **hampered** by the noise.
[M] I was glad their director told them that they were too **disruptive** and had to stop.

[M] How is the **collaboration** between the shipping and production departments progressing?
[W] There were some initial difficulties, but overall both departments have been very **open to** working more closely together.
[M] They really have **concentrated** on setting and reaching their goals.

[M] Whoever **opts** for that office will be responsible for the cleaning crew.
[W] Is that the reward for **moving up**?
[M] No, but that person will be **adjacent** to all the supplies and the time clocks.

Word Families

verb	collaborate	If we collaborate on this project, you will be sure to receive credit.
noun	collaboration	Collaboration often brings about results that no one could have predicted.
adjective	collaborative	The new project is a collaborative effort among several departments.

verb	disrupt	Try not to disrupt the meeting being held in the sales department.
noun	disruption	I'm sorry for the disruption, but this phone call is very important.
adjective	disruptive	Having to temporarily move the offices proved to be very disruptive and sales decreased during that quarter.

verb	opt	When we moved offices, I opted for the one without a window.
noun	option	Presented with several options, we chose the one that required the least amount of effort.
adjective	optimal	For optimal efficiency, department lunch breaks should be staggered.

verb	scrutinize	The auditor carefully scrutinized the financial records.
noun	scrutiny	Employees under constant scrutiny tend to perform worse than those employees who have more freedom.
adjective	inscrutable	You can never tell what she is thinking, since her facial expressions are inscrutable.

Choose the word that best completes the sentence.

1. After close _____ of the options, the managers chose an advertising company to do all the publicity for the new campaign.
   (A) scrutinize
   (B) scrutinizing
   (C) scrutiny
   (D) scrutable

2. The data entry clerk is so accustomed to working by herself that I really doubt if she is capable of _____ on this project.
   (A) collaborated
   (B) collaborating
   (C) collaborator
   (D) collaborates

3. The constant flow of traffic by the researcher's desk proved to be very _____.
   (A) disruptive
   (B) disrupts
   (C) disruption
   (D) disrupted

4. The _____ time for the meeting is tomorrow morning at nine.
   (A) opt
   (B) option
   (C) optimal
   (D) optimize

Short Talk

Read the following passage and write the appropriate form of the new words in the blanks below.

adjacent	conducive	inconsiderate	open to
collaboration	disruptive	lobby	opting
concentrate	hampered	move up	scrutinized

The layout of any office has an important influence on the atmosphere and operations in the company. The shipping department most likely will not be located next to the customer service department. The noise would be too (5.) _____. Likewise, locating a kitchen (6.) _____ to the (7.) _____ would be (8.) _____ for office visitors and clients. The marketing department is often situated close to the sales department due to their necessary (9.) _____.

Employee productivity may be (10.) _____ or improved by the arrangement of workers and departments. Employees vie for corner offices as they (11.) _____ the corporate ladder. They want to be accessible to top management, but not so close that everything that they do is being (12.) _____. At the same time, many companies are (13.) _____ for open work spaces versus traditional offices. Open spaces are more (14.) _____ to team projects, where employees interact freely. However, some employees feel that such an environment makes it difficult to (15.) _____. Employees know under which conditions they work the best. If employers are willing to listen and are (16.) _____ suggestions, they can take advantage of office space and help employees to realize their full potential.

Choose the underlined word or phrase that should be rewritten and rewrite it.

17. Moving up to another position will remove Ms. Sams from the scrutinize of her current boss and will allow her to concentrate on other options.
    A / B / C / D
    _____

18. The new office layout is more conducive to collaborated between the different departmental teams.
    A / B / C / D
    _____

19. The manager was open to any ideas about how to lessen the disrupted from the construction in the lobby, which was hampering the staff's work.
    A / B / C / D
    _____

20. After much scrutiny of the layout designs, the president opted for an open work space, knowing that some employees might have difficulty concentrating and find the decision inconsideration of their needs.
    A / B / C / D
    _____

Board Meetings
and Committees

Words to learn

adhere to
agenda
bring up
conclude
go ahead
goal
lengthy
matter
periodically
priority
progress
waste

1. **adhere to** v., to follow; to pay attention to
   a. The chairman never adhered to his own rules.
   b. The best committee members are those who adhere to the time limits and speak only when they have something important to add.

2. **agenda** n., a list of topics to be discussed
   a. The board was able to cover fifteen items on the agenda.
   b. The agenda was sent out three weeks ago so that everyone could prepare for the meeting.

3. **bring up** v., to introduce a topic
   a. Just as the meeting was about to finish, the manager brought up a controversial issue.
   b. No one brought up the resignation of the director.

4. **conclude** v., to stop; to come to a decision
   a. The committee members concluded the meeting early so that they could finish their budgets.
   b. After long discussions, the board has concluded that the project has to be canceled.

5. **go ahead** v., to proceed with; n., permission to do something
   a. Five of the six members felt that they should go ahead with the plan.
   b. The manager was just waiting for the go ahead from her boss before mailing the report.

6. **goal** n., objective, purpose
   a. Employees are expected to analyze and evaluate their annual goals.
   b. The director had to report to the committee that his department would not reach its goal of 35 percent growth.

7. **lengthy** adj., long in time, duration, or distance
   a. After lengthy discussions, the chairperson was reelected for another term.
   b. The report was so lengthy that members had to take it home and read it over the weekend.

8. **matter** n., an item, issue, topic of interest
   a. If there are no other matters to discuss, we will conclude the meeting.
   b. This is not the place to bring up personal matters.

9. **periodically** adv., from time to time
   a. The group tried to meet periodically.
   b. Periodically, new members were nominated to the committee.

10. **priority** n., something of importance, something that should be done before other things
    a. Since the remaining issues were not a priority, the group decided to move them to the next week's agenda.
    b. The manager was ineffective because she was unable to set priorities.

11. **progress** n., a movement forward; v., to move forward on something, especially work or a project
    a. The executive committee asked each group to present a report showing their progress for the year.
    b. Progress is being made on the annual report; we expect to see a finished product by next week.

12. **waste** v., not to use wisely; n., not worthwhile
    a. Without a leader, the group members wasted time and energy trying to organize themselves.
    b. The meeting wasn't a waste of time, but the members had hoped to accomplish more than they did.

Short Conversations

Read the following conversations and see how the new words are used.

[W]   That meeting was such a **waste** of time.
[M]   You're right, it was too **lengthy** and we didn't accomplish anything.
[W]   We didn't even talk about the most important **matters**.

[W]   What is on today's **agenda**?
[M]   Well, the first thing is to cover next year's **goals**.
[W]   I'm glad to hear that that is a **priority**.

[M]   We have made a lot of **progress** in a very short period of time.
[W]   If we continue like this, we should get the **go ahead** for the big project.
[M]   Let's make sure we **adhere** to the schedule and stay on track.

[M]   Our supervisors have **concluded** that we aren't a very efficient department.
[W]   Well, maybe we should meet **periodically** to try to improve things.
[M]   And we could **bring up** different issues that need to be discussed.

Word Families

verb	conclude	To conclude, we must all focus on the year ahead of us and the challenges that we will face.
noun	conclusion	Unfortunately, the conclusion of the meeting was that they needed to downsize their workforce.
adjective	conclusive	There is no conclusive evidence to back up the report.

noun	period	The sales reports for the current period are excellent.
adjective	periodic	They received periodic updates from the overseas licensees.
adverb	periodically	The employee checked his messages periodically during the week-long seminar.

verb	prioritize	Once the team members learned to prioritize their work, they were much more productive.
noun	priority	The committee member has difficulties setting priorities for herself.
adjective	prior	The prior meetings had not included the new manager.

verb	progress	Everyone was surprised at how quickly the meeting had progressed.
noun	progression	The quick progression of events didn't surprise anyone.
adjective	progressive	The new president is very progressive and is always looking for ways to improve the business.

Choose the word that best completes the sentence.

1. The original members of the committee met _____ for lunch or dinner.
   (A) period
   (B) periods
   (C) periodically
   (D) periodic

2. As the chairman stood to give his _____, everyone in the room was listening.
   (A) conclusion
   (B) conclude
   (C) conclusive
   (D) concluding

3. Even as they _____ through the hundreds of pages of supporting material, the committee was still not convinced that the project was justified.
   (A) progression
   (B) progressed
   (C) progresses
   (D) progressive

4. As her first _____, the committee chairwoman wanted to attract new, energetic members to the group.
   (A) prior
   (B) priority
   (C) prioritize
   (D) prioritized

Short Talks

Read the following passage and write the appropriate form of the new words in the blanks below.

adhered to	concluded	lengthy	priority
agenda	go ahead	matters	progress
brought up	goals	periodically	waste

Committee meetings are a frequent and necessary event at almost every company. In order for meetings to be productive and not viewed as a (5.) _____ of time, they should be run efficiently. Critical to the success of any meeting is the (6.) _____. Everyone who attends the meeting should be aware of the agenda and be prepared to discuss the (7.) _____ at hand and the (8.) _____ to be accomplished. To avoid (9.) _____ discussions, time frames should be set and (10.) _____.

The meeting is called to order by the chairperson. Attendance is taken and agenda items are (11.) _____ one by one. In general, (12.) _____ topics should be at the beginning of the agenda, to make sure that the attendees are able to discuss them fully and make timely decisions. Once the (13.) _____ is given for a plan or project, a plan of action is developed. The committee must then (14.) _____ check up on the (15.) _____ of that plan. The meeting is (16.) _____ without any outstanding issues and a date for the next meeting is set.

Choose the underlined word or phrase that should be rewritten and rewrite it.

17. The chairman was incapable of <u>adhere</u> to the <u>agenda</u> and his meetings were typically <u>lengthy</u> and <u>inconclusive</u>.
    A   B   C   D
    _____

18. After they received the <u>go ahead</u>, the team drew up an <u>agenda</u> and met <u>periodically</u> to check on each member's <u>progression</u>.
    A   B   C   D
    _____

19. Even after the <u>matter</u> was given <u>prioritize</u> status, the results proved to be <u>inconclusive</u> and the project a <u>waste</u> of money.
    A   B   C   D
    _____

20. The most important new <u>matter</u> were <u>brought up</u> and integrated with the existing <u>priorities</u> and <u>goals</u>.
    A   B   C   D
    _____

Quality Control

1. **brand** n., an identifying mark or label; a trademark
    a. Consumers often buy highly advertised brands of athletic shoes.
    b. All brands of aspirin are the same.

2. **conform** v., to match specifications or qualities
    a. The quality control manager insisted that every product that left the plant conform to the company's rigorous standards.
    b. Our safety standards conform to those established by the government.

3. **defect** n., an imperfection or flaw
    a. Because of a defect in stitching, the entire suit was thrown out.
    b. One way to sell a product with a defect is by labeling it as such and reducing the price.

4. **enhance** v., to make more attractive or valuable
    a. The reason behind quality control is to enhance the company's reputation for superior products.
    b. A stylish color enhances the appeal of a car.

5. **garment** n., an article of clothing
    a. Every garment must be carefully inspected for defects before it is shipped.
    b. The garment workers are accountable for production mistakes.

6. **inspect** v., to look at closely; to examine carefully or officially
    a. A quality control agent who does not inspect every product carefully can ruin his company's reputation.
    b. Children's car seats are thoroughly inspected and tested for safety before being put on the market.

7. **perceive** v., to notice; to become aware of; to see
    a. In her job in quality control, Marie perceived herself as the protector of her company's good name.
    b. Every employee who enjoys profit sharing perceives his job as quality control.

8. **repel** v., to keep away; to fight against
    a. Umbrellas that do not repel water should never be passed through quality control.
    b. Faulty products repel repeat customers.

9. **take back** v., to return something; to withdraw or retract
    a. Good quality control significantly limits the number of products taken back for a refund.
    b. The quality inspector took the shoddy work back to the assembly line to confront the workers.

10. **throw out** v., to dispose of
    a. It is cheaper to throw out shoddy products than to lose customers.
    b. The factory decided to throw out hundreds of lightbulbs that might have been damaged, rather than lose customers.

11. **uniform** adj., consistent in form or appearance.
    a. A successful company will ensure uniform quality of its products.
    b. Standardized products are uniform in appearance and quality.

12. **wrinkle** n., a crease, ridge, or furrow, especially in skin or fabric
    a. A wrinkle that is ironed into a permanent-press product will annoy the consumer each time the garment is worn.
    b. A wrinkle in the finish can be repaired more economically before a sale than after.

Short Conversations

Read the following conversations and see how the new words are used.

[M] What does the company do with the clothes with **defects** in them?
[W] Sometimes the company changes the **brand** name and sells them in discount stores.
[M] Don't people who buy them **take** them **back** for a refund?

[M] In quality control, it is important to ensure **uniform** quality.
[W] But some of our best products have **defects**.
[M] That is why we have to **inspect** them so carefully.

[M] When the designer **garments** have defects, we sell them for less in outlet stores.
[W] Some people **perceive** defects where there aren't any.
[M] That's true, but it is our job to be certain that every piece **conforms** exactly to the designer's specifications.

[M] A designer label **enhances** the perceived value of the clothes.
[W] I am **repelled** by wearing a fancy label, but I like to know that my clothes are top quality.
[M] You save money because you can get so much use out of quality clothes before they wear out and you **throw** them **out**.

Word Families

verb	inspect	We must inspect every product before we sell it.
noun	inspection	Each employee must conduct a careful inspection.
noun	inspector	The inspector leaves his identification number on the product to ensure accountability.

verb	repel	A quality raincoat can repel rain and keep you dry.
noun	repellent	Testing insect repellent is never a pleasant task.
adjective	repellent	Testing stain removers can be repellent to workers because of the toxic fumes.

verb	perceive	The worker perceived that the stitching on the seams could not withstand normal strain.
noun	perception	Customers' perception of quality is often based on their experience with a given store or brand.
adjective	perceptive	Perceptive workers are excellent quality control inspectors.

verb	defect	Disgusted by the poor quality of products at the factory, the employee defected to a plant that took pride in its work.
noun	defect	Even a small defect can cause a product to fail.
adjective	defective	Good quality control employees will notice defective machinery before a serious breakdown occurs.

Choose the word that best completes the sentence.

1. Rebecca is known as _____ #321 among her quality control co-workers.
   (A) inspect
   (B) inspection
   (C) inspector
   (D) inspecting

2. Agnes was _____ by the odor of the waterproofing.
   (A) repel
   (B) repellent
   (C) repelled
   (D) repelling

3. An employee who _____ his job as important performs better than one who wants only a pay-check.
   (A) perceives
   (B) perceived
   (C) perceptive
   (D) perception

4. _____ equipment on a new car is not only costly, but also dangerous.
   (A) Defect
   (B) Defector
   (C) Defective
   (D) Defection

Short Talk

Read the following passage and write the appropriate form of the new words in the blanks below.

brand	enhance	perceive	throws out
conform	garment	repel	uniform
defects	inspect	take back	wrinkle

Alex is excited about his new job with Parapluie Rain Wear. As quality control manager, his job is to make sure that his company's goods (5.) _____ to standardized quality criteria and are free from (6.) _____. Before any (7.) _____ leaves the factory, Alex must (8.) _____ it. He knows that if he (9.) _____ a damaged garment before a customer sees it, he will (10.) _____ his company's reputation and increase the demand for their products. Alex must ensure that all products meet certain criteria: A customer who buys a raincoat that does not (11.) _____ rain will probably (12) _____ the raincoat to the store and buy another (13.) _____. The same is true if the seams are not sewn tightly or the color is not (14.) _____. Alex knows that, in addition to keeping out rain, the product must be attractive to look at and to touch. It should not (15.) _____ easily, and it should last a long time. Alex knows that it is important for customers to (16.) _____ his company's goods as quality products so that his company will profit—and he can get a raise.

Choose the underlined word or phrase that should be rewritten and rewrite it.

17. Ms. Nell <u>inspected</u> every <u>brand</u> of jeans that her company manufactured and <u>threw out</u> any with <u>defective</u>.
   　　　　　A　　　　　　 B　　　　　　　　　　　　　　　　　　　　　　　　　 C　　　　　　　　 D

   _____

18. When the <u>inspect</u> checked the <u>garments</u>, he found a few with <u>wrinkles</u>, which he <u>took back</u> to the presser.
   　　　　　　 A　　　　　　　　 B　　　　　　　　　　　　　　　 C　　　　　　　 D

   _____

19. The color of the <u>garment</u> <u>enhancing</u> its visual appeal, its <u>water-repellent</u> nature made
   　　　　　　　　　　 A　　　 B　　　　　　　　　　　 C
   it practical, and its <u>brand</u> made it fashionable.
   　　　　　　　　　　 D

   _____

20. When one of the <u>inspectors</u> found evidence of a leak in the most expensive <u>brand</u> of duplicating machines, he
   　　　　　　　　　 A　　　　　　　　　　　　　　　　　　　　　　　　　　　 B
   was <u>repellent</u> by the idea of having to <u>throw out</u> the equipment.
   　　　 C　　　　　　　　　　　　　　 D

   _____

Product Development

Words to learn

anxious
ascertain
assume
decade
examine
experiment
logical
research
responsibility
solve
supervisor
systematic

1. **anxious** adj., worried
   a. The developers were anxious about the sales forecast for the new product.
   b. The graphic designers tried to be calm during their presentation, but you could tell they were anxious it would not be well received.
2. **ascertain** v., to discover; to find out for certain
   a. A necessary part of product development is to ascertain whether the product is safe.
   b. A customer survey will help to ascertain whether there is a market for the product.
3. **assume** v., to take upon oneself; to believe to be true
   a. The young man felt ready to assume the new responsibilities of his promotion.
   b. When the manufacturing company bought the research lab, it also assumed its outstanding debts.
4. **decade** n., a period of ten years
   a. After a decade of trying, the company finally developed a vastly superior product.
   b. Each decade seems to have its own fad products.
5. **examine** v., to interrogate; to scrutinize
   a. Before marketing a new product, researchers must carefully examine it from every aspect.
   b. Good researchers have to examine every possible option, including some that seem bizarre.
6. **experiment** v., to try out a new procedure or idea; n., a test or trial
   a. Product developers must conduct hundreds of experiments in their research.
   b. After designing a new product, researchers continue experimenting to determine whether it has other uses.
7. **logical** adj., formally valid; using orderly reasoning
   a. It is only logical for a research and development team to concentrate on one or two new products at a time.
   b. In addition to logical thinkers, a good research and development team should include a few dreamers.
8. **research** n., the act of collecting information about a particular subject.
   a. Part of the research the team does is to determine whether similar products are already on the market.
   b. For toy manufacturers, research can be pure fun.
9. **responsibility** n., a task
   a. The product development department has a huge responsibility to be sure that the product is safe, even if used improperly.
   b. Another responsibility of product development is to ensure that there will be a demand for the product.
10. **solve** v., to find a solution, explanation, or answer
    a. Researchers find that every time they solve one problem, two more result.
    b. One of the biggest problems to solve is why people would want to own the new product.
11. **supervisor** n., an administrator in charge
    a. The department supervisor has to balance his department's responsibilities in order to keep the president satisfied with its progress.
    b. A good supervisor gets his team to work with him, not just for him.
12. **systematic** adj., methodical in procedure; organized
    a. Once the creative development is completed, the department needs to put in place a systematic approach for making the idea a reality.
    b. Any researcher knows that creative thinking is necessary, but systematic analysis is indispensable.

Short Conversations

Read the following conversations and see how the new words are used.

[M] How did your team **ascertain** that the market needed another stuffed toy?

[W] Product Development started with the **assumption** that stuffed toys have a successful history.

[M] Just because they have been popular for the last four or five **decades** doesn't mean they will last forever.

[M] We need to **examine** the data for our Binky Doll sales before we decide to modify the original product for a new generation.

[W] Several companies have successfully **experimented** with modifications, such as bright colors and noise-makers.

[M] Consumers today are **anxious** about inflation, so our next modification should be to make the doll cheaper.

[W] Don't you think it's **logical** to come out with a drug for every mood?

[M] Logical, perhaps, but not true. Our market **research** shows people are less likely to take drugs that affect their mood.

[W] No! You mean people are going to take **responsibility** for their own moods?

[W] Once our researchers **solve** the problem with the electronic circuit, we'll be ready to test-market our new VCRs.

[M] If they'd taken a more **systematic** approach to the problem, the VCRs would be on the market by now.

[W] Don't tell me. Tell their **supervisor**.

Word Families

noun	anxiety	The level of anxiety was high when the experimental car underwent road tests.
adjective	anxious	If you feel anxious, sit down and try to relax.
adverb	anxiously	The stockholders anxiously awaited the release of the new drug that, if successful, would make their stocks more valuable.

noun	responsibility	Although the ultimate responsibility falls on the supervisor, every employee shares it.
adjective	responsible	The researcher responsible for passing the defective product has joined the cafeteria workers' assembly line.
adverb	responsibly	Product designers must act responsibly when they consider how a product might be misused.

verb	experiment	The product developer had experimented with improving electronic equipment since she was in the sixth grade.
noun	experimentation	Hi-tech companies are constantly involved in experimentation with new products in order to stay ahead of their competitors.
adjective	experimental	The new computer was experimental, so you could try it at the store, but you couldn't buy one.

verb	assume	Product developers should assume nothing that research does not support.
noun	assumption	Most consumers make the assumption that, unless they are warned otherwise, the products they buy are safe.
adjective	assumed	The assumed results should be kept confidential until the product is retested.

Choose the word that best completes the sentence.

1. The product development team were _____ that the competition would produce a similar product and get it on the market before they did.
   (A) anxious
   (B) anxiously
   (C) anxiousness
   (D) anxiety

2. The new employee accepted _____ for not discovering a trademarked toy exactly like his own company's.
   (A) responsible
   (B) responsibility
   (C) responsibly
   (D) response

3. The _____ model of the new car drew attention wherever it was shown.
   (A) experiment
   (B) experimentation
   (C) experimental
   (D) experimenting

4. The designer made the _____ that people are attracted to boxes in primary colors.
   (A) assumption
   (B) assumed
   (C) assuming
   (D) assume

Short Talk

Read the following passage and write the appropriate form of the new words in the blanks below.

anxious	decade	logical	solve
ascertain	examining	researched	supervisor
assume	experiments	responsible	systematic

Michael was worried about his promotion. He needn't have been (5.) _____ though. He had worked in the Product Development Division for nine and a half years, almost a (6.) _____. He knew the department inside out. Now, however, he would be the director. As a member of the department, he had only to do what his (7.) _____ told him. As the director, he would be the person (8.) _____ for the success of his department. Fears are not always (9.) _____; in fact, they are often illogical.

As his first task, he decided to conduct a (10.) _____ analysis of the steps required to develop new products, and to organize the tasks into a logical order. The first step in developing new products would be to (11.) _____ what kind of products the market needed and what problems existed with the products currently being used.

The second task would be to find out how best to examine these problems and determine what kind of research would be needed to (12.) _____ the problems. It would be better to say, reexamine these problems, since most of these unsolved problems had been thoroughly (13.) _____ over the years.

The third task would be to look at the quality and characteristics of the competition's products. By (14.) _____ the competition's products, he would know where he should improve. And the final task would be to decide how to gather the most substantial information from the fewest number of (15.) _____. Michael smiled and sat back to read over his list. Confident that he had a good team and a good plan, he felt ready to (16.) _____ his new job

---

Choose the underlined word or phrase that should be rewritten and rewrite it.

17. For more than a <u>decade</u> the young woman had <u>systematically</u> <u>experimented</u> with ways to generate more
        A   **B**   **C**
    power from trash, to <u>solve</u> two problems at once.
             D

    _____

18. When the new manager <u>assumed</u> his new <u>responsible</u>, he <u>anxiously</u> called in his employees to help him to
             A   **B**   **C**
    <u>solve</u> some problems with safety issues on the recently developed toy line.
     D

    _____

19. <u>Research</u> is always based on <u>assumptions</u>, which are <u>examined</u> to <u>ascertaining</u> their validity.
      A   **B**   **C**   **D**

    _____

20. To <u>examination</u> whether his <u>supervisor's</u> ideas were on target, one of the team members developed a <u>systematic</u>
       A   **B**   **C**
    plan to <u>ascertain</u> whether a hidden defect existed.
         D

    _____

Renting and Leasing

Words to learn

apprehensive
circumstance
condition
due to
fluctuate
get out of
indicator
lease
lock into
occupancy
option
subject to

1. **apprehensive** adj., anxious about the future
    a. Most new home buyers are apprehensive about their decision.
    b. The mortgage lender was apprehensive about the company's ability to pay.

2. **circumstance** n., a condition; a situation
    a. Under the current economic circumstances, they will not be able to purchase the property.
    b. If the circumstances change in the near future and we have new properties, we will be sure to call you.

3. **condition** n., the state of something; a requirement
    a. Except for some minor repairs, the building is in very good condition.
    b. There are certain conditions that are unique to leasing a property.

4. **due to** prep., because of
    a. Due to the low interest rates, good office space is difficult to find.
    b. He didn't believe that the low prices were due only to the neighborhood.

5. **fluctuate** v., to go up and down; to change
    a. No one is very comfortable making a large investment while the currency values fluctuate almost daily.
    b. Prime business areas fluctuate with local economies, crime rates, and cost of living indices.

6. **get out of** v., to escape; to exit
    a. The agent wasn't sure if the executives could get out of their prior real estate arrangement.
    b. The company wanted to get out of the area before property values declined even further.

7. **indicator** n., a sign, a signal
    a. If the economy is an accurate indicator, rental prices will increase rapidly in the next six months.
    b. The results of the elections were seen as an important indicator of the stability in the area.

8. **lease** n., a contract to pay to use property for an amount of time; v., to make a contract to use property
    a. With the lease expiring next year, they need to start looking for a new location as soon as possible.
    b. They decided to lease the property rather than buy it.

9. **lock into** v., to commit; to be unable to change
    a. The company locked itself into a ten-year lease that they didn't want.
    b. Before you lock yourself into something, check all your options.

10. **occupancy** n., the state of being or living in a certain place
    a. The occupancy rate in the building has never fallen below 85 percent.
    b. The lawyers signed the papers and the company took occupancy of the new building.

11. **option** n., a choice, an alternative
    a. You could arrange the lease with an option to buy after a certain amount of time.
    b. With the real estate market so tight right now, you don't have that many options.

12. **subject to** adj., under legal power; dependent
    a. This contract is subject to all the laws and regulations of the state.
    b. The go-ahead to buy is subject to the president's approval.

Short Conversations

Read the following conversations and see how the new words are used.

[M] I understand that we may be able to **get out of** our unfortunate situation.
[W] Yes, under certain **conditions**, a clause in your contract may not be valid.
[M] I just don't want to be **subjected** to any lawsuit.

[W] According to all the **indicators**, now is the time to buy.
[M] Are you sure that you want to make such a large commitment now? You seem **apprehensive**.
[W] If we don't buy now, interest rates may start to **fluctuate**.

[W] Under the **circumstances**, the company isn't currently in a position to make a decision.
[M] But if we don't sign this **lease** now, someone else will take the property.
[W] We simply can't **lock** ourselves **into** a lease when the future is so uncertain.

[M] As of the first of the year, we will take **occupancy** of the first and second floors.
[W] I understand that we also have first **option** on the third floor.
[M] That was **due to** great negotiating by our real estate team.

Word Families

verb	apprehend	The rental agent's lawyer tried to make the lessor apprehend that the contract was too restrictive.
noun	apprehension	The air was thick with apprehension as the landlord met with the tenants.
adjective	apprehensive	The tenants were apprehensive about the conditions of their rental agreement.

verb	condition	The president conditioned her acceptance on two factors that were spelled out in the letter of agreement.
noun	condition	They decided to rent the space, under the condition that the price would not be raised for the next two years.
adjective	conditional	If you give a conditional go-ahead, we will start drawing up the plans.

verb	indicate	As was indicated in the terms of the lease, any changes to the property must be approved by the owners.
noun	indicator	The state of local schools is a good indicator of the health of the economy.
noun	indication	The management team had every indication that the tenants were planning to stay for the near future.

verb	fluctuate	As interest rates began to fluctuate, many investors became nervous and took their money out of the real estate market.
noun	fluctuation	Construction is sensitive to any fluctuations in the economy.
gerund	fluctuating	Any additional fluctuating on prices will not be accepted.

Choose the word that best completes the sentence.

1. The real estate agent couldn't determine how to best work with a company that placed so many _____ on everything that they did.
    (A) conditional
    (B) condition
    (C) conditioned
    (D) conditions

2. The president was _____ about adding more space to the factory.
    (A) apprehend
    (B) apprehensive
    (C) apprehension
    (D) apprehended

3. The buyer _____ with a nod of his head that he was placing a bid on the property.
    (A) indicates
    (B) indication
    (C) indicated
    (D) indicator

4. _____ as it does, I don't understand how anyone can depend on that country's market to provide a safe investment.
    (A) Fluctuated
    (B) Fluctuating
    (C) Fluctuation
    (D) Fluctuate

Short Talk

Read the following passage and write the appropriate form of the new words in the blanks below.

apprehensive	due to	indicator	occupancy
circumstances	fluctuations	lease	options
condition	get out of	lock into	subject to

Starting a new business is both an exciting and frightening undertaking. Most new business owners are (5.) _____ about their ability to make all the decisions that arise during the course of opening a business. One of the first issues that will arise is whether to buy or (6.) _____ property. In order to evaluate the options, business owners research the current real estate market. (7.) _____ rates are a good (8.) _____ of the overall business climate. Prices per square foot will increase as the occupancy rate increases.

Economic change is part of the business climate. There are often large (9.) _____ in prices within a given city. These fluctuations are (10.) _____ many factors like the (11.) _____ of the building, the surrounding neighborhood, access to public transportation, and business projections for the area.

Because there is so much uncertainty in starting a business, many owners do not want to (12.) _____ themselves _____ a long-term lease. Many negotiate clauses in their contracts to (13.) _____ a lease under certain (14.) _____. They want to insure the prices and conditions of a property before making a large commitment. Leases often provide more flexibility than buying a property. They like to leave their (15.) _____ open. They don't like to be (16.) _____ the whims of the market place.

Choose the underlined word or phrase that should be rewritten and rewrite it.

17. Under the conditions of this leased, you have virtually no flexibility and are locked into occupying this space for
          A   B   C   D
    at least ten years.

    _____

18. The circumstances under which we committed to the occupancy made us apprehension about the lease.
         A   B   C   D

    _____

19. We are subjected to price fluctuating that are due to outside conditions.
          A   B   C   D

    _____

20. Because they had the option to buy in the contract, they were able to get out on an unfavorable leasing
                    A   B
    arrangement and were not subject to any penalties.
       C   D

    _____

Word Review #6   Lessons 26–30 Management Issues

Choose the word that best completes the sentence.

1. The owner of the new company personally
   _____ every expense.
   (A) scrutiny
   (B) scrutinize
   (C) scrutinized
   (D) scrutinizing

2. Several employees will _____ on
   designing the office for efficiency.
   (A) collaborate
   (B) collaborated
   (C) collaborating
   (D) collaboration

3. When there is a problem with company policy, it
   should be _____ before the board of
   directors.
   (A) bring up
   (B) bring in
   (C) brought up
   (D) brought in

4. The quality control department felt it was making
   good _____ when the number of defects
   declined.
   (A) progress
   (B) progressed
   (C) progressing
   (D) progressive

5. _____ goods can ruin the future of a
   new company.
   (A) Defect
   (B) Defects
   (C) Defective
   (D) Defection

6. The public's _____ of a company
   depends on how solidly the company stands
   behind its products.
   (A) perceive
   (B) perceptive
   (C) perceived
   (D) perception

7. The market research matched our
   _____.
   (A) assumes
   (B) assuming
   (C) assumed
   (D) assumptions

8. Determining the safeness of a particular appli-
   ance requires a _____ investigation of the
   electrical components.
   (A) system
   (B) systems
   (C) systematic
   (D) systematize

9. When _____ office space, it is wise to insist
   upon an option to renew.
   (A) lease
   (B) leasing
   (C) leased
   (D) lessor

10. _____ a lease might be expensive.
    (A) Getting in
    (B) Getting on
    (C) Getting off of
    (D) Getting out of

Choose the underlined word or phrase that should be rewritten and rewrite it.

11. Those who arrange the office should <u>concentrate</u> on creating a space that is <u>conducive</u> to work, free of
                                                  A   **B**

    <u>disrupting</u>, and <u>unhampered</u> by nonessential foot traffic.
     C   **D**

    _____

12. Efficient managers <u>adherence to</u> the <u>agenda</u>, keep <u>goals</u> in focus, and avoid <u>lengthy</u> meetings.
                            A   **B**   **C**   **D**

    _____

13. The interior designer tried to <u>enhance</u> the appearance of the <u>lobby</u> by <u>throw out</u> the old furniture that
                                      A   **B**   **C**

    unfortunately belonged to the <u>lessor</u>.
                                       D

    _____

14. Sometimes <u>circumstantial</u> force a <u>supervisor</u> to become <u>locked into</u> a commitment that is hard to <u>get out of</u>.
                      A   **B**   **C**   **D**

    _____

15. Product development <u>responsibilities</u> include <u>ascertain</u> what is needed, <u>examining</u> options, and <u>researching</u>
                                A   B   C   D
the competition.

———————————

16. A committee that does not <u>concentrate</u> on <u>priorities</u> often <u>wasting</u> time wallowing through an <u>agenda</u>.
                                    A   B   C   D

———————————

17. Although the board members meet <u>periodically</u> and could have finished <u>matters</u> at the next meeting, they
                                              A   B
decided to <u>go ahead</u> and not <u>conclusion</u> until all issues were addressed.
                 C   D

———————————

18. Before taking <u>occupancy</u> of a commercial site, check whether poor maintenance <u>conditions</u> are <u>due to</u> faulty
                      A   B   C
plumbing or electrical wiring that does not <u>conformation</u> to code.
                                              D

———————————

19. If you <u>opt</u> for <u>move up</u> the corporate ladder, be prepared for some <u>anxious</u> moments when you <u>assume</u> your
          A   B   C   D
new responsibilities.

———————————

20. An effective quality control <u>supervisor</u> of a reputable <u>brand</u> will ensure that products <u>uniformity</u> <u>conform</u> to their
                                       A   B   C   D
set standards.

———————————

Selecting a Restaurant

1. **appeal** adj., to be attractive or interesting
    a. The colorful vegetable made the dish look appealing.
    b. Eating at the new restaurant appealed to everyone in the group.

2. **arrive** v., to reach a destination
    a. By the time our meal arrived, it was cold.
    b. Frank arrived at the restaurant only minutes after Claudia left.

3. **compromise** n., a settlement of differences in which each side makes concessions
    a. The couple made a compromise and ordered food for take out.
    b. Will leaving out the green peppers compromise the taste of this dish?

4. **daring** adj., to have the courage required
    a. Kobi had more daring tastes than the rest of his family.
    b. Ordering the raw squid seemed quite a daring thing to do.

5. **familiar** adj., often encountered or seen; common
    a. It's nice to see some familiar items on the menu.
    b. The chef blends the familiar tastes with the unusual.

6. **guide** n., one who leads, directs, or gives advice
    a. The guide led our tour group to a small restaurant only known to the locals.
    b. I don't know where to go, so why don't we consult the guidebook.

7. **majority** n., the greater number or part
    a. The majority of the group wanted to try the new Chinese restaurant.
    b. Claude was in the majority, so he was very pleased with the decision.

8. **mix** v., to combine or blend into one mass; n., a combination
    a. The daring chef mixed two uncommon ingredients.
    b. The mix of bright colors on the plate was very pleasing.

9. **rely** v., to have confidence in; to depend on
    a. I have always relied on the restaurant advice this guidebook gives.
    b. I seldom rely on the restaurant reviews in the paper when choosing a restaurant.

10. **secure** v., to get possession of; to obtain
    a. Despite the popularity of the restaurant, Max was able to secure reservations for this evening.
    b. The hostess secured us another chair, so we could eat together.

11. **subjective** adj., particular to a given person; highly personal; not objective
    a. Food preferences are subjective and not everyone agrees on what tastes good.
    b. The reviews in this guidebook are highly subjective, but fun to read.

12. **suggest** v., to offer for consideration or action
    a. Can I make a suggestion about what to order?
    b. I suggest you think about the specials, since they are very good today.

Short Conversations

Read the following conversations and see how the new words are used.

[W]   Did you get any good **suggestions** for a restaurant for this weekend?
[M]   The **majority** of people in my office enjoyed the new seafood restaurant.
[W]   Well, we can always **rely** on the opinion of the masses.

[W]   The woman who writes the weekly restaurant reviews for the newspaper has published a **guide** to local restaurants.
[M]   That won't be too helpful. I don't think the same food **appeals** to her as appeals to me.
[W]   I know what you mean. There is a lot of **subjectivity** in reviewing restaurants.

[M]   I'm tired of the same kind of food all the time. Let's go somewhere with a really **daring** menu.
[W]   I like **familiar** foods and I'm not as willing as you are to try new dishes.
[M]   We'll go somewhere with a **mix** of old favorites and exciting specials.

[M]   What time do you think we'll **arrive** at the restaurant?
[W]   I'd like to say by 6 P.M., but I know that's early for you. Can we **compromise** and say by 7 P.M.?
[M]   Sounds good. I'll go ahead and **secure** a reservation for 7 P.M.

Word Families

verb	mix	The chef was famous for mixing unfamiliar ingredients.
noun	mixture	The texture of the vegetable mixture was too lumpy for my taste.
adjective	mixable	Oil and water are not mixable.

verb	rely	We will rely on the hostess's recommendations.
noun	reliability	The reliability of deliveries became a problem for the manager.
adjective	reliable	Hiring a reliable staff is the first priority for every restaurant manager.

verb	guide	The hostess guided us to our table.
noun	guidance	Li asked the waiter for guidance in selecting the wine.
adjective	guidable	Finding the patrons to be very guidable, the waiter steered them to the most expensive items on the menu.

verb	suggest	Can I suggest a good wine to go with the entrée?
noun	suggestion	Clark asked his boss for a suggestion for a good place to eat.
adjective	suggestible	The patrons were in a suggestible mood, and were easily convinced to have dessert.

Choose the word that best completes the sentence.

1. If you need some _____ on what to order, be sure to consult your server.
   - (A) guide
   - (B) guides
   - (C) guided
   - (D) guidance

2. Your father is in the kitchen _____ a batch of his famous chocolate chip cookies.
   - (A) mixture
   - (B) mixed
   - (C) mix
   - (D) mixing

3. This guidebook is several years old, so I would question its _____.
   - (A) rely
   - (B) reliance
   - (C) reliability
   - (D) relying

4. I have always found Lola's restaurant _____ to be very good, so I continue to seek her guidance.
   - (A) suggestions
   - (B) suggest
   - (C) suggestive
   - (D) suggestible

Short Talk

Read the following passage and write the appropriate form of the new words in the blanks below.

appeal	daring	majority	secure
arrive	familiar	mix	subjective
compromise	guidance	relies	suggestion

When Atul is trying to impress business contacts who are potential new clients, he takes them to the best restaurant in town. He hopes this will help (5.) _____ a new contract for his telecommunications business.

It's hard to determine which restaurants are best. Atul (6.) _____ on newspaper and magazine reviews. He also asks his friends and colleagues for (7.) _____. They are happy to make a (8.) _____.

Food tastes are (9.)_____. Although Atul likes to be (10.) _____ and take risks, he knows that the food should (11.) _____ to a variety of palates. He wants the (12.) _____ of his guests to be happy. He usually decides to (13.) _____ on a restaurant that offers a menu with a (14.) _____ of (15.) _____ standards and some exciting specials.

When he calls to book the table, he tells the person taking the reservation what time his party will (16.) _____ and the number of people he needs seating for.

Choose the underlined word or phrase that should be rewritten and rewrite it.

17. The <u>majority</u> of diners like to order <u>familiar</u> food from the menu, but the waiter will be happy to
    A   B
    <u>suggestion</u> specials for those with more <u>daring</u> tastes.
    C   D

    _____

18. Although different tastes <u>appeal</u> to different palates, it is still a good plan to <u>rely</u> on the <u>guidance</u> of friends
    A   C   B
    who have recently eaten out, despite the <u>subjective</u> of their opinions.
    D

    _____

19. Your guests may feel more <u>secure</u> if you take them to a restaurant with a menu that <u>mixture</u> <u>familiar</u> favorites
    A   B   C
    and <u>daring</u> trendy dishes.
    D

    _____

20. Fabrice didn't like Mimi's <u>suggestion</u> for a restaurant and Mimi didn't like his, so they <u>relied</u> on a restaurant
    A   B
    <u>guide</u> to come up with a <u>compromised</u>.
    C   D

    _____

Lesson 32

Eating Out

Words to learn

basic
complete
excite
flavor
forget
ingredient
judge
mix-up
patron
predict
random
remind

1. **basic** adj., serving as a starting point or basis
   a. The new restaurant offers a very basic menu.
   b. The restaurant manager ordered enough basic supplies to get through the first month.

2. **complete** adj., having all necessary or normal parts, components, or steps
   a. The new restaurant offers a complete menu of appetizers, entrees, and desserts.
   b. The tasty dessert was the perfect completion to the meal.

3. **excite** v., to arouse an emotion
   a. Exotic flavors always excite me.
   b. I get excited when I try a new restaurant.

4. **flavor** n., a distinctive taste
   a. Fusion cooking is distinguished by an interesting mix of flavors.
   b. The cook changed the flavor of the soup with a unique blend of herbs.

5. **forget** v., to be unable to remember
   a. The waiter forgot to bring the rolls, annoying the customer.
   b. Don't forget to tell your friends what a great meal you had tonight.

6. **ingredient** n., an element in a mixture
   a. The chef went to the farmer's market to select the freshest ingredients for tonight's menu.
   b. I was unfamiliar with some of the ingredients in the dish.

7. **judge** v., to form an opinion
   a. Hector was not familiar with Asian cooking, so he was unable to judge if the noodles were cooked correctly.
   b. The restaurant review harshly judged the quality of the service.

8. **mix-up** n., a confusion; v., (mix up) to confuse
   a. There was a mix-up in the kitchen so your order will be delayed.
   b. The amateur chef mixed up the ingredients and ruined the dish.

9. **patron** n., a customer, especially a regular customer
   a. Once the word was out about the new chef, patrons lined up to get in to the restaurant.
   b. I used to patronize the restaurant until the management changed.

10. **predict** v., to state, tell about, or make known in advance
    a. I predicted this restaurant would become popular and I was right.
    b. Kona was unable to predict what time Andy, who is always late, would show up at the restaurant.

11. **random** adj., having no specific pattern, purpose, or objective
    a. We made random selections from the menu.
    b. We asked the waiter to bring us several appetizers, letting him choose them at random.

12. **remind** v., to cause to remember
    a. Ms. Smith was annoyed at having to remind the waitress to bring the check.
    b. I left the client a reminder that we are meeting for dinner tomorrow evening.

Short Conversations

Read the following conversations and see how the new words are used.

[M] This restaurant **reminds** me of one we visited last year on vacation.
[W] I think they use many of the same **ingredients** in the dishes.
[M] Yes, the **flavor** of the dishes is similar.

[M] The waiter **forgot** to offer us water.
[W] He didn't even **complete** my order.
[M] Don't get **excited**. I **predict** he'll come back.

[W] Even though the menu here is **basic**, the food is highly rated.
[M] The chef uses spices at **random**, I hear.
[W] It's hard for me to **judge**. I just know what I like to eat.

[W] The server **mixed up** everyone's orders.
[M] Don't upset the **patrons**; that's the first rule of good service.
[W] I haven't **forgotten** the rules. You don't have to remind me.

Word Families

verb	complete	The meal could not be completed without dessert.
noun	completion	The coffee was the last item ordered and brought the meal to completion.
adverb	completely	The chef forgot that the dessert was in the oven and completely ruined it.

verb	forget	Don't forget to bring us the check.
adjective	forgetful	The forgetful waitress put a burden on the rest of the staff.
adjective	forgettable	The meal was bland and forgettable.

verb	predict	I predict that this restaurant will be a success.
noun	prediction	The manager's prediction came true, and the chef was named to the "Top 100" list.
adverb	predictably	Predictably, because the waiter neglected to write down the order, he forgot some necessary items.

verb	excite	The chef knows how to excite his patrons.
noun	excitement	You can feel the excitement in the air.
adjective	exciting	Being here is really exciting.

Choose the word that best completes the sentence.

1. Would you like to _____ your meal with an after-dinner drink?
   (A) complete
   (B) completed
   (C) completely
   (D) completeness

2. I've already _____ what the last table of guests ordered.
   (A) forget
   (B) forgetful
   (C) forgotten
   (D) forgetfulness

3. No one could have _____ how successful the restaurant would become.
   (A) predictive
   (B) predictably
   (C) predictable
   (D) predicted

4. I've had enough _____ for the day.
   (A) excite
   (B) exciting
   (C) excitement
   (D) excites

Short Talk

Read the following passage and write the appropriate form of the new words in the blanks below.

basic	flavor	judged	predict
complete	forget	mix up	random
excite	ingredients	patrons	remind

The key to a happy meal is that everyone should enjoy eating what they ordered. Before the waiter takes your order, you can ask him for a recommendation or you can select at (5.) _____ from the menu.

Good service is part of the overall enjoyment of the meal. The waiter should make the (6.) _____ feel welcome and comfortable. Good waiters can (7.) _____ what you need, like more water, without having to be asked for it. It's easy for a waiter to (8.) _____ something, but you should not have to (9.) _____ a waiter more than once to bring you something. Nor do you want the waiter to (10.) _____ the food orders. You should get what you ordered, and your order should be (11.) _____.

The quality of the food is the primary way restaurants are (12.) _____. The food should taste and look wonderful. Your plate of food should (13.) _____ all your senses and be fragrant and colorful. Even the most (14.) _____ or familiar dishes can taste different from restaurant to restaurant. A chef can bring out a distinct (15.) _____ in a dish, depending on the (16.) _____ he or she uses.

Choose the underlined word or phrase that should be rewritten and rewrite it.

17. The restaurant <u>patrons</u> ordered at <u>random</u> from the menu, so when the waiter <u>mix up</u> their orders, they had
         A   B   C
    <u>forgotten</u> what they ordered.
     D

    _____

18. The chef prepared a <u>basic</u> dish with daring <u>ingredients</u> that gave it an exotic <u>flavor</u> none of us could have
             A   B   C
    <u>prediction</u>.
     D

    _____

19. Before we <u>completed</u> our entrée, we had to <u>reminder</u> our waiter that we needed bread; we wondered how he
            A   B
    could <u>forget</u> such a <u>basic</u> component of the meal.
       C   D

    _____

20. Some of the most <u>exciting</u> and <u>flavor</u> dishes contain only <u>basic</u> <u>ingredients</u>.
                A   B   C   D

    _____

Ordering Lunch

1. **burdensome** adj., of or like a burden; onerous
   a. The secretary found her tedious assignments burdensome.
   b. The burdensome load made the deliveryman's back ache.

2. **common** adj., widespread, frequent, usual
   a. It is common for the office manager to be designated to order lunch for business meetings.
   b. The sandwich choices were quite common—turkey, ham, and beef.

3. **delivery** n., the act of conveying or delivering
   a. The caterer hired a courier to deliver the package.
   b. The restaurant is reluctant to make deliveries, but makes an exception for our office.

4. **elegant** adj., exhibiting refined, tasteful beauty
   a. It's important that the meal be elegant.
   b. The lunch we ordered was not elegant, but it was hearty.

5. **fall to** v., to become one's responsibility
   a. The task of preparing the meal fell to the assistant chef when the chief chef was ill.
   b. The menu was in French, so ordering for us fell to Monique, who spoke French.

6. **impress** v., to affect strongly, often favorably
   a. I was impressed with how quickly they delivered our lunch.
   b. If you want to impress the new staff member, order her a nice lunch.

7. **individual** adj., by or for one person; special; particular
   a. We had the delivery man mark the contents of each individual order.
   b. The jaunty whistle of the delivery woman marked her individual style.

8. **list** n., a series of names, words, or other items; v., to make a list
   a. The office manager compiled a list of everyone's order.
   b. The phone book lists all the restaurants in this area that deliver.

9. **multiple** adj., having, relating to, or consisting of more than one part
   a. The delivery person was not able to keep track of the multiple order, causing a food mix-up.
   b. It takes multiple steps to get into this building, which frustrates all our employees.

10. **narrow** v., to limit or restrict; adj., limited
    a. Etseko narrowed the restaurant possibilities down to three.
    b. The restaurant has a narrow range of choice, but can offer fast delivery.

11. **pick up** v., to take on passengers or freight
    a. The delivery man picks up lunch orders on his motor scooter.
    b. If you ask me nicely, I will pick up the order on my way home.

12. **settle** v., to make compensation for, to pay; to choose
    a. We settled the bill with the cashier.
    b. After much debate, we finally settled on the bistro on the corner.

Short Conversations

Read the following conversations and see how the new words are used.

[W] Will you please arrange for an **elegant** lunch during the regional manager's visit?
[M] That's such an annoying **burden**. Why don't you just go to a restaurant?
[W] I need to show our **impressive** sales data during lunch and can't show slides at a restaurant.

[W] Here's a **list** of 12 restaurants in the area.
[M] Let's **narrow** this list to two or three and then ask the staff to make a final selection.
[W] First, let's double-check that they all offer free **delivery** to this building.

[M] I'm so annoyed. I've sent **multiple** E-mail notices to staff asking for their votes for lunch choices.
[W] I think you are trying too hard to pamper people's **individual** tastes and preferences. Just make a decision.
[M] Why does this job always **fall to** me?

[M] Do caterers usually charge a fee for **picking up** the dirty dishes after an event?
[W] It's **common** to charge extra for that, but I know of one caterer who will pick up for free.
[M] That **settles** it. As far as I am concerned, we can use the cheaper caterer.

Word Families

noun	in common	The two secretaries keep a file of restaurant menus in common to facilitate placing an order.
adjective	common	It is a common practice for restaurants to deliver.
adverb	commonly	It was commonly known that the sandwich shop had slow deliverymen.

noun	elegance	The elegance of the surroundings was accentuated by the wonderful meal the caterers delivered.
adjective	elegant	Delores set an elegant table that was sure to impress.
adverb	elegantly	The tasty appetizers were elegantly served from silver platters.

verb	impress	I am favorably impressed by how quickly the pizza was delivered.
noun	impression	She gave the impression that the food would be delivered within the hour.
adjective	impressionable	I have an impressionable child, so I don't like him to see deliverymen running red traffic lights.

verb	individualize	The take-out shop does not allow you to individualize your order by asking for substitutions.
noun	individual	The portions are large enough to feed two individuals.
adverb	individually	The individually marked boxes made it easy for us to claim our orders.

Choose the word that best completes the sentence.

1. It is a _____ practice in this building for staff to meet the delivery person in the lobby to pick up their orders.
   (A) commonness   (C) common
   (B) commonly   (D) in common

2. Despite being served in disposable containers, the meal had an _____ touch.
   (A) elegant   (C) elegantly
   (B) elegance   (D) elegancy

3. Our office manager was so _____ by the speed of the delivery, she decided to order from them again.
   (A) impressive   (C) impression
   (B) impressed   (D) impressionable

4. Let's order _____ so we can all get what we want for lunch.
   (A) individualize   (C) individually
   (B) individualist   (D) individual

Short Talk

Read the following passage and write the appropriate form of the new words in the blanks below.

burdensome	elegant	individual	narrow
common	falls to	list	pick up
delivered	impress	multiple	settled

As the office manager, it usually (5.) _____ Lucia to order the food for a working lunch or an office party. Lucia finds ordering food for a working lunch to be especially (6.) _____. First, in order to avoid placing (7.) _____ small orders from different food establishments, she must (8.) _____ down the choice to one kind of food. The most (9.) _____ choices are sandwiches and (10.) _____ pizzas.

Once she has (11.) _____ on a good choice, she calls a restaurant or other food service on her approved (12.) _____. Usually she needs the food (13.) _____ so she does not have to leave the office and (14.) _____ the order herself.

In case of a more formal lunch, where her boss is trying to (15.) _____ new clients, for example, Lucia will call a catering service that can provide a more (16.) _____ meal.

Choose the underlined word or phrase that should be rewritten and rewrite it.

17. At a lunch to win the new advertising account, we served each potential new client an <u>individual</u> **A** specialty dessert; this <u>elegant</u> **B** touch <u>impressive</u> **C** those attending and helped <u>settle</u> **D** any questions about our staff's level of creativity.

   _____

18. The <u>delivery</u> **A** service is unique in that it will <u>pick up</u> **B** various orders from <u>multiples</u> **C** restaurants, making it unnecessary for everyone to <u>narrow</u> **D** their choice to one type of food.

   _____

19. Ordering food for work lunches is a <u>burden</u> **A** that <u>falls on</u> **B** the office manager, so he sends us a <u>list</u> **C** of the choices and asks us to vote for our preference and then orders the most <u>commonly</u> **D** response.

   _____

20. I think it is easiest to <u>narrow</u> **A** the choices to a small <u>list</u> **B** of sandwiches, which will appeal to <u>individual</u> **C** tastes and can be <u>delivery</u> **D** without becoming cold, like pizza.

   _____

Cooking as a Career

1. **accustom to** v., to become familiar with, to become used to
   a. Chefs must accustom themselves to working long hours.
   b. Sean was not accustomed to eating spicy foods, but he was developing a taste for them.

2. **apprentice** n., a student worker in a chosen field
   a. Instead of attending cooking school, Raul chose to work as an apprentice with an experienced chef.
   b. The cooking school has an apprentice program that places students in restaurants to gain work experience.

3. **culinary** adj., relating to the kitchen or cooking
   a. The chef was widely known for his culinary artistry.
   b. His interest in culinary arts drew him to a commercial foods program.

4. **demanding** adj., requiring much effort or attention
   a. Theodore was exhausted by his demanding job in the restaurant.
   b. Paolo was able to handle multiple requests from demanding customers without becoming frantic.

5. **draw** v., to cause to come by attracting
   a. We hope the new restaurant will draw other business to the area.
   b. Matthew was drawn to a career in cooking.

6. **incorporate** v., to unite one thing with something else already in existence
   a. Coca incorporated the patron's suggestions into her new menu.
   b. Here are the fresh greens for you to incorporate into a salad.

7. **influx** n., a flowing in
   a. An influx of new chefs is constantly needed to fill open jobs.
   b. Due to the rise in popularity of cooking as a career, cooking schools report an influx of applications.

8. **method** n., a procedure
   a. Gloria perfected a simple method for making croissants.
   b. Many chefs borrow cooking methods from a variety of cultures and incorporate them into their cooking style.

9. **outlet** n., a means of release or gratification, as for energies, drives, or desires
   a. Even before he became a professional baker, Jacob used baking as an outlet for frustration.
   b. Many people find cooking to be a hands-on outlet for their creativity.

10. **profession** n., an occupation requiring considerable training and specialized study
    a. Cooking is considered as much a profession as is law or medicine.
    b. Lulu took up cooking as her profession and is very happy with her decision.

11. **relinquish** v., to let go; to surrender
    a. People find it hard to relinquish their accustomed food preferences and try something new.
    b. After Claude married Kiki, he had to relinquish his exclusive hold on the kitchen and learn to share the joys of cooking.

12. **theme** n., an implicit or recurrent idea; a motif
    a. The caterers prepared food for a party with a tropical island theme.
    b. The restaurant's food and decor demonstrated its southwestern theme.

Short Conversations

Read the following conversations and see how the new words are used.

[M] This soup is delicious. What **culinary** secret have you discovered?
[W] It's fennel, an herb I've become **accustomed** to using lately.
[M] I also like how it's **incorporated** into the squash casserole.

[M] There's been a large **influx** of new chefs recently.
[W] I've noticed that, too. They're **demanding** large salaries, too.
[M] Good chefs manage to **draw** customers into restaurants.

[M] How do young people get started in the cooking **profession**?
[W] Most chefs serve as **apprentices** under an experienced chef.
[M] Cooking is a good **outlet** for a certain kind of creativity.

[M] Let's go to Oriental Taste for lunch; the chef there uses Asian cooking methods.
[W] I bow to your expertise. I **relinquish** to you my option to choose a restaurant.
[M] You'll enjoy yourself. The restaurant has an Asian **theme** with Asian music and videos.

Word Families

verb	apprentice	Instead of attending cooking school, Michael decided to apprentice to a master chef.
noun	apprentice	The new group of apprentices will start working any day now.
noun	apprenticeship	The apprenticeship was a grueling period, but George learned a lot.

verb	incorporate	Take these items and incorporate them into a stew.
noun	incorporation	The restaurant was the incorporation of every good idea the chef had thought of in his career.
gerund	incorporating	Chef Tao was famous for incorporating different cooking styles into one.

noun	profession	The number of people choosing cooking as a profession has risen over the past decade.
adjective	professional	She was professional in her approach to dealing with the problem of late deliveries.
adverb	professionally	Although the customer was rude and loud, the waiter handled the situation very professionally.

noun	method	The chef discovered a more efficient method of peeling boiled eggs.
noun	methodology	Even the order of adding ingredients is an unappreciated aspect of cooking methodology.
adjective	methodical	The head cook was not so artistic as methodical in preparing standard dishes.

Choose the word that best completes the sentence.

1. The student accepted a six-month _____ with a famous chef.
   (A) apprentice
   (B) apprenticed
   (C) apprenticing
   (D) apprenticeship

2. I love this chef's cooking style, which _____ so many different tastes.
   (A) incorporation
   (B) incorporates
   (C) incorporating
   (D) incorporator

3. The restaurant is well known for the coolly detached _____ of its staff.
   (A) professionalism
   (B) professional
   (C) professionalize
   (D) professionally

4. The experienced chef was _____ about the way he prepared his award-winning dish.
   (A) method
   (B) methodical
   (C) methodically
   (D) methodology

Short Talk

Read the following passage and write the appropriate form of the new words in the blanks below.

accustomed	demanding	influx	profession
apprenticeship	drawn	methods	relinquish
culinary	incorporate	outlet	themes

When people start thinking about careers, they may be looking for an (5.) _____ for their creativity. Many people are (6.) _____ to cooking as a career and see it as a (7.) _____, not merely a trade. The restaurant business is (8.) _____ and needs a constant (9.) _____ of new talent.

Chefs (10.) _____ ingredients and (11.) _____ of cooking from around the world into successful menus. Most chefs offer meals that are variations on standard (12.) _____. They will try to stretch their patrons' range of food tastes by taking food that is still recognized as traditional and infuse it with something new, like a rare spice or seasoning. People (13.) _____ to eating certain tastes and textures aren't going to (14.) _____ their preferences immediately.

Chefs attend (15.) _____ school or train in restaurants with experienced chefs, in an (16.) _____. For those of you who like hands-on creativity, being a chef might be a good choice.

Choose the underlined word or phrase that should be rewritten and rewrite it.

17. Regular patrons recognized the chef's unique <u>culinary</u> style, which <u>incorporated</u> both traditional and
    A B
    unconventional <u>methodological</u>, and were <u>drawn</u> to the innovative menu.
    C D

    _____

18. While he was still a young <u>apprentice</u>, the chef found that the cooking <u>professional</u> was a good <u>outlet</u> for his
    A B C
    <u>demand</u> for hands-on creativity.
    D

    _____

19. The <u>influx</u> of immigrants into this country over the centuries has meant that diners had to <u>relinquishing</u> menus
    A B
    to which they had grown <u>accustomed</u> to make room for different cooking <u>methods</u>.
    C D

    _____

20. Chefs draw from cultural <u>themes</u> and cooking <u>methods</u> of many national origins, which they <u>incorporation</u> into
    A B C
    meals that expand the tastes that one is <u>accustomed</u> to.
    D

    _____

Events

Words to learn

assist
coordinate
dimensions
exact
general
ideal
lead time
plan
proximity
regulation
site
stage

1. **assist** v., to give help or support to
   a. Bonnie hired a secretary to assist her with the many details of the event.
   b. The hotel manager was able to assist us with some last-minute advice.

2. **coordinate** v., to adjust or arrange parts to work together
   a. Benet tried to coordinate all departments to make sure the event ran smoothly.
   b. The colors of the flowers were ordered to coordinate with the colors in the corporate logo.

3. **dimension** n., a measure of width, height, or length
   a. What are the dimensions of the ballroom?
   b. We need the dimensions of the meeting rooms before we can determine how many chairs each will hold.

4. **exact** adj., characterized by accurate measurements or inferences
   a. We will need an exact head count by noon tomorrow.
   b. The exact measurements of the room are unknown, but we can guess.

5. **general** adj., involving only the main features rather than precise details
   a. We have a general idea of how many guests will attend.
   b. In general, about half the guests will bring their spouses.

6. **ideal** adj., imaginary; existing as a perfect model
   a. The ideal location for the concert would have plenty of parking.
   b. Lucy had imagined the ideal setting for her wedding, so no site could live up to her expectations.

7. **lead time** n., the time between the initial stage of a project and the appearance of results
   a. The lead time for reservations is unrealistic.
   b. We will need to give the caterer enough lead time to cut the cake.

8. **plan** n., a scheme for making something happen; v., to formulate a scheme
   a. The plan is to gather tomorrow to discuss the menu.
   b. Planning their wedding was a source of tension for the young couple.

9. **proximity** n., the state, quality, sense, or fact of being near or next to; closeness
   a. The fans were worried by the proximity of the storm clouds.
   b. An important factor in selecting the site was its close proximity to a parking garage.

10. **regulation** n., rules, laws, or controls; v., to control
    a. We followed all the state regulations for food safety.
    b. The site staff closely regulates how many cars can be brought on the grounds.

11. **site** n., a place or setting
    a. Once we saw the site, we knew it would be perfect for the event.
    b. The on-site manager was most helpful.

12. **stage** v., to exhibit or present
    a. The gazebo outside was the perfect location from which to stage the cutting of the cake.
    b. A historic house can be the perfect site to stage a small reception.

Short Conversations

Read the following conversations and see how the new words are used.

[M] I've found the **ideal** location for our wedding reception.
[W] Will we be able to **coordinate** all the details?
[M] It's **exactly** what we wanted, and the manger will help us with the details.

[M] We have very strict **regulations** about serving food and alcohol at the museum.
[W] I'm sure you do. In fact I'm surprised you'll let us **stage** a reception here.
[M] We are one of the few **sites** in town that will allow parties.

[W] The site staff can offer you plenty of **assistance** in **coordinating** details.
[M] That's helpful. I'm trying to **plan** everything in advance.
[W] It's important to start early and have as much **lead time** as possible.

[M] Do you think the **dimensions** of the hall are large enough to hold your group?
[W] We're expecting about 5000 attendees. That's **generally** the number that come.
[M] No, this hall is too small, but there's another in close **proximity** and together they could accommodate all of you.

Word Families

verb	generalize	When we generalize, we must be aware of the many exceptions.
adjective	general	I need a general idea of what you want before I can provide specific answers.
adverb	generally	Although I cannot speak for every case, generally it is less expensive to buy in quantity.

verb	assist	Let me assist you with planning your next event.
noun	assistance	Dennis's idea of assistance is to call a professional firm for advice.
noun	assistant	In light of the number of events she had to run this year, Annu asked her boss for an assistant.

verb	idealize	Rhoda idealized the location until she could no longer see any flaws in it.
noun	ideal	The ideal of a perfect event within your budget is difficult, but attainable.
adverb	ideally	Ideally, the site would be within our budget and have an outdoor area.

verb	regulate	The state will regulate the food-handling precautions.
noun	regulation	Please obey the state regulations regarding serving alcohol to minors.
adjective	regulatory	Even though it is private, the country club's kitchen is subject to the rules of regulatory agencies.

Choose the word that best completes the sentence.

1. Do you need our _____ with any of the evening's details?
   (A) assist
   (B) assisting`
   (C) assistance
   (D) assistant

2. When the event planner saw the hotel ballroom, she knew that the size wasn't _____, but the price was right.
   (A) ideal
   (B) ideally
   (C) idealize
   (D) idealist

3. Like restaurants, caterers are subject to _____ concerning safe food handling.
   (A) regulate
   (B) regulations
   (C) regulatory
   (D) regulating

4. _____ speaking, the event was poorly organized.
   (A) General
   (B) Generally
   (C) Generality
   (D) Generalizations

Short Talk

Read the following passage and write the appropriate form of the new words in the blanks below.

assist	exact	lead time	regulations
coordinated	general	planning	site
dimensions	ideally	proximity	stage

Planning an event is not simple. There are hundreds of details that have to be (5.) _____, whether it is a wedding or a business conference. Early in the (6.) _____ process, you need to decide on the (7.) _____. If you know where you want to (8.) _____ the event, you should contact the site representative for an (9.) _____ description of the facility. The staff will provide you with information about room (10.) _____; food and beverage arrangements, including whether there are local (11.) _____ or restrictions for serving alcoholic beverages; and required (12.) _____ for reserving the site.

If you decide that the first site is not (13.) _____ suited for your specific requirements, a guidebook will (14.) _____ you in finding an alternative setting. In considering location, you should also think about its (15.) _____ to public transportation.

With a (16.) _____ idea of how many people will attend, and how much money you can spend, you can narrow down the available sites to the ones that best accommodate the needs of your group.

Choose the underlined word or phrase that should be rewritten and rewrite it.

17. The hotel manger gave Natasha <u>assisting</u> in <u>planning</u> her first reception, especially in <u>coordinating</u> all the
                        A   B   C
    details and preparing the <u>site</u>.
                         D

    _____

18. Boris wanted to <u>stage</u> a fund-raising event, but the <u>ideally</u> locations either did not have the <u>dimensions</u> to
                 A   B   C
    accommodate the crowd he expected, or they were not in reasonable <u>proximity</u> to downtown.
                                                               D

    _____

19. In choosing a <u>site</u> for the reception, Ms. Benson had special criteria that had to be met, including close
                 A
    <u>proximity</u> to public transportation, so she needed a lot of <u>lead time</u> to meet her <u>exactly</u> needs.
    B   C   D

    _____

20. In order to <u>coordination</u> the event, we had to have a <u>general</u> idea of how many guests would attend, and <u>plan</u>
                 A   B   C
    an <u>ideal</u> menu to satisfy the needs and tastes of everyone who attended.
        D

    _____

Word Review #7   Lessons 31–35 Resaurants and Events

Choose the word that best completes the sentence.

1. The aroma coming from the restaurant was so
_____ that the tourists did not hesitate
before entering.
(A) appeal
(B) appealed
(C) appealing
(D) appeals

2. Because the menu was not in his native language,
the visitor asked the waiter for

_____.
(A) guide
(B) guided
(C) guiding
(D) guidance

3. The waiter _____ that the customer would
enjoy the duck.
(A) predict
(B) predicted
(C) predicting
(D) prediction

4. Food critics are also expected to _____
a restaurant's service and atmosphere.
(A) judge
(B) judges
(C) judging
(D) judgment

5. The host usually _____ the check for his
guest.
(A) picks over
(B) picks on
(C) picks off
(D) picks up

6. Sometimes diners request _____,
or "separate," checks.
(A) individuality
(B) Individually
(C) individual
(D) individualize

7. The most _____ customers seem to be
the worst tippers.
(A) demand
(B) demanded
(C) demanding
(D) demandingly

8. Food preparation is not just frying hamburgers; it
is a respected _____.
(A) profess
(B) professing
(C) profession
(D) professional

9. An event planner must _____ the entire
affair, not just choose the menu.
(A) coordinated
(B) coordinating
(C) coordinator
(D) coordinate

10. The planner must also ensure that participants
observe all local _____.
(A) regulated
(B) regulations
(C) regulating
(D) regulate

Choose the underlined word or phrase that should be rewritten and rewrite it.

11. Although most of us <u>settle</u> for a <u>familiar</u> restaurant, a <u>daringly</u> diner will listen to other <u>suggestions</u>.

         A   B   C   D

_____

12. A <u>site</u> for a national <u>culinary</u> event should be in close <u>proximity</u> to <u>elegantly</u> restaurants and cooking supply

     A   B   C   D
    stores.

_____

13. <u>Ingredients</u> are not added <u>randomly</u> to a dish; a <u>mixed up</u> in the order during food preparation could change

      A   B   C
    the <u>flavor</u>.

      D

_____

14. I enjoy a restaurant that <u>mixes</u> its offerings and <u>relies</u> on flavor and <u>elegance</u> to bring <u>patronize</u> back.

                            A   B   C   D

_____

15. Although a <u>general</u> concept of the <u>ideal</u> event is all right at the beginning, the outline must be more <u>exacted</u> as
         A   **B**   **C**

    <u>planning</u> continues.
      D

    _____

16. <u>Accustom to</u> impressing patrons, the chef taught his <u>apprentice</u> how to use <u>culinary</u> tricks to <u>incorporate</u> the
       A   **B**   **C**   **D**

    best flavors and textures.

    _____

17. While even the most <u>demanding</u> chefs draw on traditional <u>methods</u>, new technology has <u>multiplied</u> ways to
                         A   **B**   **C**

    improve flavor without <u>compromise</u> quality.
                        D

    _____

18. <u>Securing</u> reservations doesn't guarantee seating on <u>arrived</u>, but it does <u>narrow</u> the chances of a long wait if
     A   **B**   **C**

    there is a sudden <u>influx</u> of diners.
                 D

    _____

19. Some restaurants require a long <u>lead time</u> for <u>staging</u> a large event, but that time will allow you to add any-
                                 A   **B**

    thing you had <u>forgetting</u> and <u>settle</u> matters you hadn't thought about.
               C   **D**

    _____

20. Offering to pay the tip while your host <u>settles</u> the bill is a way to <u>reminder</u> someone who has <u>forgotten</u> that a
                                   A   **B**   **C**

    tip, although <u>subjective</u>, should be at least 15 percent of the bill.
              D

    _____

General Travel

1. **agency** n., an establishment engaged in doing business
    a. Once we decided we wanted to go to Costa Rica for vacation, we called the travel agency to see how much flights would cost.
    b. The staff at the travel agency included brochures and sight-seeing information with the ticket.
2. **announcement** n., a public notification
    a. Did you hear an announcement about our new departure time?
    b. I expect an announcement any time now about a snow emergency at the airport.
3. **beverage** n., a drink other than plain water
    a. The flight attendant offered all passengers a cold beverage during the flight.
    b. The restaurant had a range of beverages on the drinks menu, including soft drinks and juices.
4. **blanket** n., a covering for keeping warm, especially during sleep; any full coverage; v., to cover uniformly
    a. It's going to be a cold night so I'll ask housekeeping to send an extra blanket for our bed.
    b. The snow blanketed the windshield, making it difficult to see the roads.
5. **board** v., to enter a boat, plane, or train; to furnish with meals and a place to stay
    a. The inn offers room and board at weekly rates.
    b. We will board the train for New York in ten minutes.
6. **claim** v., to take as rightful; to retrieve
    a. Please proceed directly to the baggage arrival area to claim your luggage.
    b. Lost luggage can be claimed at the airline office.
7. **delay** v., to postpone until a later time; n., the period of time during which one is delayed
    a. The bus was delayed due to inclement weather.
    b. The station was experiencing minor delays, making many people late for work.
8. **depart** v., to go away or leave; to vary from a regular course of action.
    a. After the wedding, the married couple departed for their honeymoon in Morocco.
    b. We're going to depart from our usual policy and allow you to leave work early one day a week.
9. **embark** v., to go onboard a flight or ship; to begin
    a. At the gate, the passenger was required to show her passport before she could embark upon the flight.
    b. They were nervous, but also excited, to embark on a long-awaited trip to Africa.
10. **itinerary** n., a proposed route for a journey, showing dates and means of travel
    a. He reviewed the itinerary the travel agent had faxed him before purchasing the ticket.
    b. I had to change my itinerary when I decided to add two more countries to my vacation.
11. **prohibit** v., to forbid by authority or to prevent
    a. We were prohibited from wearing causal clothes in the office.
    b. Airline regulations prohibit the passengers from having beverages open during take off and landing.
12. **valid** adj., having legal efficacy or correctness
    a. I need to make certain that my passport is valid if we plan to go overseas this December.
    b. The officer's argument for increased airport security seemed valid at the time.

Short Conversation

Read the following conversations and see how the new words are used.

[W] The travel **agent** said that you will need a visa for your trip next week.
[M] Oh dear, I don't have a **valid** passport and will need to get that renewed first.
[W] I'm afraid that may force you to **delay** your trip.

[M] Would you care for another **beverage**?
[W] Is there time? According to my **itinerary**, we should be landing soon.
[M] We've been delayed. Would you like a **blanket** so you can take a nap?

[M] Does the flight **depart** at 7:15 or 7.30?
[W] Your **embarkation** card should have the flight time on it.
[M] Because use of electronic equipment is **prohibited** during the flight, I want to be sure I have time to fax some documents before we board.

[W] I hope I don't have to wait a long time to **claim** my bags at the baggage area.
[M] The captain **announced** that the flight was half empty so it shouldn't take very long.
[W] Good. I was **prohibited** from bringing more than one bag **onboard** so I had to check the other one.

Word Families

verb	announce	The captain announced that the flight would be landing in approximately 15 minutes.
noun	announcement	The flight attendant made an announcement reminding the passengers that this was a no-smoking flight.
noun	announcer	The announcer gave the instructions for boarding, in three languages.

verb	board	You can't board the flight without an embarkation card.
noun	board	The board of directors met to discuss problems with the striking pilots.
adjective	onboard	The onboard telephone was expensive to use, but a true time-saver.

verb	delay	Please don't delay me; I need to get to my gate immediately.
noun	delay	The delay in takeoff times was caused by a bad storm.

verb	validate	You can get your parking ticket validated at the concierge desk.
noun	validation	The restaurant received three stars, which is quite a validation of the chef's skills.
adjective	valid	Your ticket is no longer valid because it was issued over a year ago.

Choose the word that best completes the sentence.

1. When it's time to _____ the flight, an announcement will be made.
   (A) boarded
   (B) boarding
   (C) board
   (D) boarder

2. The man had to _____ his travel plans because an emergency came up at work.
   (A) delay
   (B) delaying
   (C) delayed
   (D) delays

3. The airport applied a blanket rule that all passengers must be in possession of _____ tickets in order to enter the waiting area.
   (A) valid
   (B) validity
   (C) validate
   (D) validation

4. The desk clerk _____ the change in gate numbers at least an hour ago.
   (A) announcement
   (B) announcing
   (C) announcer
   (D) announced

Short Talk

Read the following passage and write the appropriate form of the new words in the blanks below.

agency	blanket	delayed	itinerary
announcements	board	depart	prohibited
beverage	claim	embarkation	valid

When Ms. Tan has to go on business travel, she calls the staff at her favorite travel (5.) _____. They remind her to make sure that she takes a (6.) _____ passport on her trip. Once her reservations have been made and confirmed, the travel agent will issue a ticket and an (7.) _____. Before leaving for the airport, she calls the airline to check if the flight is on time and has not been (8.)_____.

At the airport, after checking in her suitcase at the check-in counter, since she is (9.) _____ from taking more than one piece of carry-on luggage onto the plane, Ms. Tan receives her (10.) _____ card. She will present this at the gate when it is time to (11.) _____ her flight. She is told to be at the gate 15 minutes before the flight is to (12.) _____. During the flight, the attendant may offer her a (13.) _____, and she can even request a (14.) _____ if she is cold. The captain will make (15.) _____ during the flight to let the passengers know at what altitude they are flying, and when they may expect to arrive at their destination.

Once the flight has landed, Ms. Tan disembarks and must first go through customs, before proceeding to the baggage (16.) _____ area to retrieve her suitcase. After this, she will take a cab to the hotel where she is staying, so she can rest and prepare for her meeting the next day. She will also reconfirm her return flight a day or two before she leaves to return home.

Choose the underlined word or phrase that should be rewritten and rewrite it.

17. Once we heard that the <u>departing</u> flight would be <u>delaying</u> for several hours, because of the fog that <u>blanketed</u> the coast, we exercised by walking around the baggage <u>claim</u> area.

    _____

18. Because he had lost the <u>itinerary</u> that his travel <u>agent</u> had given him, Mr. Peacock looked at the <u>embark</u> card
       A   B   C
    to check the exact time that his flight would <u>depart</u>.
                                                  D

    _____

19. The man had to show the gate attendant his <u>validation</u> passport and <u>itinerary</u>, in addition to his <u>embarkation</u>
                                                A   B   C
    card, before he was allowed to <u>board</u> the flight.
                                    D

    _____

20. The <u>announcement</u> reminded all <u>boarding</u> passengers that carrying on <u>beverages</u> was <u>prohibition</u> on this
           A   B   C   D
    airline.

    _____

Airlines

1. **deal with** v. phrase, to attend to; to manage; to see to
   a. Ticket agents must deal courteously with irate customers.
   b. Sick passengers, frightened children, and rude pilots are just a few of the things cabin attendants have to deal with.

2. **destination** n., the place to which one is going or directed
   a. The Great Barrier Reef is a popular tourist destination this year.
   b. Once you have determined your desired destination, we can work toward getting the best airfare.

3. **distinguish** v., to make noticeable or different
   a. Suki was able to distinguish between the different types of jets on the runway.
   b. My travel agent has distinguished herself as being one of the best in our area.

4. **economical** adj., intended to save money, time, or effort
   a. My travel agent takes an economical approach to my travel, which I appreciate.
   b. There are a number of more economical ways to get to Tokyo from here.

5. **equivalent** adj., equal
   a. Carlos used the Internet to search for hotels of equivalent dollar value to the one recommended.
   b. The food the airline serves in coach class is equivalent to that served in first class.

6. **excursion** n., a pleasure trip; a trip at a reduced fare
   a. With some time between meetings in London, the company president enjoyed an excursion to Stonehenge.
   b. The finance officer was pleased to find an excursion for the entire consulting team.

7. **expensive** adj., marked by high prices
   a. The shops in the airport are convenient, but I think they are expensive.
   b. Mr. Jones chose the more expensive ticket because it got him to his destination sooner.

8. **extend** v., to make longer; to offer
   a. We extended our vacation by a day.
   b. Our wonderful travel agent extended the full services of her firm to us.

9. **prospective** adj., likely to become or be
   a. The airline had a reception to impress travel agents who might be prospective clients.
   b. I narrowed my list of prospective destinations to my three top choices.

10. **situation** n., the combination of circumstances at a given moment
    a. The airline suggested I check with the State Department regarding the political situation in the country I'm flying to.
    b. The vast number of different air fares available makes for a complicated situation.

11. **substantial** adj., considerable in importance, value, degree, amount, or extent
    a. In the consumer satisfaction survey, the airline I work for won by a substantial margin.
    b. There is a substantial difference in the price for the two airfares.

12. **system** n., a functionally related group of elements
    a. The airline system covers the entire world with flights.
    b. We need a better system to keep track of how much money we are spending on this vacation.

Short Conversations

Read the following conversations and see how the new words are used.

[M] If you are willing to be flexible about your **excursion**, I can get you a lower airfare.
[W] We have to reach our **destination** by noon on Sunday.
[M] I didn't realize your **situation** was so structured.

[M] The airfares to Hong Kong are too **expensive**.
[W] Let's look for a more **economical** fare for you.
[M] I will really need a **substantial** discount to make my trip possible.

[M] Here are some brochures on the **prospective** vacations you mentioned on the phone.
[W] I've seen so many travel brochures, I can't **distinguish** one from another.
[M] You need a travel agent who is used to **dealing with** holiday **excursions**.

[M] I'm **extending** my stay by two days, so I need you to change my plane reservations.
[W] Unfortunately, our **system** of pricing fares does not allow me to put you on another flight without a surcharge.
[M] I was hoping to get a fare **equivalent** to the one I've already paid for.

Word Families

verb	distinguish	I can't distinguish any difference in the two airlines, since their fares are the same.
adjective	distinguishable	The airline's planes were easily distinguishable by the bright logo on the planes' tails.
adverb	distinguishably	Even though you have paid a lower fare, we won't be distinguishably different than the other passengers on the plane.

verb	economize	We no longer fly first class, since our company is trying to econmize.
noun	economy	When I sit in economy, I often get the middle seat.
adjective	economical	Without hesitation, we chose the more economical of the two airline tickets.

noun	expense	To stay within our travel budget, we must keep all our expenses as low as possible.
adjective	expensive	Only the most expensive fares were still available.
adverb	expensively	The first-class seats are for those who travel expensively but with great style.

noun	substance	I couldn't recognize the substance that was on my meal tray and that the airlines called dinner.
adjective	substantial	Ms. Qin found there was a substantial difference in the price quoted for the plane ticket, depending on which day she flew.
adverb	substantially	There is substantially no difference in the quality of food served in first class and in economy class.

Choose the word that best completes the sentence.

1. Let me point out the features of our service that _____ our airline from our competitors.
   (A) distinguishably
   (B) distinguishable
   (C) distinguishing
   (D) distinguish

2. I think the proposal for plane tickets is too _____ and want you to renegotiate the costs with the airline.
   (A) expensiveness
   (B) expensively
   (C) expensive
   (D) expenses

3. Let's shop around until we find a more _____ airfare.
   (A) economical
   (B) economize
   (C) economy
   (D) economically

4. Unless you find a _____ difference in the fare, I would book seats on the airline with which you have frequent-flyer miles.
   (A) substance
   (B) substantial
   (C) substantially
   (D) substantiality

Short Talk

Read the following passage and write the appropriate form of the new words in the blanks below.

deal with	equivalent	extending	situation
destination	excursion	indistinguishable	substantial
economical	expensive	prospective	system

If you travel, you most likely will have to (5.) _____ flying. Flying is the quickest, most convenient means of travel between countries, and often between different parts of one country. Flying is (6.) _____, but when all costs are taken into account for traveling any (7.) _____ distance, air travel is usually less expensive than driving by car. It is also the most (8.) _____ way to go in terms of time. You'll miss the scenery en route, but you'll have more time at your vacation (9.) _____ with air travel.

Airlines sell seats at a variety of prices under a (10.) _____ of requirements and restrictions. Full-fare tickets are the most expensive, but give you the most flexibility in terms of making changes. A (11.) _____ traveler can buy a ticket up to takeoff time as long as a seat is available.

Fares change rapidly, and even travel experts find it difficult to keep up. The changing (12.) _____ is due to many factors, including increased competition. As a general rule, the less you pay for the ticket, the more restrictions you can expect. If you are trying to save money, look for (13.) _____ fares. These are the airline's (14.) _____ of a special sale. Most excursion fares are for round-trip travel and have strict regulations and a minimum and maximum length of stay, so don't count on (15.) _____ your vacation or staying less time than required. However, once you are on the plane, you are (16.) _____ from passengers who paid higher fares.

Choose the underlined word or phrase that should be rewritten and rewrite it.

17. For travelers looking for <u>economical</u> fares, you get <u>substantially</u> savings with special <u>excursion</u> rates to your
          A   **B**   **C**
    <u>destination</u>.
    D

    _____

18. Due to the <u>expense</u> of flights to our travel <u>destination</u>, our travel agent suggests we <u>extensive</u> our stay to get
         A   **B**   **C**
    the most out of the difficult <u>situation</u>.
               D

    _____

19. The airline <u>system</u> is so complex that it is difficult to <u>distinguishable</u> between <u>equivalent</u> fares on different air-
        A   **B**   **C**
    lines; that is why most people appreciate the expertise of a travel agent used to <u>dealing</u> with the airlines.
               D

    _____

20. A <u>prospect</u> traveler may need to compromise to get an <u>economical</u> <u>excursion</u> fare to a vacation
      A   **B**   **C**
    <u>destination</u>.
    D

    _____

Lesson 38

Trains

Words to learn

comprehensive
deluxe
directory
duration
entitle
fare
offset
operate
punctual
relatively
remainder
remote

1. **comprehensive** adj., covering broadly; inclusive
   a. The conductor has a comprehensive knowledge of rail systems from all over the world.
   b. Our travel agent gave us a comprehensive travel package, including rail passes.

2. **deluxe** adj., noticeably luxurious
   a. My parents decided to splurge on deluxe accommodations for their trip.
   b. The train station is not near any of the deluxe hotels, so we will have to take a taxi.

3. **directory** n., a book or collection of information or directions
   a. We consulted the directory to see where the train station was located.
   b. By calling directory assistance, Mr. Scannel was able to get the phone number for the train station.

4. **duration** n., the time during which something lasts
   a. Mother lent me her spare jacket for the duration of the trip.
   b. Despite our personal differences, my roommate and I agreed to be as pleasant as possible for the duration of the train ride.

5. **entitle** v., to allow or qualify
   a. During the holiday rush, a train ticket entitled the passenger to a ride, but not necessarily a seat.
   b. Because the train line had made a mess of Pedro's reservations for a sleeping room, he felt entitled to a free upgrade to a better room.

6. **fare** n., the money paid for transportation
   a. The train fare has increased since I rode last.
   b. Pay your fare at the ticket office and you will get a ticket to board the train.

7. **offset** v., to counterbalance
   a. The cost of the hotel room offset the time savings we gained by taking the train instead of the plane.
   b. By reducing her transportation costs once in the United States, Mrs. Sato offset the cost of getting to this country.

8. **operate** v., to perform a function
   a. The train operates on a punctual schedule.
   b. The train only operates in this area at the height of the tourist season.

9. **punctual** adj., prompt
   a. Please be on time; the train leaves punctually at noon.
   b. The train is usually punctual; I can imagine what is delaying it.

10. **relatively** adv., somewhat
    a. The train is relatively empty for this time of day.
    b. The train station has been relatively busy for a weekday.

11. **remainder** n., the remaining part
    a. The Alaskan frontier has train service in the summer, but for the remainder of the year the tracks are impassable.
    b. We will move you to a less expensive room and credit the remainder of what you've already paid to your charge card.

12. **remote** adj., far removed
    a. I was surprised to find train service to such a remote location.
    b. We took the train out of the city and found a remote hotel in the country for the weekend.

Short Conversations

Read the following conversations and see how the new words are used.

[M] I can't believe this train is so crowded! We'll be standing for the **duration** of the trip.

[W] I always thought that buying a **fare entitled** me to a seat.

[M] They should **operate** more trains on busy holidays like today.

[M] Take a look at the **directory** to see exactly what time the next train to New York leaves.

[W] Do you think the trains are **punctual**?

[M] I would think that **operating** on time would be the basis of any transportation company.

[M] I would like to take the train to visit my parents, but they live in a **remote** part of the state.

[W] I sympathize. I wish there were a more **comprehensive** train system in this country.

[M] Taking a plane is an option and the time saved just might **offset** the cost of the ticket.

[M] We would like to upgrade our accommodations for the **remainder** of the trip.

[W] I'm afraid that all the sleeping chambers we have available are **relatively** the same.

[M] That's a shame. We were hoping to secure a **deluxe** room.

Word Families

noun	comprehensiveness	Due to the comprehensiveness of the train system, the complete timetable was a thick document.
adjective	comprehensive	Due to the comprehensive reach of the rail system, the train can take you to every major city and many smaller ones.
adverb	comprehensively	The surveyors comprehensively studied the terrain before planning the site for the new train tracks.

verb	operate	Trains don't operate in this town after the summer tourism season is over.
noun	operation	The train system is a massive operation with thousands of large and small stations across the country.
adjective	operational	As the operational expenses for the train system rose, the managers were forced to either cut services or raise prices.

noun	punctuality	The Swiss trains are legendary for their punctuality.
adjective	punctual	For a transportation service to have any credibility, it must be punctual.
adverb	punctually	The conductor arrived punctually at the train station

noun	remoteness	The remoteness of the state park was part of its attraction, but since it's not served by a train line, I couldn't get to it.
adjective	remote	The remote cabin in the woods can only be reached by car; the nearest train station or airport is more than 100 miles away.
adverb	remotely	I wasn't remotely interested in taking a cross-country trip by train since I can't stand to be confined for a long time.

Choose the word that best completes the sentence.

1. Do you have a _____ map that shows all the station stops west of the Mississippi?
   (A) comprehension   (C) comprehensive
   (B) comprehensively   (D) comprehensiveness

2. The train has stopped because of a malfunction, but we expect it to be _____ again within minutes.
   (A) operational   (C) operation
   (B) operate   (D) operationally

3. John has a bad habit of not being _____, so I always am anxious when we travel together for fear of missing a train.
   (A) punctualness   (C) punctually
   (B) punctual   (D) punctuality

4. With this traffic, there isn't even a _____ chance that we will get to the train station on time.
   (A) remotely   (C) remoteness
   (B) remote   (D) remotest

Short Talk

Read the following passage and write the appropriate form of the new words in the blanks below.

comprehensive	duration	offset	relatively
deluxe	entitle	operate	remainder
directories	fares	punctual	remote

Trains are among the best ways to see a lot of a country in a (5.) _____ short amount of time. In addition to the consideration of time, traveling by train allows you to really see the country you are passing through. You need only get to the station on time; after that you can relax and watch from the window.

Most trains are on time and run on a (6.) _____ schedule. Routes, schedules, and (7.) _____ are listed in a timetable available at a train station, in many travel (8.) _____, or posted on the World Wide Web. Directories that are (9.) _____ list all the trains, the cities they serve, the stations they depart from, and the class of services available. A few (10.) _____ travel destinations are accessible only during the peak tourist season; the train does not (11.) _____ there the (12.) _____ of the year.

The fare is based on how far you travel and the quality of your accommodations. The basic fare buys you a seat for the (13.) _____ of the trip. To be more precise, an unreserved seat guarantees a passenger transportation only; seats are allocated on a first-come, first-served basis. On busy holidays, it is possible that you could stand for at least some of your trip. For long trips, you will want to reserve a seat.

If you are traveling overnight, the cost of your room accommodation will depend on how (14.) _____ your room is. Although taking the train is less expensive than flying, the savings may be (15.) _____ by the cost of booking a sleeping room.

Travelers coming to the United States can take advantage of special rates not available in the United States. These passes (16.) _____ the bearer to unlimited coach travel on trains for a fixed period of days, usually a month.

Choose the underlined word or phrase that should be rewritten and rewrite it.

17. If the train is <u>punctuality</u> to the time schedule listed in the <u>directory</u>, we can <u>offset</u> the previous delay and be
    A   B   C
    back on schedule for the <u>remainder</u> of the trip.
                             D
    _____

18. The lesser <u>fare</u> does not necessarily <u>entitle</u> you to a seat, so there is a <u>remotely</u> chance you will have to stand
              A   B   C
    when the train <u>operates</u> on a busy holiday.
                   D
    _____

19.. The train has a <u>comprehensively</u> array of sleeping accommodations, ranging from <u>deluxe</u> suites to <u>relatively</u>
                      A   B   C
    small rooms, with a range of <u>fares</u>.
                                 D
    _____

20. The transcontinental train ride, which is 12 days in <u>duration</u>, <u>operating</u> through some of the more <u>remote</u> parts
                                                          A   B   C
    of Canada; then the <u>remainder</u> of your trip is in the beautiful city of Vancouver.
                        D
    _____

Hotels

1. **advance** n., a move forward
   a. Clarissa booked the bridal suite in advance of the hotel's official opening.
   b. Every advance in technology was evident throughout the hotel's computerized functions.

2. **chain** n., a group of enterprises under a single control
   a. Budget-priced hotel chains have made a huge impact in the industry.
   b. The hotel being built in Seoul is the newest one in the chain.

3. **check in** v., to register at a hotel; to report one's presence
   a. Patrons check in at the hotel immediately upon their arrival.
   b. To know that the conference guests have arrived, we ask them to check in at the registration desk.

4. **confirm** v., to validate
   a. Jorge called the hotel to confirm that he had a room reservation.
   b. We automatically send a postcard to let you know that your travel dates have been confirmed.

5. **expect** v., to consider probable or reasonable
   a. You can expect a clean room when you check in at a hotel.
   b. Mr. Kim expected that the bed linens would be changed daily.

6. **housekeeper** n., someone employed to do domestic work
   a. Eloise's first job at the hotel was as a housekeeper and now she is the manager.
   b. The desk clerk is sending the housekeeper to bring more towels to your room.

7. **notify** v., to report
   a. They notified the hotel that they had been delayed in traffic and would be arriving late.
   b. Lydia notified the hotel in writing that she was canceling her reservation.

8. **preclude** v., to make impossible; to rule out
   a. The horrible rainstorm precluded us from traveling any further.
   b. The unexpected cost of the room precluded a gourmet dinner for the travelers.

9. **quote** v., to give exact information on; n., a quotation
   a. We were quoted a price of $89 for the room for one night.
   b. Call ahead and get a price quote for a week-long stay.

10. **rate** n., the payment or price according to a standard
    a. The rate for the hotel room is too high considering how few services are available on-site.
    b. The sign in the lobby lists the seasonal rates.

11. **reserve** v., to set aside
    a. I know I reserved a room for tonight, but the hotel staff has no record of the reservation in the system.
    b. The bride and groom reserved a block of rooms at the hotel for guests coming to their wedding from out of town.

12. **service** n., useful functions
    a. The hotel has a number of luxury services like the on-site gym, sauna, pool, and beauty salon.
    b. Mr. Rockmont called room service to order a late-night snack.

Short Conversations

Read the following conversations and see how the new words are used.

[M] Mrs. Kim called to **confirm** her stay this weekend.
[W] She made a **reservation** several weeks ago.
[M] Yes, she took advantage of the special **rate** we advertised for the winter holidays.

[M] What is our hotel **chain's** policy on canceling reservations?
[W] If we have been notified of your cancellation at least 24 hours in **advance**, we will refund any deposit.
[M] That's good news, because the customer **expects** to have his deposit returned.

[M] The customer in Room 334 says he was **quoted** a room rate of $89 per night.
[W] Why didn't he say something when he **checked in** at the registration desk?
[M] Maybe he was too busy asking about the different hotel **services** available.

[M] We'd like to use our room in **advance** of the check-in time.
[W] I'm sorry, but that would **preclude** the staff from cleaning your room and making the bed.
[M] Then, please **notify** us when the housekeeper is through.

Word Families

verb	confirm	It is wise to confirm your reservation before you leave for your trip.
noun	confirmation	The confirmation code given to Suzanne when she booked her room made it easy for her to resolve her problem.
adjective	confirmed	The concierge had the confirmed helpful manner that is necessary in her position.

verb	expect	We expect to reach our destination by dinner.
noun	expectation	The guest's expectations were not met, so he complained to the manager.
adjective	expectant	The expectant travelers, loaded with luggage, left the hotel for their scheduled flight.

verb	quote	When customers ask for the room rate, just quote them the prices listed on this sheet.
noun	quotation	The quotation given to me didn't make sense, so I called again to verify it.
adjective	quotable	Our manager instructed us that the current room rates would be quotable only until the end of the month, when a rate increase would go into effect.

verb	reserve	We reserved a room well in advance.
noun	reservation	Seeing the crowds on the highway, I decided to pull over and telephone the hotel to make a reservation.
noun	in reserve	Like many other businesses, a hotel must keep some cash in reserve to pay for emergencies.

Choose the word that best completes the sentence.

1. Gladys _____ her reservation by calling in advance.
   (A) confirmation
   (B) confirmed
   (C) confirming
   (D) confirmative

2. The Chamber of Commerce had high _____ for the amount of business the new hotel would bring to the town.
   (A) expectancy
   (B) expected
   (C) expect
   (D) expectations

3. I expect the rate that I was _____ over the phone and I will not accept any changes.
   (A) quoted
   (B) quotation
   (C) quotable
   (D) quotes

4. Since we had made our _____ so far in advance, we saved considerably on the room rate.
   (A) reserve
   (B) reservation
   (C) reserved
   (D) reservable

Short Talk

Read the following passage and write the appropriate form of the new words in the blanks below.

advance	confirm	notify	rates
chains	expect	preclude	reservations
check in	housekeeper	quoted	service

People stay in hotels for business and personal travel. But with room rates being so high, many travelers are staying home. Since high costs can (5.) _____ travel, smart travelers know they can save money and get the best (6.) _____ for a room by making (7.) _____ well in (8.) _____ of the beginning of their trip. When you make a reservation, the hotel staff will ask you to (9.) _____ them as soon as there is any change in your travel plans. To avoid any surprises, it's a good idea to call and (10.) _____ the availability of your room and the rate you were (11.) _____.

In selecting a hotel, first think about the kinds of (12.) _____ you will need or like to have. You naturally (13.) _____ a clean, well-lit room. You naturally expect that a (14.) _____ will clean your room daily even in the smallest hotels. Large hotel (15.) _____ offer the most services, such as a pool, health club, or money exchange. The front desk clerks will tell you about such services when you (16.) _____ at the hotel.

Choose the underlined word or phrase that should be rewritten and rewrite it.

17. By making <u>reserve</u> three months in <u>advance</u>, Cleo was able to take advantage of a special <u>rate</u> that was
         A   B   C
    cheaper than the price <u>quoted</u> in the hotel brochure.
                          D

    _____

18. With multiple locations in every major city, the dominant hotel <u>chains</u> offer low <u>rates</u> and extensive <u>services</u>
                                             A   B   C
    that many small hotels are <u>preclusion</u> from offering.
                               D

    _____

19. Even before you <u>check in</u> at the registration desk, you can <u>expectation</u> that the hotel <u>housekeeper</u> has made
                        A   B   C
    your room ready in <u>advance</u> of your arrival.
                       D

    _____

20. Before departing for his trip, Jacques called the hotel in <u>advance</u> to <u>confirm</u> the <u>rate</u> and to make sure the staff
                                               A   B   C
    had been <u>notification</u> that he needed a wheelchair-accessible room.
         D

    _____

Lesson 40

Car Rentals

1. **busy** adj., engaged in activity
   a. Alfred was busy getting ready for his vacation.
   b. The airport was busy, with people catching planes and heading for car rental companies.

2. **coincide** v., to happen at the same time
   a. My cousin's wedding coincided with a holiday weekend, so it was a perfect time to rent a car and go for a drive.
   b. Sean was hoping that the days for the special discount on car rentals would coincide with his vacation, but they did not.

3. **confusion** n., a lack of clarity, order, or understanding
   a. There was some confusion about which rental discount coupons applied to which car rental agency.
   b. To avoid any confusion about renting the car, Yolanda asked her travel agent to make the arrangements on her behalf.

4. **contact** v., to get in touch with
   a. Manuel contacted at least a dozen car rental agencies to get the best deal.
   b. Last night I was contacted by my travel agent who said he had found a better price on a car rental.

5. **disappoint** v., to fail to satisfy the hope, desire, or expectation of
   a. Leila was disappointed to discover that no rental cars were available the weekend she wished to travel.
   b. I hate to disappoint you, but I can't allow you to rent a car unless you have a major credit card.

6. **intend** v., to have in mind
   a. I never intended to drive to Los Angeles until my brother suggested we do it together.
   b. Do you intend to return the car to this location or to another location?

7. **license** n., the legal permission to do or own a specified thing
   a. First, I'll need to see your driver's license and a major credit card.
   b. You will need a license in order to run this business.

8. **nervous** adj., easily agitated or distressed; uneasy or apprehensive
   a. Lonnie is nervous about driving in the city, so I volunteered to drive that part of the trip.
   b. I looked around nervously the entire time I was in the dark parking garage.

9. **optional** adj., not compulsory or automatic
   a. Check this box if you wish to have this optional insurance.
   b. Having a driver's license is not optional.

10. **tempt** v., to be inviting or attractive to
    a. I am tempted by the idea of driving across the country instead of flying.
    b. Gina is tempted to rent the smaller car to save a few dollars.

11. **thrill** n., the source or cause of excitement or emotion
    a. The thought of renting a sports car gave John a thrill.
    b. Just taking a vacation is thrill enough, even if we are driving instead of flying.

12. **tier** n., a rank or class
    a. The car rental company had a few tiers of cars, each one costing more than the previous tier.
    b. If you are on a budget, I suggest you think about renting a car from our lowest tier.

Short Conversations

Read the following conversations and see how the new words are used.

[M] I'm sorry to **disappoint** you, but we don't have any rental cars available.
[W] I didn't realize that a holiday **coincided** with our vacation.
[M] This holiday weekend has been especially **busy**.

[M] Would you like to have collision insurance on the rental car? It's **optional** coverage.
[W] I doubt very much that we'll have an accident, but I'd feel less **nervous** if we had the coverage.
[M] No one ever **intends** to have an accident, so it's probably wise to have the extra insurance coverage.

[M] In addition to the compact cars and sedans, we also have a **tier** of luxury cars, such as sports cars and convertibles.
[W] Please don't **tempt** me with a convertible. I should stick with a budget car.
[M] You know your needs, but I don't want you to miss the **thrill** of driving along the ocean with the top down.

[M] The car rental agency won't rent a car to me until I've had my driver's **license** for at least six months.
[W] They just want to be sure you are an experienced driver. Did you **contact** more than one agency?
[M] I've called at least six companies, and each has different restrictions and prices. I'm **confused** by all the information.

Word Families

verb	coincide	This year, my vacation coincides with a national holiday, which will make renting a car more expensive.
noun	coincidence	By coincidence, I ran into an old friend in line waiting to rent a car.
adverb	coincidentally	Coincidentally, we are offering a special discount if you are over age 65.

noun	intention	I have every intention of paying by cash even though I reserved the car with my credit card.
adjective	intent	Intent on avoiding an accident, Zola drove cautiously through the rush hour traffic.
adverb	intently	The tourist intently studied the road map.

noun	nervousness	I hope my nervousness did not show when I was filling out the forms.
adjective	nervous	This was Jane's first time renting a car, so she was somewhat nervous.
adverb	nervously	Mr. Lane nervously parallel parked the rental car between two others in the parking garage.

verb	tempt	Can I tempt you to rent a larger car with a special discount?
noun	temptation	The temptation to drive the sports car fast was too great for Karl to resist.
adjective	tempting	As tempting as it sounds to drive to Florida, I think I'd rather fly.

Choose the word that best completes the sentence.

1. I don't think it is a _____ that the special discount rate for renting a car expires right before the holiday weekend.
   (A) coincidental   (C) coincidence
   (B) coincidentally   (D) coincide

2. Due to the detour and the lack of good directional signs, the frustrated driver drove _____ through several city blocks, looking for the new exit.
   (A) confuse   (C) confusion
   (B) confusedness   (D) confusedly

3. Tito _____ drove the rental car through the crowded garage following the signs to the car rental return location.
   (A) nerve   (C) nervous
   (B) nervousness   (D) nervously

4. The new car rental company _____ me to try them by offering a discount coupon toward my next rental.
   (A) tempted   (C) temptation
   (B) tempting   (D) temptress

Short Talk

Read the following passage and write the appropriate form of the new words in the blanks below.

busy	contacted	license	tempted
coincided	disappointment	nervous	thrill
confused	intended	optional	tier

Many travelers taking a driving vacation simply rent a car. Yoko called ahead to rent a car at her vacation destination. Although she was (5.) _____ to book a car once she arrived at her destination, Yoko was (6.) _____ about not having a reservation. Her vacation (7.) _____ with a holiday, so she knew many other people would also be renting cars. Yoko wanted to avoid the (8.) _____ of finding that a car was not available at this (9.) _____ travel time.

There are a lot of car rental firms, so Yoko (10.) _____ several of them to compare rates and requirements. At each company she called, she learned she would need a valid driver's (11.) _____ and a major credit card to rent a car.

Yoko was somewhat (12.) _____ by the many different rates for renting cars. Some companies offered substantial discounts provided that the car was reserved for a certain number of days. One company offered her a great daily rate, but it was based on a three-day rental. Since she only (13.) _____ to rent the car for two days, the discount did not apply to her. Also, the base price did not cover (14.) _____ costs, like collision insurance or gas refills.

Another factor influencing the rate was the type of car. Rentals are based on a (15.) _____ price system. The more luxurious or sporty, or the larger the car, the higher the daily rate. Since Yoko needed only a small reliable car, she found a reasonable rate—although she would have liked the (16.) _____ of driving a convertible!

Choose the underlined word or phrase that should be rewritten and rewrite it.

17. Due to the busy weekend, by coincidence both a government and a religious holiday, travelers who had not
    A   **B**
    reserved ahead were disappointment when they contacted car rental agencies and found no cars available.
                          C   **D**

    _____

18. I'm sure the car rental agent did not intend to confuse me with the various insurance coverage options, but
                                    A   **B**   **C**
    I was nervousness weighing my options and became overwhelmed.
         D

    _____

19. Carlos, confusion by the signs directing him to the rental car drop-off location, nervously drove around the many
              A   **B**
    levels of the parking garage until he finally used his cell phone to contact a busy agent and get directions.
                                                          C   **D**

    _____

20. After inspecting the customer's credit card and driver's license, Luisa tried to temptation the customer into
                                                          A   **B**
    renting a more expensive car by promoting the thrill of a sports car ride, but he chose a car from the rental
                                              C
    agency's budget tier.
                   D

    _____

Word Review #8   **Lessons 36–40 Travel**

Choose the word that best completes the sentence.

1. When _____ your luggage, be sure to check the name on the tag.
   (A) claim
   (B) claimed
   (C) claimant
   (D) claiming

2. The plane's _____ was delayed until the wings were defrosted.
   (A) depart
   (B) departed
   (C) departure
   (D) departing

3. Many airlines _____ courtesy discounts to senior citizens.
   (A) extend
   (B) extending
   (C) extension
   (D) extensive

4. It is easier to _____ making reservations if you are specific about your requirements.
   (A) deal in
   (B) deal from
   (C) deal out
   (D) deal with

5. Trains are generally more _____ than airlines.
   (A) punctuality
   (B) punctually
   (C) punctual
   (D) punctuate

6. Some travel agencies _____ on a very tight budget.
   (A) operating
   (B) operation
   (C) operates
   (D) operate

7. Even if you pay cash, you need a credit card just to _____ to a hotel.
   (A) check in
   (B) checks in
   (C) checking in
   (D) checked in

8. Sometimes when you arrive, there is no room for you, even with a _____ reservation.
   (A) confirm
   (B) confirms
   (C) confirmed
   (D) confirmation

9. Without a reservation, renting a car could be a big _____.
   (A) disappoint
   (B) disappointed
   (C) disappointing
   (D) disappointment

10. No one will allow someone who isn't a _____ driver to rent a car.
    (A) license
    (B) licensed
    (C) licensing
    (D) licensee

Choose the underlined word or phrase that should be rewritten and rewrite it.

11. Before <u>reservation</u> a hotel room, ask the agent to <u>quote</u> the lowest <u>rate</u>; then make a <u>confirmed</u> reservation.
          A   B   C   D
    _____

12. An airline can be <u>economical</u> and still <u>distinguishing</u> itself with more comfortable <u>blankets</u> or a wider choice of
                            A   B   C
    <u>beverages</u>.
    D
    _____

13. Before <u>boarding</u>, check the <u>valid</u> of your passport, that you have an extra copy of your <u>itinerary</u>, and that you
            A   B   C
    are not carrying any <u>prohibited</u> items.
                               D
    _____

14. The rental agency was so <u>busy</u> that people caught in the <u>confusion</u> were <u>tempted</u> to <u>contacting</u> another
                                    A   B   C   D
    agency.
    _____

15. Finding an <u>economically</u> <u>excursion</u> fare does not mean that your trip must be <u>substantially</u> different from a
                  A   B   C
    more <u>expensive</u> one.
         D
    _____

16. If your hotel accommodations do not meet your <u>expecting</u>, <u>notify</u> the <u>housekeeper</u>, who will immediately
                                                      A   **B**   **C**
<u>service</u> the room.
  D
_____

17. Trains offer <u>comprehensive</u> services at very different <u>fares</u>, from the <u>deluxe</u> to the <u>relativity</u> basic.
                  A   **B**   **C**   **D**
_____

18. Travel agencies are <u>notified</u> in <u>advance</u> of bargains and regular <u>announcing</u> about dangerous <u>situations</u>.
                           A   **B**   **C**   **D**
_____

19. No matter what the rental rate, when you start selecting <u>options</u> equipment, you should be a little <u>nervous</u>
                                                   A   **B**
about whether the value is <u>equivalent</u> to the <u>expense</u>.
                           C   **D**
_____

20. At the point of <u>embarkation</u>, listen for <u>announcements</u> about when you may <u>board</u> or whether there will be a
                  A   **B**   **C**
<u>delayed</u>.
  D
_____

Lesson 41

Movies

Words to learn

attain
combine
continue
description
disperse
entertainment
influence
range
release
represent
separate
successive

1. **attain** v., to achieve
   a. The movie quickly attained cult status.
   b. The director attained his goal of an Academy Award.

2. **combine** v., to come together
   a. The director combined two previously separate visual techniques.
   b. The new production company combines the talents of three of Hollywood's best known teams.

3. **continue** v., to maintain without interruption
   a. The film continues the story set out in an earlier film.
   b. The search for a star will continue until one is found.

4. **description** n., a representation in words or pictures
   a. The description of the film did not match what we saw on screen.
   b. The critic's description of the film made it sound very appealing.

5. **disperse** v., to spread widely, to scatter
   a. The reporters dispersed after the press agent cancelled the interview with the film director.
   b. The crowd outside the movie premiere would not disperse until they had seen the movie stars.

6. **entertainment** n., a diverting performance or activity
   a. The movie was provided for our entertainment.
   b. There was no entertainment for children of guests at the hotel.

7. **influence** v., to alter or affect
   a. The editor's style influenced a generation of film editors.
   b. The producer was able to influence the town council to allow her to film in the park.

8. **range** n., the scope
   a. The range of the director's vision is impressive.
   b. What is the price range you are willing pay for a ticket to the premiere?

9. **release** v., to make available to the public; to give permission for performance
   a. The film was finally released to movie theaters after many delays.
   b. The producers of the film are hoping to release it in time for the holidays.

10. **represent** v., to typify
    a. The actor represented the ideals of the culture.
    b. The hungry child in the film represented the world's poverty.

11. **separate** adj., detached; kept apart
    a. Movie-making combines several separate processes.
    b. The financial and artistic teams are usually in separate divisions.

12. **successive** adj., following in order
    a. The script went through successive rewrites.
    b. Somehow the successive images were interrupted and had to be edited again.

137

Short Conversations

Read the following conversations and see how the new words are used.

[M] I was amazed at how the film **represented** good and evil through symbols.
[W] The **descriptions** were much more graphic on film than in the novel.
[M] The film was certainly able to **attain** a high degree of suspense.

[M] Did you find the latest movie as **entertaining** as the previous ones?
[W] Oh, yes. I can see how the actress has been **influenced** by light situation comedies on television.
[M] She certainly has developed a broader **range** of styles in the past two years.

[M] This movie is a sequel to an earlier film and **continues** the themes of the first movie.
[W] I saw them both years ago and on **successive** nights. Now, I've confused both of them.
[M] The movie we'll see tonight was **released** in theaters for only a short time and wasn't as popular.

[M] We need to do more editing on the sound for this film, but the sound engineers **dispersed** before we could do the final edits.
[W] Will the sound track be on the image track or will it be on a **separate** track?
[M] They're usually **combined**. This film will be subtitled, though, not dubbed.

Word Families

verb	attain	The film quickly attained a reputation as a "must-see" movie.
noun	attainment	The technical attainments in the movie's special effects were laudable.
adjective	attainable	The director's goal of having an unlimited budget was not attainable.

verb	continue	Continue giving out movie passes until I tell you to stop.
noun	continuation	The continuation of the film will be shown after the intermission.
adjective	continual	The actors' continual demands slowed down the pace of production.

verb	describe	Please describe the new movie theater to me.
noun	description	The description of Africa in the film was not as I remembered it.
adjective	descriptive	The writer's descriptive account of the war is shocking and saddening.

verb	entertain	The comedian worked hard to entertain the children in the hospital.
noun	entertainment	Movies are one of the most popular forms of entertainment.
adjective	entertaining	The light comedy was entertaining, if not memorable.

Choose the word that best completes the sentence.

1. Do you think this actor will _____ the heights of his famous father?
   (A) attain
   (B) attaining
   (C) attainable
   (D) attainment

2. A sequel is a _____ of a story set in motion by a previous film.
   (A) continuity
   (B) continuing
   (C) continuation
   (D) continues

3. Each director has a uniquely _____ style of storytelling.
   (A) descriptive
   (B) describe
   (C) description
   (D) descriptively

4. _____ is one of the fastest growing sectors of the economy.
   (A) Entertained
   (B) Entertainment
   (C) Entertain
   (D) Entertainingly

Short Talk

Read the following passage and write the appropriate form of the new words in the blanks below.

attain	descriptions	influence	represent
combines	dispersement	range	separate
continues	entertaining	released	successive

The popularity of the movies began early in the 20th century and (5.) _____ today. People of all ages find movies (6.) _____. Movies are a worldwide phenomenon, as the internationalism of movie distribution has affected the rapid (7.) _____ of ideas around the globe. One movie can quickly (8.) _____ other movies. But why are movies so popular?

Movies are a kind of storytelling. They try to describe an idea or record an observation about our culture. These (9.) _____ are recorded using moving visual images. Some movies portray the situation accurately and realistically, whereas other movies find visual symbols to (10.) _____ those situations.

On the most simple level, movies are a succession of moving images. These (11.) _____ images are captured on film. Directors film a wide (12.) _____ of shots—long, medium, and close up—to create a visual composition. The visual images, along with plot, characterization, and sound, produce the desired narrative. The shots are joined together in any number of combinations in a process called editing.

Making a film is a massive, complex, and expensive task that (13.) _____ art and business. Making a movie involves the talents of hundreds, and sometimes thousands, of artists, producers, and business people. It can take months, even years, for a film to be (14.) _____ into a movie theater.

Like a novel, a movie is not just a story, but a story told a certain way. A film director may want to make a movie that tells a meaningful story or one that is primarily entertaining, and will use different filming techniques to (15.) _____ that goal. It is impossible to (16.) _____ what is told in a movie from how it is told. A director's artistic vision can range from improvised to carefully controlled. Think about the complexity of a movie the next time you see one.

Choose the underlined word or phrase that should be rewritten and rewrite it.

17. Part of the <u>entertainment</u> of seeing a movie is understanding how the director <u>combination</u> a <u>range</u> of different
    A   B   C
    styles to <u>attain</u> an artistic goal.
    D
    _____

18. The director's early films, which showed the classic French <u>influential</u> of <u>combining</u> tragedy and comedy in a
    A   B
    broad <u>range</u> of story material, were finally <u>released</u> on video.
    C   D
    _____

19. The film <u>described</u> the poverty of the city in a <u>succession</u> of stark images that <u>continuation</u> the director's famil-
    A   B   C
    iar theme of how good and evil are <u>dispersed</u> throughout society.
    D
    _____

20. The award-winning film <u>combined</u> the frequently <u>separate</u> worlds of critical success and popular appeal that
    A   B
    other films fail to <u>attain</u> by <u>representation</u> the full range of human emotions.
    C   D
    _____

Theater

1. **action** n., the series of events that form the plot of a story or play
    a. The director decided that the second act needed more action and asked the playwright to review the work.
    b. The action on stage was spellbinding.

2. **approach** v. to go near; to come close to in appearance or quality; n., a way or means of reaching something
    a. The performance approaches perfection.
    b. The director's approach to the play was controversial.

3. **audience** n., the spectators at a performance
    a. The audience cheered the actors as they walked off the stage.
    b. The playwright expanded his audience by writing for film as well as for stage.

4. **create** v., to produce through artistic or imaginative effort
    a. The writer created the characters to represent the seven deadly sins.
    b. The legendary actress created the role of Blanche and no one else dared take on the part.

5. **dialogue** n., a conversation between two or more persons
    a. The actors performed the dialogue without using scripts.
    b. The written dialogue seemed great, but was hard to perform.

6. **element** n., fundamental or essential constituent
    a. The audience is an essential element of live theater.
    b. By putting together all the elements of theater into one play, he over-whelmed the critics.

7. **experience** n., an event or a series of events participated in or lived through
    a. The experience of live theater is very thrilling.
    b. Going to the theater was not part of Claude's experience growing up.

8. **occur** v., to take place; to come about
    a. The murder in the play occurs in the second act.
    b. It never occurred to me that the wife whom the character referred to was imaginary.

9. **perform** v., to act before an audience, to give a public presentation of
    a. The theater group performed a three-act play.
    b. Juan performed the role without forgetting any lines.

10. **rehearse** v., to practice in preparation for a public performance; to direct in rehearsal
    a. The players rehearsed for only three weeks before the show opened.
    b. The director rehearses with the actors ten hours each day.

11. **review** n., a critical estimate of a work or performance; v., writing a criticism of a performance
    a. The critic's influential review of the play was so negative that it sank the entire production.
    b. The newspaper sent a rank amateur to review the play.

12. **sold out** adj., having all tickets or accommodations completely sold, especially ahead of time; v., to sell all the tickets
    a. The Broadway opening was sold out months in advance.
    b. We expect that this play will be a smash and sell out quickly.

Short Conversations

Read the following conversations and see how the new words are used.

[M] Did you read the **review** of the new musical comedy that ran in yesterday's paper?
[W] I can't believe the tickets are already **sold out** for the entire run.
[M] I hear the charming **dialogue** among the characters is very funny.

[W] The staging of the play was the most **creative** I had ever seen.
[M] All the **elements** of the production—the sets, costumes, and lights—were unusual.
[W] That production was a once-in-a-lifetime **occurrence**.

[M] I won't be home for dinner because I have a **rehearsal**.
[W] How many more weeks until your first **performance**?
[M] Too few; I'll feel much better knowing that you'll be supporting me from the **audience**.

[W] The meaning of the play can be **approached** from many different levels.
[M] There was so much **action**, I think I missed the meaning. I'll have to think about it for a while.
[W] That's all part of the theater **experience**.

Word Families

verb	approach	The actress approached me with the idea for a new play.
adjective	approachable	Despite his great fame, the director was friendly and approachable.
noun	approach	The informal approach to the play was unconventional.

verb	create	The playwright created a realistic town and townspeople with the scenery and dialogue.
noun	creation	The creation of the elaborate costumes took months.
adjective	creative	The director is one of the most creative people I know.

verb	experience	The actor experienced great self-doubt before he became famous.
noun	experience	Directors bring their experience of the world onto the stage.
adjective	experienced	The experienced make-up artist transformed Maxine into an old woman in a matter of minutes.

verb	perform	The popular actress was hired to perform Shakespeare on a world tour.
noun	performance	I booked tickets for the performance the day they went on sale.
noun	performer	The performers each had three costume changes.

Choose the word that best completes the sentence.

1. The director's creativity showed in everything from her _____ to the literary quality of the play to the costumes and sets.
   (A) approaching
   (B) approach
   (C) approachable
   (D) approachability

2. As your director, I call upon you to bring your life _____ into your role.
   (A) experienced
   (B) experiencing
   (C) experiential
   (D) experience

3. I am not _____ enough to work in the theater, but I certainly enjoy attending it.
   (A) create
   (B) creativeness
   (C) creative
   (D) creativity

4. I look forward to the annual _____ of *The Nutcracker* ballet.
   (A) performance
   (B) performer
   (C) perform
   (D) performable

Short Talk

Read the following passage and write the appropriate form of the new words in the blanks below.

action	created	experiences	rehearsal
approach	dialogue	occurs	reviews
audience	elements	performance	sold out

Many people find nothing as exciting as an evening of live theater. The theater combines great works of literature written for the stage, the talents of great actors, and the efforts of hundreds of skilled artisans who work to create a mood. This mood, (5.) _____ by the actors, director, and playwright with the supporting (6.) _____ of sets, lighting, and costumes, is what makes a theatrical (7.) _____ magical. When the curtain goes up, this magic (8.) _____ right before your eyes.

The director of a play will (9.) _____ the work from his or her own artistic perspective. Each director has a different vision and this shapes how he or she directs the movement or (10.) _____ between the characters. Directors use not only their theatrical training, but real-life experiences to create a meaningful, realistic evening. Actors also bring their own artistic and personal (11.) _____ to their work. This is why every staging of a play is unique.

Plays construct another world before your eyes. Ordinary words turn into meaningful (12.) _____. Costumes and sets can be realistic or symbolic. Everything in a play looks easy, but it takes many weeks of (13.) _____ to get everything in place.

Watching a play from the (14.) _____ is great fun. To find out if a play is good, look for (15.) _____ in the newspapers or ask friends. When plays are really popular, the available seats can fill up quickly and the play will be (16.) _____.

Choose the underlined word or phrase that should be rewritten and rewrite it.

17. Under a creation hand, common elements come together to make a special experience for the audience.
    A   B   C   D
    _____

18. The reviews of the new play were all very positive, so the performing sold out quickly as audiences spread the
    A   B   C   D
    good word.
    _____

19. The action of the play was very unconventional, so its meaning could be approached from different levels;
    A   B
    when this occurrence, audiences have a lot to talk about.
    C   D
    _____

20. Even before the rehearsals were completed, the dialogues between the characters had been heard and seen
    A   B
    on television, so the performance was sold out before the reviewing ran in the papers.
    C   D
    _____

Music

Words to learn

available
broad
category
disparate
divide
favorite
instinct
preference
reason
relaxation
taste
urge

1. **available** adj., ready for use; willing to serve
    a. In order to understand all the words to the opera, Sue Lin kept an Italian dictionary available at all times.
    b. I checked the list of available compact discs before ordering.

2. **broad** adj., covering a wide scope
    a. Dominique had a broad knowledge of opera history.
    b. The history of music covers a broad range of culture and ethnicity.

3. **category** n., a division in a system of classification; a general class of ideas
    a. Jazz is one of many categories of music.
    b. The works of Mozart are in a category by themselves.

4. **disparate** adj., fundamentally distinct or different
    a. In the song, the disparate voices hauntingly join a blended chorus.
    b. Religious songs cut across disparate categories of music.

5. **divide** v., to separate into parts
    a. The music class was evenly divided between those who liked country and western music and those who do not.
    b. The broad topic of music can be divided into manageable parts, such as themes, styles, or centuries.

6. **favorite** adj., preferred
    a. Sam had long considered Mozart his favorite composer and had a wide collection of recordings of his works.
    b. Hearing the jazz trio in such a large hall is not my favorite way to enjoy them.

7. **instinct** n., an inborn pattern that is a powerful motivation
    a. The student's ability to play the cello was so natural, it seemed an instinct.
    b. The music lover followed his instincts and collected only music that he enjoyed.

8. **preference** n., someone or something liked over another or others
    a. His musical preferences were for contemporary popular music.
    b. Ms. Lanet failed to indicate her seating preference when she ordered the opera tickets.

9. **reason** n., the basis or motive for an action; an underlying fact or cause
    a. We'll never understand the reason why some music is popular and some is not.
    b. There is every reason to believe that Beethoven will still be popular in the next century.

10. **relaxation** n., the act of relaxing or the state of being relaxed; refreshment of body or mind
    a. Listening to soothing music before bedtime provides good relaxation.
    b. He played the piano for relaxation and pleasure.

11. **taste** n., the ability to discern what is excellent or appropriate
    a. Ella had the taste required to select a musical program for the visiting dignitaries.
    b. This music does not appeal to my tastes; but I'm old-fashioned.

12. **urge** v., to advocate earnestly; n., a natural desire
    a. His mother urged him to study the piano; the rest is musical history.
    b. I get the urge to play the guitar every time I pass a music store window.

Short Conversations

Read the following conversations and see how the new words are used.

[M]   I looked for my **favorite** CDs at the music store, but they were out of stock. Everything **available** was pretty dull.
[W]   With all the **disparate** music out there, how could all the CDs be boring?
[M]   I guess my **tastes** don't match those of the majority of the people buying CDs these days.

[W]   Please don't adjust the preset button on my radio.
[M]   I just want to listen to some **relaxing** music.
[W]   I just like to be able to find the music I **prefer** right away.

[M]   You have so many tapes and CDs. How do you **categorize** them so you know where they are?
[W]   I just **divide** them into the different forms of music, like all operas together, or all gospel music together.
[M]   You certainly like a **broad** range of music.

[W]   What's the **reason** for the happy expression on that girl's face?
[M]   She has the **urge** to dance, that's clear.
[W]   Her affinity for following the beat of the music seems **instinctive**.

Word Families

verb	categorize	Some singers have a broad range of styles and are difficult to categorize.
noun	category	Most of Sam's compact discs fall into the category of classical music.
adjective	categorical	The sheet music follows the categorical system used in most libraries.

adverb	favorably	The concert was favorably reviewed by the music critic.
adjective	favorite	The teenager had an extensive collection of music by all her favorite groups.
adjective	favorable	The favorable reviews of the group's new album helped to push the album up the sales charts.

verb	prefer	I would prefer tickets for Saturday's concert, but will accept Sunday tickets if that is all that is available.
noun	preference	Jazz is his preference, but he is usually happy to hear anything playing locally.
adjective	preferential	The stage manager gave the opera diva preferential treatment, fearing her famous temper.

verb	relax	After a long concert tour, the singer liked to relax by the pool.
noun	relaxation	Listening to music is an enduring form of relaxation.
adjective	relaxed	The conductor made her way to the podium, struck a relaxed pose, then raised her baton.

Choose the word that best completes the sentence.

1. I don't know how to _____ my taste in music.
    - (A) categorize
    - (B) categories
    - (C) categorical
    - (D) categorically

2. The symphony members _____ to travel abroad only once a year.
    - (A) prefer
    - (B) preferable
    - (C) preference
    - (D) preferential

3. The string quartet received a _____ comparison to the best of the genre.
    - (A) favor
    - (B) favoritism
    - (C) favorably
    - (D) favorable

4. After a hard day at work, we like to _____ to soothing music.
    - (A) relaxation
    - (B) relaxes
    - (C) relaxing
    - (D) relax

Short Talk

Read the following passage and write the appropriate form of the new words in the blanks below.

available	disparate	instinctive	relax
broad	divided	prefer	taste
category	favorite	reason	urge

Everyone loves music, it seems. And there's little (5.) _____ to wonder why. There is so much music (6.) _____ from which to choose, and there is a (7.) _____ of music to appeal to every (8.) _____. The major groups of music are (9.) _____ broadly into classical, popular, and jazz. Within these (10.) _____ groups are many other subcategories. For example, such (11.) _____ types of music as movie soundtracks, rhythm and blues, rock, and rap all fit within the category of popular music.

The (12.) _____ to make and enjoy music may be (13.) _____. Even small children will (14.) _____ certain kinds of music.

Another reason that music is so popular is the variety of settings in which one can enjoy his or her (15.) _____ kind of music. You can go to a church to hear great religious music, or to a concert hall to hear a well-known classical symphony. On another night, you might go to a small club to listen to an up-and-coming jazz group while you enjoy a drink. A few nights later, you might go with some friends to join thousands of other people in a stadium to hear your favorite rock band play in your city on a world tour. And, back at your house or apartment, you can (16.) _____ while you put in a tape or CD and listen to your favorite artists again and again in your own home.

Choose the underlined word or phrase that should be rewritten and rewrite it.

17. Although my friends have <u>urged</u> me to change my <u>taste</u> in music, I still <u>favor</u> country-western music, which is
        _A   _B   _C
     always <u>availability</u> on the radio.
              _D

     _____

18. The basic <u>categories</u> of music can be <u>division</u> into a few <u>broad</u> groups that appeal to many different musical
                _A   _B   _C
     <u>tastes</u>.
      _D

     _____

19. The <u>reasons</u> for the <u>disparate</u> kinds of music in the world reflect not only personal <u>preferable</u> but also people's
            _A   _B   _C
     <u>instinctive</u> need to express themselves.
        _D

     _____

20. Every night, Chester <u>prefers</u> to <u>relaxation</u> and forget the workday by indulging his <u>urge</u> to listen to his <u>favorite</u>
                             _A   _B   _C   _D
     music.

     _____

Museums

1. **acquire** v., to gain possession of; to get by one's own efforts
    a. The museum acquired a Van Gogh during heavy bidding.
    b. The sculptor acquired metalworking skills after much practice.

2. **admire** v., to regard with pleasure; to have esteem or respect for
    a. Raisa, admiring the famous smile, stood before the Mona Lisa for hours.
    b. The gallery was lucky to be given a collection of works by such an admired artist.

3. **collection** n., a group of objects or works to be seen, studied, or kept together
    a. The museum's collection contained many works donated by famous collectors.
    b. The museum's collection kept two full-time curators busy.

4. **criticism** n., an evaluation, especially of literary or other artistic works
    a. According to the criticism of the Victorian era, the painting was a masterpiece; now it is considered merely a minor work.
    b. The revered artist's criticism of the piece was particularly insightful.

5. **express** v., to give an opinion or depict emotion
    a. The sculptor was able to express his feelings better through the use of clay than words.
    b. The photograph expresses a range of emotions.

6. **fashion** n., the prevailing style or custom
    a. According to the fashion of the day, the languid pose of the sculpture was high art.
    b. The museum's classical architecture has never gone out of fashion.

7. **leisure** n., freedom from time-consuming duties; free time
    a. The woman took up painting in her retirement, when she had more leisure time.
    b. We can go to the permanent collection at our leisure.

8. **respond** v., to make a reply; to react
    a. You should respond to the invitation to attend the museum gala.
    b. The visitors who viewed those poignant photographs responded emotionally.

9. **schedule** n., a list of times of events; v., to enter on a schedule
    a. The museum offers a schedule of guided tours.
    b. The museum is scheduling a collection of works by Japanese masters.

10. **significant** adj., meaningful; having a major effect; important
    a. The use of lambs to symbolize innocence is significant in Western art.
    b. The rash of new acquisitions represented a significant change in the museum's policies.

11. **specialize** v., to concentrate on a particular activity
    a. The art historian specialized in Navajo rugs.
    b. The museum shop specializes in Ming vases.

12. **spectrum** n., a range of related qualities, ideas, or activities
    a. The painting crosses the spectrum from symbolic to realistic representation.
    b. The whole spectrum of artistic expression was represented in the watercolor.

Short Conversations

Read the following conversations and see how the new words are used.

[M] The art historians say that this painting is a **significant** contribution to the field. Do you like it?
[W] I don't know if I can always tell what abstract art is trying to **express**.
[M] Neither can I, but I **admire** the use of color.

[M] How will the museum staff **respond** to the charges that they have an insufficient number of works by minority artists?
[W] They are certainly embarrassed by the **criticism**.
[M] I think they should **acquire** a more diverse range of works.

[M] We have hired Ms. Jessup to mount an exhibit from our **collection** of Southeast Asian art.
[W] She's one of the best known **specialists** in Southeast Asian sculpture.
[M] There's really a broad **spectrum** of sculpture from that region.

[M] I can't believe how crowded it is in here. When did it become **fashionable** to visit the museum?
[W] Since people have more **leisure** time, I guess they like to spend it looking at art.
[M] I'll have to **schedule** another time when it is less crowded to come.

Word Families

verb	collect	The enthusiast began to collect Shaker furniture in the 1960s.
noun	collection	My parents' collection of crystal had outgrown their dining room cupboard.
noun	collector	The avid collector spent weekends at estate sales looking for rare art objects.

verb	criticize	The sculptor was criticized for his lack of perspective.
noun	critic	The art critic gave the show a poor review, which saddened the exhibition team.
noun	criticism	The writer's elegant essays on the use of light in Flemish painting were landmarks in art criticism.

verb	respond	When Mr. Hon did not respond to the invitation to the opening, we assumed he was not able to attend.
noun	response	The response to the request for assistance was overwhelming.
adjective	responsive	The director was not responsive to any of the staff's suggestions, which made them both annoyed and anxious.

verb	specialize	The art student decided to specialize in French and English paintings of the 1860s.
noun	specialist	The curator is a specialist in native Caribbean art.
adjective	specialized	The museum hired specialized personnel to adjust the humidity and light for the display of ancient books.

Choose the word that best completes the sentence.

1. Once Mimi began _____ pottery, her husband gave her pieces as gifts.
   (A) collection   (C) collecting
   (B) collectable   (D) collector

2. The curator's _____ of the museum's fund-raising plan seemed shortsighted.
   (A) criticism   (C) critical
   (B) critic   (D) criticize

3. We have been asked to _____ to the proposal by the end of the month.
   (A) responsive   (C) respond
   (B) response   (D) responding

4. After becoming a _____ in Egyptian tomb painting, the art historian lost her interest in other kinds of art.
   (A) specialize   (C) specially
   (B) specialist   (D) special

Short Talk

Read the following passage and write the appropriate form of the new words in the blanks below.

acquire	criticism	leisure	significant
admire	expressing	responded	specialize
collected	fashion	schedule	spectrum

Museums are places to view and (5.) _____ the great works of art. All large cities, and even many small cities, have good art museums in which you will find a wide (6.) _____ of paintings, sculptures, drawings, and prints.

Museums attempt to collect and display a broad range of examples of how, throughout time, men and women have (7.) _____ to what they have seen, thought, and felt by (8.) _____ themselves through materials like stone, clay, and paint, or ink and paper. The artist imposes an order on these materials that is (9.) _____. Some styles of art or particular objects are in (10.) _____ for only a while, and others earn positive (11.) _____ over time and are seen as enduring classics. Museums collect the best of these works for the public to see.

When you go to a museum, be sure to (12.) _____ plenty of time to see the art without feeling rushed. If you are lucky enough to live near a museum, you can come back again at your (13.) _____. Some museums show a broad collection of art from different times and cultures, often (14.) _____ and donated by their generous patrons. Other museums (15.) _____ in displaying art from a certain period, say from the ancient world, or by a certain group or nationality of people, like by Native Americans.

The operations of many museums are paid for by the government and these museums are often free to the public; other museums must charge each person upon entry. These fees help the museum operate and (16.) _____ more works.

Choose the underlined word or phrase that should be rewritten and rewrite it.

17. Delores <u>admired</u> the wonderful <u>collection</u> of nature photographs that seemed to <u>expressive</u> the wide <u>spectrum</u>
             A   **B**   **C**   **D**
    of design found in nature.

    _____

18. The city's newest museum, which <u>specializes</u> in art by African Americans, has <u>acquisition</u> works that are
                               A   **B**
    <u>significant</u> in how they <u>respond</u> to the American experience.
     C   **D**

    _____

19. Even though the paintings had once been very <u>fashionable</u>, art <u>critics</u> now find them to be <u>insignificant</u> and
                                   A   **B**   **C**
    unworthy of being in a museum <u>collect</u>.
                               D

    _____

20. The museum has <u>acquired</u> so many new paintings that I will have to <u>schedule</u> a day to <u>admire</u> them at my
               A   **B**   **C**
    <u>leisurely</u>.
     D

    _____

Lesson 45

Media

Words to learn

assignment
choose
constant
constitute
decisive
disseminate
impact
in depth
investigative
link
subscribe
thorough

1. **assignment** n., v., something, such as a task, that is assigned
   a. The reporter was assigned to cover the president.
   b. When the reporter is on assignment, research piles up on her desk.

2. **choose** v., to select one thing over another
   a. Alan chooses to read to *The New York Times* over the *Wall Street Journal*.
   b. I did not choose that candidate to be the editor of our student newspaper.

3. **constant** n., something that is unchanging or invariable
   a. The constant updating of information keeps reporters busy checking their facts.
   b. People constantly look to the news to keep up-to-date on what is going on in the world.

4. **constitute** v., to be the elements or parts of
   a. All the different news sources constitute the media industry.
   b. A talented staff, adequate printing facilities, and sufficient distribution points constitute a successful newspaper.

5. **decisive** adj., characterized by decision and firmness
   a. The court set a decisive precedent when it allowed the newspaper to print the controversial story.
   b. Newspaper editors must be decisive when determining which stories go on the front page.

6. **disseminate** v., to scatter widely; to distribute
   a. The media disseminates news across the world.
   b. The computer virus was disseminated through the newsroom by reporters sharing terminals.

7. **impact** n., a strong, immediate impression
   a. The story of the presidential scandal had a huge impact on the public.
   b. The impact of the news coverage is yet to be known.

8. **in depth** adj., in complete detail; thorough
   a. The newspaper gave in-depth coverage of the tragic bombing.
   b. Ivan worked for months on a story that covered in depth the spread of the disease and its effect on the population.

9. **investigative** adj., specializing in uncovering and reporting hidden information
   a. He is one of the most famous investigative reporters.
   b. The amount of fact-checking needed to run a hard-hitting investigative story is time-consuming.

10. **link** n., an association; a relationship
    a. The computer links will take you to today's headlines.
    b. The father-daughter team of reporters is just one example of many family links at this newspaper.

11. **subscribe** v., to receive a periodical regularly on order
    a. Jill subscribes to a gardening magazine.
    b. Brian bought his friend a magazine subscription for his birthday.

12. **thorough** adj., exhaustively complete
    a. The reporters were thorough in their coverage of the event.
    b. The story was the result of thorough research.

Short Conversations

Read the following conversations and see how the new words are used.

[M] Would you **choose** to work for television news instead of a newspaper?
[W] No way! Newspapers can cover a story much more **thoroughly** than television news.
[M] That's certainly a **decisive** answer.

[M] Does the Internet **constitute** a legitimate media vehicle?
[W] If an organization **disseminates** news to the public, it is considered a news outlet.
[M] I think many people find it convenient to **link** the news right from their computers.

[M] I don't think I can complete my **assignment** by the deadline.
[W] I'm feeling the pressure of **constantly** having to perform on deadline. My reporting is starting to suffer.
[M] I doubt that our **subscribers** know what we go through to put out a paper every day.

[M] Why did you decide to become an **investigative** reporter?
[W] I was excited about the chance to provide an **in-depth** look at topics of interest.
[M] Your reports certainly have had an **impact** on the profession of journalism.

Word Families

verb	choose	No one was surprised when the student decided to choose a career in journalism.
noun	choice	It's your choice whether we use a color or black and white photo.
adjective	choosy	The editor was famous for being choosy about whom she wanted on her staff.

verb	investigate	Alban was excited about his first chance to investigate a story.
noun	investigation	The investigation into the president's past was covered by the media worldwide.
adjective	investigative	After turning up details in the crime that even the police had missed, Helen became well known as an investigative reporter.

verb	subscribe	I subscribe to the local newspaper to stay current.
noun	subscription	Buying a subscription to the magazine was much less expensive than buying individual issues.
noun	subscribers	The magazine went out of business because it did not have enough subscribers.

noun	thoroughness	A newspaper cannot survive long without a reputation for thoroughness.
adjective	thorough	Toshi is famous for her thorough and fair reporting of the issues.
adverb	thoroughly	The reporter thoroughly checked all his facts to avoid any potential embarrassment.

Choose the word that best completes the sentence.

1. I don't want to pressure you, but you need to _____ the reporter who will cover the mayor's race this year.
   (A) chosen   (C) choose
   (B) choosy   (D) choice

2. The reporters followed the official _____ by interviewing all the witnesses to the crime.
   (A) investigate   (C) investigative
   (B) investigation   (D) investigational

3. I need to renew my _____ for cable television, but I can't find the form.
   (A) subscribing   (C) subscriber
   (B) subscription   (D) subscribe

4. The editor was impressed with how _____ the reporter was in getting the details from his sources.
   (A) thorough   (C) thoroughly
   (B) thoroughness   (D) thoroughbred

Short Talk

Read the following passage and write the appropriate form of the new words in the blanks below.

assignments	constitutes	impact	links
chooses	decisions	in-depth	subscribes
constant	disseminated	investigative	thoroughly

Chen likes to get his news from the paper. Lemma turns on the television to find out what's going on in the world. Eve (5.) _____ to more magazines than she can keep track of, whereas Kobi (6.) _____ to listen to radio talk shows that cover issues (7.) _____ to tap into what's going on in the world. All these people are touched by the media.

What is the media? What (8.) _____ the media? The media consists of all the ways that news and information is (9.) _____ to a mass audience. The media covers everything from hard news, which is (10.) _____ reporting, to stories that are purely entertaining, such as whether your favorite movie star was on the "Best Dressed/Worst Dressed" list. Whether in print or broadcast on TV, the stories are the product of the reporting of many journalists who write the stories, and editors who give out the (11.) _____, assess the quality of the writing and research, and make the (12.) _____ about where and when the stories run.

The news has an immediate (13.) _____. The Internet puts global news onto the personal computer on your desk. Almost all browsers have (14.) _____ to up-to-the-minute news stories from various news services. You can get (15.) _____ news updates from a variety of sources via your personal computer, providing you with the most up-to-date and (16.) _____ coverage.

Choose the underlined word or phrase that should be rewritten and rewrite it.

17. The <u>decision</u> and <u>thorough</u> way the reporter handled every <u>assignment</u> made her a natural candidate for the
         A   B   C
    <u>investigative</u> news desk.
      D

    _____

18. The avid reader was so impressed with the <u>in-depth</u> information the magazine <u>disseminated</u> about terrorist
                                        A   B
    training camps that he immediately became a <u>subscriber</u> in order to ensure he had a <u>constancy</u> supply of news.
                                            C   D

    _____

19. The media, which is <u>comprised</u> of newspapers, magazine, television and radio news, and Internet news ser-
                          A
    vices, <u>investigator</u> and <u>disseminates</u> news in an impartial fashion and serves as our <u>link</u> to the world.
          B   C   D

    _____

20. The TV anchor knew the <u>impact</u> the tragic story would have so he <u>assignment</u> a junior reporter to develop a
                                   A   B
    <u>thorough</u>, <u>in-depth</u> story on the tragedy.
      C   D

    _____

Word Review #9   Lessons 41–45 Entertainment

Choose the word that best completes the sentence.

1. Movies are probably the most popular form of
   _____ in the United States.
   (A) entertain
   (B) entertained
   (C) entertaining
   (D) entertainment

2. Television has seriously _____ society.
   (A) influence
   (B) influenced
   (C) influencing
   (D) influential

3. Actors can spend too much time _____ as
   well as too little.
   (A) rehearse
   (B) rehearsed
   (C) rehearsing
   (D) rehearsal

4. Even when a show is _____, it is sometimes
   possible to get in.
   (A) sell out
   (B) sell on
   (C) sold off
   (D) sold out

5. Orchestra music is wonderfully conducive to
   _____.
   (A) relaxation
   (B) relaxed
   (C) relaxes
   (D) relax

6. There is no good or bad music, only that which
   does or does not appeal to your _____.
   (A) taste
   (B) tastes
   (C) tasted
   (D) tasting

7. New _____ are one of the most excit-
   ing aspects of museum work.
   (A) acquire
   (B) acquisitions
   (C) acquires
   (D) acquisitive

8. Sometimes I look at a famous painting and won-
   der why it is considered more
   _____ than the ones on
   either side of it.
   (A) signify
   (B) signified
   (C) significant
   (D) significantly

9. The Internet _____ information faster than
   any other medium.
   (A) disseminate
   (B) disseminates
   (C) dissemination
   (D) disseminating

10. In any news medium, the only news is what the
    editor _____ is news.
    (A) decide
    (B) decides
    (C) decision
    (D) decisions

Choose the underlined word or phrase that should be rewritten and rewrite it.

11. The <u>dialogue</u> between <u>collectors</u> and art <u>specialize</u> <u>influences</u> the shape of a museum's collection.
        A   B   C   D
    _____

12. The <u>range</u> of <u>critical</u> of the film reflects the <u>tastes</u> of a diverse <u>audience</u>.
        A   B   C   D
    _____

13. <u>Critics'</u> <u>reviews</u> have a great <u>impacted</u> on the <u>entertainment</u> industry.
      A   B   C   D
    _____

14. Music is <u>available</u> in a <u>broad</u> range of <u>categories</u> to suit individual <u>prefers</u>.
            A   B   C   D
    _____

15. Some writers <u>choose</u> to specialize in <u>in-depth</u> <u>investigated</u> <u>assignments</u>.
            A   B   C   D
    _____

16. Rave <u>reviewed</u> can <u>create</u> <u>sold-out</u> <u>performances</u> for the run of the show.

     A   B   C   D

   _____

17. I prefer to <u>admire</u> art <u>collections</u> at <u>leisurely</u>, especially paintings that have an <u>impact</u> on me.

       A   B   C   D

   _____

18. Some critics <u>express</u> <u>criticisms</u> that reflect their <u>instinctive</u> <u>responsive</u>, not analysis.

        A   B   C   D

   _____

19. Many newspapers have on-line <u>links</u> to <u>constantly</u> updates or <u>in-depth</u> analysis; some send a news summary

               A   B   C

to <u>subscribers</u>.

  D

   _____

20. Editors face constant <u>decisions</u> about what <u>constituting</u> news, and <u>schedule</u> stories according to their <u>instinct</u>

          A   B   C   D

and experience.

   _____

Doctor's Office

1. **annual** adj., yearly
   a. I try to schedule my annual physical right after my birthday.
   b. A number of tests are provided annually by my insurance plan.
2. **appointment** n., arrangements for a meeting; a position in a profession
   a. To get the most out of your appointment, keep a log of your symptoms and concerns.
   b. The psychiatrist holds an academic appointment at the university hospital as well as having a private practice.
3. **assess** v., to determine the value or rate of something
   a. The physical therapist assessed the amount of mobility Ms. Crowl had lost after her stroke.
   b. The insurance rate Mr. Victor was assessed went up this year after he admitted that he had started smoking again.
4. **diagnose** v., to recognize a disease; to analyze the nature of something
   a. After considering the patient's symptoms and looking at his test results, the doctor diagnosed the lump as benign.
   b. She diagnosed the problem as a failure to follow the directions for taking the medication.
5. **effective** adj., producing the desired effect; being in effect
   a. The improved images showed the effectiveness of the new X-ray machine.
   b. The new policies, effective the beginning of the fiscal year, change the amount charged to see the physician.
6. **instrument** n., a tool for precise work; the means whereby something is achieved
   a. The pediatrician tried not to frighten the children with her strange-looking instruments.
   b. The senior physician carried his instruments in a black leather bag.
7. **manage** v., to handle; to deal with; to guide
   a. The head nurse's ability to manage her staff through a difficult time caught the hospital administrator's attention.
   b. By carefully managing their limited resources, the couple found the money for the elective surgery.
8. **prevent** v., to keep from happening; to hinder
   a. By encouraging teenagers not to smoke, doctors are hoping to prevent many cases of cancer.
   b. His full caseload prevented the doctor from taking on new patients.
9. **recommend** v., to present as worthy; to endorse
   a. The professor recommended her former student for the job in the medical practice.
   b. The doctor recommended that Edwin take off at last a week to rest and regain his health.
10. **record** v., to set down in writing; n., an official copy of documents
    a. Ms. Han typed a written request for her medical records.
    b. The official records kept in the city archives showed that an unusually high number of babies are born in the summer months.
11. **refer** v., to direct for treatment or information; to mention
    a. I was referred to this specialist by the family practice nurse.
    b. As soon as Agnes referred to the failed treatment, everyone's mood soured.
12. **serious** adj., weighty
    a. The impact of the serious news could be read on everyone's face.
    b. For her dissertation, she made a serious study of women's health care needs in developing nations.

Short Conversations

Read the following conversations and see how the new words are used.

[M]   I'm glad to see that you remembered to schedule your **annual** physical.
[W]   I was surprised that it took so long to get an **appointment**.
[M]   Sometimes I can **manage** to see patients sooner if they really need to be seen.

[M]   I'm **recommending** that you see a specialist at the university hospital for another test.
[W]   Heavens, that sounds **serious**. Am I okay?
[M]   I often **refer** patients with your condition to specialists who have more experience than I do in the latest treatment options.

[M]   That **instrument** you just put in my ear is cold!
[W]   Sorry, but it's the best way to **diagnose** why you have ringing in your ears.
[M]   As big as it is, I would hope it is **effective**.

[M]   Why do you take such detailed **records** of your patients' histories?
[W]   By looking very carefully at their lifetime of health problems, we can better **assess** what is going wrong with them.
[M]   I hope that means we can **prevent** some diseases by knowing who gets them.

Word Families

verb	assess	He was able to assess her health problems with the help of her detailed medical history.
noun	assessment	The specialist's assessment of the patient's condition was consistent with the general practioner's.
adjective	assessable	That medical condition is not assessable by this laboratory test.

verb	diagnose	Her symptoms are overlapping, making it difficult to diagnose the exact cause of her chest pain.
noun	diagnosis	Phil did a much better job of taking care of himself once his father had a diagnosis of lung cancer.
adjective	diagnostic	The new X-ray suite has all the latest diagnostic equipment.

verb	prevent	By stopping smoking now, you may be able to prevent lung cancer.
noun	prevention	He made a career of disease prevention through mass vaccinations.
adjective	preventive	Eloise took preventive steps against gum disease by more thorough toothbrushing.

verb	recommend	I recommend that you have this test annually starting at age 40.
noun	recommendation	Against my doctor's recommendation, I decided to purchase the generic brand of medication.
adjective	recommendable	There is nothing particularly recommendable about this therapy over the other therapy I mentioned.

Choose the word that best completes the sentence.

1. Luckily, the test results show no _____ damage from the accident.
    (A) assess   (C) assessing
    (B) assessment   (D) assessable

2. This is not an easy _____ to make without the benefit of numerous test results.
    (A) diagnosis   (C) diagnostic
    (B) diagnose   (D) diagnosed

3. The most effective way to treat illness is to _____ it from ever occurring.
    (A) prevention   (C) preventing
    (B) preventable   (D) prevent

4. My doctor _____ that I carry a lighter purse to avoid back strain.
    (A) recommendation   (C) recommends
    (B) recommendable   (D) recommending

Short Talk

Read the following passage and write the appropriate form of the new words in the blanks below.

annually	diagnosing	manage	record
appointment	effective	preventing	refer
assessment	instruments	recommend	serious

   Sooner or later, everyone needs to go to the doctor's office. In fact, it's in your best interest to see your doctor at least (5) _____. The better he or she knows you and your health, the more (6.) _____ your doctor can be. Most people need help in (7.) _____ routine medical problems they are experiencing, such as symptoms of colds and the flu, allergies, rashes, and ear aches. Other times, people visit a doctor for help in (8.) _____ health problems from ever occurring, through lowering their risk of heart attack or stroke by dieting or exercising.

   When you arrive for your (9.) _____, the doctor's office staff will have ready a (10.) _____ of all your visits, so that the doctor has a complete reference of your health. The visit will begin with an (11.) _____ of your general health and a discussion of any problems that are of concern you.

   The doctors may use a variety of (12.) _____ to get a closer look at you. The doctor will (13.) _____ your problem and (14.) _____ a treatment plan. The doctor may prescribe medication, (15.) _____ you to a specialist more experienced in treating your condition, or order tests to gain more information. In (16.) _____ cases, he or she may send you to the hospital for care.

Choose the underlined word or phrase that should be rewritten and rewrite it.

17. Li had visited his doctor <u>annually</u>, and his thorough medical <u>record</u> helped the new doctor <u>assessment</u> Li's
                    A   B   C
     overall health and <u>recommend</u> a weight loss strategy.
                          D

     _____

18. The doctor's <u>instruments</u>, such as scopes and lights for seeing into ears and down throats, help the doctor
                  A
     make an accurate <u>diagnose</u> in the office, without <u>referring</u> patients to a lab for further tests, thus eliminating
                            B   C
     further <u>appointments</u>.
             D

     _____

19. An emergency room is most <u>effectiveness</u> in treating a <u>serious</u> problem, like a heart attack, because it has
                                A   B
     many technical and staff resources to <u>diagnose</u> and <u>manage</u> a crisis.
                                      C   D

     _____

20. Working with your doctor, you can <u>prevent</u> or minimize health problems with a plan that <u>recommendation</u>
                                     A   B
     certain screening tests that can <u>diagnose</u> disease early when its is most easily <u>managed</u>.
                                    C   D

     _____

Lesson 47

Dentist's Office

1. **aware** adj., having knowledge
    a. I was not aware that flossing my teeth could prevent a buildup of plaque.
    b. My dentist made me aware that I should have an appointment twice a year.

2. **catch up** v., to bring up to date
    a. My dentist likes to take time to catch up before she starts the examination.
    b. The dental assistant caught up on her paperwork in between patients.

3. **distraction** n., the act of being turned away from the focus
    a. To provide a distraction from the noise, Luisa's dentist offered her a pair of earphones.
    b. My dentist is kind enough to provide distractions like television, which take my mind off the procedure.

4. **encouragement** n., inspiration or support
    a. The perfect checkup was certainly encouragement to keep up my good dental hygiene.
    b. Let me offer you some encouragement about your crooked teeth.

5. **evident** adj., easily seen or understood; obvious
    a. The presence of a wisdom tooth was not evident until the dentist started to examine the patient.
    b. Unfortunately, his poor dental hygiene is evident from a distance.

6. **habit** n., a customary manner or practice
    a. The toddler's father stressed the importance of toothbrushing in hopes of establishing a good habit.
    b. The patient had a habit of grinding his teeth during his sleep.

7. **illuminate** v., to provide or brighten with light
    a. The dark recesses of the mouth can only be seen clearly when illuminated with a lamp.
    b. Let me turn on more lights to properly illuminate the back teeth.

8. **irritate** v., to chafe or inflame, to bother
    a. The broken tooth rubbed against my tongue, irritating it.
    b. Hannah's gums are irritated by foods that are very cold or very hot.

9. **overview** n., a summary; a survey; a quick look
    a. I did a quick overview of your teeth and they look in good shape.
    b. An overview of your dental records shows a history of problems.

10. **position** n., the right or appropriate place
    a. Let me tilt your head to a more comfortable position for you.
    b. The position of the chair can be adjusted to a range of heights.

11. **regularly** adv., occurring at fixed intervals
    a. She brushes regularly after every meal.
    b. I have to remind my son regularly to brush his teeth.

12. **restore** v., to bring back to an original condition
    a. The cleaning restored the whiteness of my teeth.
    b. I will talk to my dentist about whether she knows any procedure to restore the parts of my teeth that I have ground away.

Short Conversations

Read the following conversations and see how the new words are used.

[M] One of my teeth has developed a rough edge that is **irritating** the inside of my cheek.
[W] You need to call your dentist and make him **aware** of your problem.
[M] I'm having a **regular** appointment soon, so I'm trying to avoid scheduling an emergency appointment.

[M] A quick **overview** of your dental records shows there's cause for concern.
[W] I don't care about cavities. I just want you to **restore** the shine to my teeth.
[M] Your best chance is to kick the **habits** of smoking and drinking coffee. They both dull the teeth.

[M] Now that we've **caught up** on your family news, let's see how your teeth are doing.
[W] I need to be **encouraged** to floss more often.
[M] From the amount of tartar between your teeth, I'd say that problem was very **evident**.

[M] I'll have to adjust this bright light to better **illuminate** your back teeth.
[W] Let me change my **position**. The light is in my eyes.
[M] No. Don't move your head. Shift your eyes by watching the TV screen. Maybe the program will **distract** you.

Word Families

verb	distract	The child is frightened by the instruments. Try to distract his attention while I get ready.
noun	distraction	The soothing background music was a pleasant distraction from the drilling sounds at the dentist's office.
adjective	distracted	The distracted patient left the office without paying her bill.

noun	evidence	The dentist found evidence of decay on my wisdom tooth.
adjective	evident	My lack of dental hygiene was evident without a checkup.
adverb	evidently	Proper flossing evidently worked, since my gums are now in good health.

noun	habit	I'm trying to start the habit of flossing at least once a day.
adjective	habitual	His habitual coffee drinking stained his teeth.
adverb	habitually	Jack is habitually late for his appointments, which forced the receptionist to scold him.

verb	irritate	My dentist was late for my appointment, which irritated me, especially since he did not apologize.
noun	irritation	I have an irritation on the inside of my mouth that won't heal.
adjective	irritable	The baby grew irritable when she was teething.

Choose the word that best completes the sentence.

1. I don't want to _____ you, but there is a phone call waiting for you at the front desk.
   (A) distractedly
   (B) distractible
   (C) distraction
   (D) distract

2. Knowing his _____ tidiness, I'm not surprised to learn that David flosses three times a day.
   (A) habit
   (B) habitual
   (C) habitually
   (D) habitualness

3. An _____ at the gum line can be nothing serious or the symptom of a larger problem.
   (A) irritate
   (B) irritable
   (C) irritation
   (D) irritability

4. It was _____ from the X-rays that I needed dental work.
   (A) evident
   (B) evidently
   (C) evidence
   (D) evidential

Short Talk

Read the following passage and write the appropriate form of the new words in the blanks below.

aware	encourage	illuminates	position
catch up	evident	irritates	regularly
distraction	habit	overview	restores

At least twice a year, Toshiro makes an appointment with his dentist. He's (5.) _____ that taking good care of his teeth and seeing a dentist can help prevent the buildup of tarter and plaque that could cause serious problems later.

The dentist starts the appointment by looking over Toshiro's chart, which details all the work that has been done on his teeth, as a way to (6.) _____ on Toshiro's dental health. Toshiro brushes (7.) _____, but is not so regular about daily flossing. His dentist is trying to (8.) _____ a better flossing (9.) _____, by demonstrating some easy-to-use techniques.

When the dentist is ready to look into Toshiro's mouth, she adjusts the height and (10.) _____ of the chair to make sure she can see all of Toshiro's teeth. A bright light (11.) _____ Toshiro's eyes, but (12.) _____ the dark places in the back of his mouth. The dentist does a quick (13.) _____ of Toshiro's mouth, looking for any obvious problems, such as a cavity or a broken tooth. The dentist asks if Toshiro has been having any problems, like tooth pain, bleeding, or soreness.

Sometimes, problems in the mouth are quite (14.) _____ and can be seen by the dentist's trained eye. But other times, the dentist will take X-rays to make certain there are no problems in areas she cannot see, such as under the gum line or inside a tooth.

The dentist then goes to work, repairing any damage. She then (15.) _____ the natural color to his teeth with a thorough cleaning. The noise of the drills and cleaners can upset some patients, so Toshiro's dentist is kind enough to supply earphones to provide a (16.) _____.

Choose the underlined word or phrase that should be rewritten and rewrite it.

17. Most parents are <u>aware</u> that they can prevent dental problems by <u>encouragement</u> their children to get in the
                 A   **B**
    <u>habit</u> of brushing <u>regularly</u>.
     C   **D**

    _____

18. You cannot <u>catch up</u> overnight for months of bad dental <u>habits</u>; the damage to your teeth is already <u>evident</u>
              A   **B**   **C**
    and it will be hard to <u>restoration</u> them to health.
                         D

    _____

19. The sound of the drill <u>irritated</u> the patient, so her dentist gave her earphones to <u>distraction</u> her, a <u>habit</u> she
                              A   **B**   **C**
    <u>encouraged</u> him to repeat.
       D

    _____

20. The dentist settled Marcus into a <u>position</u> where the light could <u>illuminate</u> his back teeth; although the intensity
                                        A   **B**
    of the light is <u>irritation</u>, it makes problems with the back teeth more <u>evident</u>.
               C   **D**

    _____

Health Insurance

1. **allow** v., to let do or happen; to permit
    a. My insurance does not allow me to choose my own hospital.
    b. The health plan made an exception by allowing me to go directly to a dermatologist.

2. **alternative** n., the choice between two mutually exclusive possibilities
    a. To lower the cost of health insurance, my employer chose an alternative method of insuring us.
    b. I'd like to know the alternative to this treatment before I agree to it.

3. **aspect** n., a feature element; an appearance
    a. The right to chose their own doctor is an important aspect of health coverage for many people.
    b. The aspect of HMOs that people most dislike is the lack of personal service.

4. **concern** v., to be of interest or importance to
    a. Whenever I have health concerns, I call my doctor.
    b. Salman is concerned by the rising cost of health care.

5. **emphasize** v., to stress
    a. The nurse emphasized the importance of eating a balanced diet.
    b. The new plan places more emphasis on wellness by reimbursing for health club memberships.

6. **incur** v., to acquire or come into
    a. I incurred substantial expenses that my health plan does not cover.
    b. Dominic incurs the cost of a co-payment at each doctor's visit.

7. **personnel** n., a group of employees or workers
    a. The office manager insisted that she needed more personnel to finish the project on time.
    b. The employee went to see the director of personnel about taking an extended leave of absence.

8. **policy** n., a set of rules and regulations
    a. Company policy did not provide for overtime pay.
    b. The company's insurance policy did not cover cosmetic surgery.

9. **portion** n., a section or quantity within a larger thing; a part of a whole
    a. A portion of my benefits is my health care coverage.
    b. I am keeping a record of the portion of my income I spend on health care.

10. **regardless** adv., in spite of
    a. Regardless of the cost, we all need health insurance.
    b. I keep going to the same doctor, regardless of the fact that she does not take my pain seriously.

11. **salary** n., a fixed compensation paid regularly for work done; one's pay
    a. The receptionist believed that he worked too hard for such a small salary.
    b. The technician was pleased to have a raise in salary after only six months on the job.

12. **suitable** adj., appropriate to a purpose or an occasion
    a. The insurance was not suitable for a young family, as it had no well-baby care.
    b. I have finally found a health plan that is suitable for my needs.

Short Conversations

Read the following conversations and see how the new words are used.

[M] Does the health plan **allow** me to see a specialist immediately, or do I have to see my primary care provider first?

[W] If you go without your primary care provider's referral, you will **incur** a higher percentage of the total cost.

[M] So, I would pay an increased **portion** of the bill.

[M] I'm not happy about being forced to switch to an **alternative** health plan. I like the traditional plan.

[W] Come on, some of the new benefits of the new **policy** are great. We get a cash payback if we stay with a gym for a year as part of the preventive health program.

[M] I'll have to admit I like that **aspect** of the plan.

[M] With all these choices, it's hard to pick the most **suitable** coverage for my family.

[W] Does your **salary** determine the cost of your insurance premium?

[M] I don't know, but I want the best care, **regardless** of the cost.

[M] We hope you choose us as your company's health care provider, since we place an **emphasis** on the patient, not the cost.

[W] Our company needs a **policy** that will appeal to all of our **personnel**.

[M] I appreciate your **concerns** and I'm sure we can satisfy all of your personnel's needs.

Word Families

verb	allow	The insurance policy did not allow multiple prescription refills.
noun	allowance	The policy is liberal in its allowance for optometry services.
adjective	allowable	A maximum of two dental visits is allowable under the plan.

verb	alternate	We alternate turns in taking the kids to the doctor.
noun	alternative	Our medical insurance was too expensive, so we sought a cheaper alternative.
adverb	alternatively	Alternatively, we could just stop having health insurance, but that's not my favorite option.

verb	emphasize	The plan representative emphasized the need for a second medical opinion.
noun	emphasis	The emphasis of the health plan is on staying well.
adjective	emphatic	Hassan made an emphatic appeal to the medical insurance director.

verb	suit	I'm dropping my health plan because it does not suit my needs.
adjective	suitable	Not every kind of health insurance is suitable for every family.
adverb	suitably	The errors on my insurance statement were caught and suitably fixed.

Choose the word that best completes the sentence.

1. You should investigate to see if there are any _____ to costly hospital stays.
   (A) alternate
   (B) alternatively
   (C) alternatives
   (D) alternating

2. Office policy does not _____ employees to leave the office for medical appointments.
   (A) allow
   (B) allowing
   (C) allowable
   (D) allowance

3. I'm really pleased that my health plan provider is paying for my gym membership as a way to _____ its concern for my health.
   (A) emphasis
   (B) emphasize
   (C) emphatic
   (D) emphasizing

4. The employee's goal is to find her family _____ health coverage.
   (A) suit
   (B) suitable
   (C) suitably
   (D) suitability

Short Talk

Read the following passage and write the appropriate form of the new words in the blanks below.

allow	concerns	personnel	regardless
alternatives	emphasize	policy	salary
aspect	incurs	portion	suitable

The cost and availability of health insurance is one of the greatest (5.) _____ of company (6.) _____. A covered employee should be familiar with the terms and conditions of the insurance (7.) _____. Although the insured pays a (8.) _____ of the cost of his or her coverage through (9.) _____ deductions, the employer generally covers most of the cost.

Self-employed persons can arrange for their own insurance or join an association of those performing similar work in order to get lower premiums. Traditionally, the insurance carrier will (10.) _____ most of the charges related to medical care, although the insured might be responsible for a small portion.

Although the company or association negotiates the most (11.) _____ terms they can, most experts (12.) _____ that employees should be on the lookout for (13.) _____ that might better suit their needs. (14.) _____ of the cost of premiums, the most important (15.) _____ of good health insurance is that it meets the needs of the insured and (16.) _____ the least possible cost for necessary procedures.

Choose the underlined word or phrase that should be rewritten and rewrite it.

17. One <u>aspect</u> of the health plan that Vivianne likes is the <u>emphasize</u> on wellness; this means the plan will pay a

    A   B
    large <u>portion</u> of her annual physical, allowing her to keep more of her <u>salary</u>.

    C   D

_____

18. <u>Concerned</u> about <u>incurred</u> large costs for health premiums, employers found ways to lower the cost, such as

  A   B
    having <u>personnel</u> contribute more to the premium and aligning with <u>alternative</u> providers like HMOs.

     C   D

_____

19. The HMOs will not <u>allow</u> their subscribers to use medical <u>personnel</u> they do not find <u>suitability</u>; for example,

                   A   B   C
    seeing a specialist without a referral is discouraged, <u>regardless</u> of the cause.

                                                  D

_____

20. Finding a <u>suitable</u> health <u>policy</u> is difficult, since most place the <u>emphasis</u> on cost and are not <u>concern</u> with

        A   B   C   D
    the quality of care.

_____

Lesson 49

Hospitals

Words to learn

admit
authorization
designate
escort
identify
mission
permit
pertinent
procedure
result
statement
usual

1. **admit** v., to permit to enter
   a. The injured patient was admitted to the unit directly from the emergency room.
   b. The staff refused to admit the patient until he had proof of insurance.
2. **authorization** n., the act of sanctioning
   a. To speed up getting a room, her doctor advised that she bring an extra copy of her insurance company's authorization for services.
   b. The nurse could not submit an authorization over the phone; it had to be done in writing.
3. **designate** v., to indicate or specify
   a. The labels on the bags of blood designated the type of blood the bags contained.
   b. On her admittance form, Grandmother designated Aunt Tessa as her chief decision-maker.
4. **escort** n., a person accompanying another to guide or protect
   a. Let's see if there is an escort available to take you to the parking garage.
   b. You cannot leave the unit on your own; you'll have to wait for an escort.
5. **identify** v., to ascertain the name or belongings of
   a. The tiny bracelet identified each baby in the nursery.
   b. Your medical records are all marked with your patient number to identify them in case of a mix-up.
6. **mission** n., an inner calling to pursue an activity or perform a service
   a. The hospital chaplain took as his mission to visit every patient admitted each day.
   b. The nurse explained that the mission of everyone in the unit was to make sure the patients got well as soon as possible.
7. **permit** v., to allow
   a. Smoking is not permitted anywhere inside the hospital.
   b. Would you check with the nurse to see if I am permitted to eat before surgery?
8. **pertinent** adj., having relevance to the matter at hand
   a. You should mention any pertinent health issues to the staff before you are admitted for surgery.
   b. The patient's health record contained pertinent information, like the dates of all his inoculations.
9. **procedure** n., a series of steps taken to accomplish an end
   a. The surgical procedure can now be done in half the amount of time it took even five years ago.
   b. Call the hospital to schedule this procedure for tomorrow.
10. **result** n., an outcome
    a. Your lab results won't be ready for hours.
    b. The scientific results prove that the new procedure is not significantly safer than the traditional one.
11. **statement** n., an accounting showing an amount due; a bill
    a. The billing statement was filed with the insurance company last month.
    b. Check with your doctor's office for an original statement; we cannot process a faxed copy.
12. **usual** adj., ordinary, expected
    a. It is not usual for that kind of surgery to be performed on an outpatient basis.
    b. The insurance company refuses to pay for services it does not consider customary or charges that are not usual.

Short Conversations

Read the following conversations and see how the new words are used.

[M]   Your mother needs a surgical **procedure** to treat her condition.
[W]   Will she need to be **admitted** for an overnight hospital stay?
[M]   Not at all. We **usually** perform this type of surgery on an outpatient basis.

[M]   I'm not at all happy with the care my wife received here. Is there someone **designated** to handle our problem?
[W]   Our **mission** is to deliver complete satisfaction. What was your problem?
[M]   The hospital **identified** my wife incorrectly in the computer system. Now all of her records are mixed up.

[M]   When you come to the hospital next week, please bring all your **pertinent** insurance records with you.
[W]   I know I need an **authorization** number from my health plan.
[M]   We'll need that number for all your billing **statements**.

[M]   Your final set of test **results** looks perfect. You are all set to go home.
[W]   Am I **permitted** to check out now?
[M]   Yes. I'll call an orderly to **escort** you to your waiting family.

Word Families

verb	admit	The patients lined the hospital corridors waiting to be admitted.
noun	admittance	Your admittance to the hospital is dependent on your showing proof that you can pay the bills.
noun	admission	Take these records down to Admissions and have them duplicate the files for you.

verb	designate	The hospital administrator designated a team to create an emergency preparedness plan.
noun	designation	The designation of the hospital as one of the best in the region certainly helped its marketing efforts.
noun	designator	The national health service is the sole designator of which hospitals will get the grants.

verb	identify	If you will identify your valuables, the nurse will give them back to you.
adjective	identifiable	The red cross on the hospital's helicopter landing pad was identifiable from the air.
noun	identification	Please remember to bring some form of identification with you when you check in at the hospital.

verb	permit	I can't permit more than one visitor at a time in the intensive care unit.
adjective	permissible	It is not permissible to smoke inside the hospital.
noun	permission	Mohammed got his insurance company's permission to stay another day in the hospital.

Choose the word that best completes the sentence.

1. As a precaution, it's wise to _____ someone in your family to make health care decisions for you in case there is a time that you cannot.
   (A) designation (C) designator
   (B) designate (D) designated

2. Your X-rays will have your name and social security number printed on them, so we can easily _____ them as yours.
   (A) identifiably (C) identifiable
   (B) identification (D) identify

3. Before we can begin the surgery, we will need your signed _____ authorizing us to perform the procedure.
   (A) permit (C) permission
   (B) permissive (D) permissible

4. Before my father was _____ to the hospital, he had to undergo a series of tests.
   (A) admit (C) admittance
   (B) admitted (D) admissions

Short Talk

Read the following passage and write the appropriate form of the new words in the blanks below.

admitting	escort	permitted	results
authorization	identification	pertinent	statement
designated	mission	procedures	usually

Hospitals have a (5.) _____ to provide patients with high-quality medical care. Everyone on staff will make sure that you get the best possible treatment for your condition.

When you arrive at the hospital, you should have with you all the (6.) _____ information needed to be admitted, like your insurance information and copies of X-rays and other test (7.) _____, even if they were taken at another facility. Bring your insurance card and any referral or (8.) _____ form from your doctor. You should also have some form of (9.) _____ with a photo. You will also need to sign an agreement regarding treatment consent. Once you arrive, there is usually a concierge who will assist you with the (10.) _____ process.

Many elective surgeries and other (11.) _____ are (12.) _____ done on the same day. Usually a hospital staff member will (13.) _____ you to the exit and make sure you get into the car safely. After you leave the hospital, you will receive a (14.) _____ from the hospital for the charges your insurer does not cover. Your insurance policy will outline any amount for which you may be responsible.

You will find that smoking is not (15.) _____ in any hospital building. Often, hospitals have (16.) _____ smoking areas outside for patients, families, and staff who wish to smoke.

Choose the underlined word or phrase that should be rewritten and rewrite it.

17. Jose's <u>authorization</u> for the surgical <u>procedure</u> had expired, so the hospital would not <u>admission</u> him until they
    A   B   C
    had <u>permission</u> to do so from his health plan.
    D

    _____

18. When delayed test <u>results</u> became a <u>usually</u> occurrence, the hospital administrator <u>identified</u> it as a problem
    A   B   C
    that could damage the <u>mission</u> of the hospital.
    D

    _____

19. In an official <u>statement</u>, the hospital <u>authorized</u> all nursing units to <u>designation</u> a staff member to <u>escort</u>
    A   B   C   D
    patients to their cars.

    _____

20. The <u>admissions</u> office asked Ruby for all her <u>pertinent</u> personal data, such as <u>identification</u> and health plan
    A   B   C
    <u>authorized</u>, before she could check into her hospital room.
    D

    _____

Pharmacy

1. **consult** v., to seek advice or information of
   a. The doctor consulted with a specialist before writing a new prescription.
   b. May I consult with you about a drug interaction case I have?

2. **control** v., to exercise authoritative or dominating influence over
   a. To control the cost of this medication, you may get the generic version.
   b. Please take your medication every day to control your high blood pressure.

3. **convenient** adj., suited or favorable to one's purpose; easy to reach
   a. Is this a convenient location for you to pick up your prescription?
   b. The convenience of a pharmacy in the same building as my doctor is hard to beat.

4. **detect** v., to discover or ascertain
   a. My doctor put me through some simple tests to detect if I have asthma.
   b. I have to keep track of my sleep patterns to detect how many times I get up in the night.

5. **factor** n., a contribution to an accomplishment, a result, or a process
   a. Taking medications as directed is an important factor in getting well.
   b. Could my cat be a factor contributing to my asthma?

6. **interaction** n., an influence; a mutual activity
   a. My pharmacist was concerned about the interaction of the two medications I was prescribed.
   b. The interaction between the patient and the doctor showed a high level of trust.

7. **limit** n., the point beyond which something cannot proceed
   a. My prescription has a limit of three refills.
   b. My health plan authorization sets a limit on which health care providers I can see without their permission.

8. **monitor** v., to keep track of
   a. The nurse practitioner carefully monitors the number of medications her patients are taking.
   b. The patient had weekly appointments so that the doctor could monitor her progress.

9. **potential** adj., capable of being but not yet in existence; possible
   a. To avoid any potential side effects from the medication, be sure to tell your doctor all the drugs you are currently taking.
   b. Given the potential delay in getting reimbursed by the health plan, why don't we just fill one prescription today?

10. **sample** n., a portion, piece, or segment that is representative of a whole
    a. The pharmacist gave Myra a few free samples of the allergy medication.
    b. A sample of the population taking the new medicine was surveyed to determine whether it caused side effects.

11. **sense** n., a judgment; an intellectual interpretation
    a. The doctor had a good sense about what the problem was but wanted to get a second opinion.
    b. I got the sense it would be better to get my prescription filled right away.

12. **volunteer** n., one who performs a service without pay; v., to perform as a volunteer
    a. My doctor volunteered to call the drugstore, so my medication would be waiting for me.
    b. The volunteers would bring the filled prescriptions from the pharmacy to the homes of the shut-ins.

Short Conversations

Read the following conversations and see how the new words are used.

[M] Will this pill **control** my runny nose?
[W] You should be able to **detect** a change within two days.
[M] I'll try the **samples** and, if they work, I'll fill the prescription you wrote.

[M] The doctor has **volunteered** to call in a prescription for you. What pharmacy do you use?
[W] The one near my house is **convenient**, but my husband will be picking up the prescription for me. Can I ask him which he'd prefer?
[M] Sure. Why don't you **consult** with him and let me know.

[M] This prescription has the **potential** to lower your blood pressure, but only in conjunction with the other things we talked about earlier.
[W] I know I need to **limit** my salt intake and get more exercise.
[M] That's right. Drugs are only one **factor** in your recovery.

[M] I get the **sense** that you are concerned about the number of medications I am taking.
[W] I'm concerned about the amount and the **potential** for harmful drug **interactions**.
[M] I really appreciate a pharmacist taking the time to **monitor** my medications.

Word Families

verb	consult	Beatrice consulted her pharmacist about the number of different medications she is taking.
noun	consultation	Let me arrange a consultation with a specialist to discuss your heart problem and some possible medications.
adjective	consultative	This is a consultative process and you probably won't have a definitive answer immediately.

noun	convenience	The convenience of a 24-hour neighborhood pharmacy is not to be underestimated.
adjective	convenient	Many people shop there because of its convenient location.
adverb	conveniently	The pharmacy is conveniently located on my way home from work.

verb	detect	The laboratory test detected the presence of medication in his blood.
noun	detection	Early detection of diseases usually means that medications can be more effective.
adjective	detectable	After he took his medication faithfully for a few months and exercised more, Jack's disease was no longer detectable.

verb	volunteer	The pharmacist volunteers his services monthly at the free clinic for homeless people.
noun	volunteerism	In the spirit of volunteerism, the doctors are donating free samples of medication to the relief project.
adjective	voluntary	Your compliance with this new policy is completely voluntary, but we think it is in the public interest that you do so.

Choose the word that best completes the sentence.

1. Would you please schedule the patient for a medical _____ tomorrow afternoon?
   (A) consult
   (B) consultation
   (C) consulting
   (D) consultative

2. Your prescription will be ready in an hour, if that's _____ with you.
   (A) conveniences
   (B) conveniently
   (C) convenience
   (D) convenient

3. The procedure _____ a slight problem, but the doctor assured us not to be alarmed.
   (A) detected
   (B) detect
   (C) detection
   (D) detectable

4. We desperately need _____ to help at the free clinic next month.
   (A) voluntary
   (B) volunteer
   (C) volunteers
   (D) volunteerism

Short Talk

Read the following passage and write the appropriate form of the new words in the blanks below.

consulting	detection	limit	samples
control	factors	monitor	sense
convenient	interactions	potential	volunteers

Yoko is having trouble with seasonal allergies this fall. After (5.) _____ with her doctor, they decide she should take medication on a regular basis to (6.) _____ her symptoms. Her doctor recommends the medication he thinks will work best and offers her a handful of (7.) _____ at no charge. For her long-term needs, Yoko will need to have a prescription filled. Her doctor (8.) _____ to call the pharmacy Yoko uses to order a supply, which will (9.) _____ the time she spends waiting for the prescription to be filled.

Yoko is new in town and does not know which pharmacy she wants to use. She knows that there is a drugstore near her apartment and one near where she works, but does not remember the operating hours for either. Yoko knows that (10.) _____ hours and location are important (11.) _____ in selecting a pharmacy. Although she can fill different prescriptions at different drugstores, it makes more (12.) _____ to Yoko to fill all of her medications at one location.

Occasionally, some drugs will have harmful (13.) _____. Usually, your doctor will prevent a drug interaction problem before it starts. But, if you see more than one doctor, it is hard to (14.) _____ the various medications you are taking. Having all your prescriptions filled at one location increases the chances that the pharmacist will detect a (l5.) _____ drug interaction problem. This timely (l6.) _____ can save your life.

Choose the underlined word or phrase that should be rewritten and rewrite it.

17. By consultative with her pharmacist, Lydia was able to establish a computer record that monitored the kinds of drugs she took to prevent the potential for harmful interactions.
    A   B
    C   D

_____

18. The limited pharmacy hours were not convenient for me, so I was grateful when my doctor voluntary to give
    A   B   C
    me free drug samples.
    D

_____

19. Gladys's symptoms grew increasingly difficult to control, so her doctor wrote a prescription for a convenience
    A   B
    strap-on heart monitor that would immediately detect an irregular heartbeat.
    C   D

_____

20. It made sense to Sanjay that the pharmacist should monitor drug interactive and other factors that could be
    A   B   C   D
    harmful.

_____

Word Review #10   Lessons 46–50 Health

Choose the word that best completes the sentence.

1. Your doctor's _____ are as important as his prescriptions.
   (A) recommend
   (B) recommended
   (C) recommending
   (D) recommendations

2. Dentists are as concerned with your dental _____ as the current condition of your teeth.
   (A) habits
   (B) habitual
   (C) habitually
   (D) habituated

3. To avoid _____ any additional charges, you should ask to be discharged from the hospital.
   (A) incur
   (B) incurs
   (C) incurred
   (D) incurring

4. It is as fast and efficient to _____ with your pharmacist as with your physician.
   (A) consult
   (B) consulting
   (C) consulted
   (D) consultation

5. Although an annual checkup is important, you should also make an _____ whenever you have a health concern.
   (A) appoint
   (B) appointed
   (C) appointment
   (D) appointments

6. A dentist can perform dental _____ as well as routine maintenance.
   (A) restore
   (B) restored
   (C) restoring
   (D) restoration

7. A good medical insurance will _____ preventive health programs as well as treatment.
   (A) emphasize
   (B) emphasis
   (C) emphasizing
   (D) emphasized

8. The most difficult part of hospitalization is being _____.
   (A) admit
   (B) admitted
   (C) admissions
   (D) admitting

9. A pharmacist will _____ whether a new prescription has the potential to interact with another.
   (A) monitor
   (B) monitors
   (C) monitoring
   (D) monitored

10. I don't understand most of what I read in a hospital's billing _____.
    (A) state
    (B) stated
    (C) stating
    (D) statement

Choose the underlined word or phrase that should be rewritten and rewrite it.

11. Your pharmacist is a <u>conveniently</u> <u>factor</u> in <u>monitoring</u> your prescription <u>record</u>.
                         A   B   C   D

    _____

12. At your <u>annual</u> <u>appointment</u>, your doctor can most <u>effective</u> <u>diagnose</u> you if you tell her everything.
              A   B   C   D

    _____

13. Any doctor can help you to <u>management</u> your medical health: to <u>prevent</u> risky behavior, eliminate bad <u>habits</u>,
                                     A   B   C
    or <u>refer</u> you to a specialist.
       D

    _____

14. Before being <u>admission</u> to a hospital, you need to have all <u>pertinent</u> documents as <u>evidence</u> of insurance
                       A   B   C
    <u>authorization</u>.
       D

    _____

15. <u>Regardless</u> of how minor, any <u>procedure</u> can <u>resulting</u> in <u>serious</u> complications.
       A   B   C   D

    ———————————————

16. Once a doctor <u>assesses</u> your condition, his <u>alternatives</u> include <u>referral</u> you to another physician
                 A   B   C

    or <u>recommending</u> special exercise or diet.
         D

    ———————————————

17. Even when a dental problem is not <u>evident</u>, a dentist's powerful <u>illumination</u> and specialized <u>instruments</u>
                                 A   B   C

    can make him <u>awareness</u> of a potential problem.
               D

    ———————————————

18. Some insurance <u>policies</u> do not <u>allowed</u> for certain procedures <u>designated</u> cosmetic instead of <u>restorative</u>.
                   A   B   C   D

    ———————————————

19. Some physicians <u>voluntarily</u> information about generic drugs or give <u>samples</u>, always alert to <u>potential</u>
                   A   B   C

    <u>interactions</u>.
      D

    ———————————————

20. <u>Distracting</u> by multiple <u>policy</u> regulations, insurance <u>personnel</u> do not always respond accurately to a patient's
      A   B   C

    <u>concerns</u>.
      D

    ———————————————

Answer Key

Lessons 1–5 General Business
Lesson 1 Contracts: 1. D 2. A 3. D 4. B 5. agreement
6. parties 7. specifies 8. obligates 9. assurance
10. establishment 11. determine 12. provide 13. resolve
14. engaging 15. abide by 16. cancel 17. A, resolution
18. C, determine 19. C, cancel 20. A, establishes

Lesson 2 Marketing: 1. C 2. A 3. A 4. D 5. product
6. market 7. persuaded 8. consumers 9. attract
10. satisfied 11. current 12. inspire 13. convince
14. compared 15. competes 16. fad 17. B, inspire
18. B, persuade 19. D, compared 20. B, attracting

Lesson 3 Warranties: 1. B 2. C 3. A 4. D 5. promise
6. required 7. frequently 8. consider. 9. characteristics
10. vary 11. coverage 12. implies 13. expire 14. protect
15. reputations 16. consequences 17. D, expired
18. D, vary 19. A, consequences 20. A, consider

Lesson 4 Business Planning: 1. A 2. C 3. D 4. C
5. develop 6. primary 7. avoid 8. strength 9. substitute
10. strategy 11. evaluation 12. offered 13. risks 14. gathering
15. demonstrate 16. address 17. B, demonstrate
18. D, offering 19. D, evaluate 20. B, risks

Lesson 5 Conferences: 1. B 2. C 3. D 4. A 5. associations
6. get in touch 7. take part in 8. sessions 9. attending
10. select 11. arrangements 12. accommodate 13. hold
14. overcrowded 15. location 16. register 17. B, registered
18. A, selecting 19. C, holding 20. C, attendees

Word Review #1: 1. C 2. D 3. D 4. B 5. A 6. B 7. A 8. B
9. A 10. A 11. B, inspire 12. A, select 13. D, satisfy
14. D, resolve 15. B, selecting 16. C, implies 17. B, assurance
18. A, attract 19. B, registered 20. B, product

Lessons 6–10 Office Issues
Lesson 6 Computers: 1. A 2. B 3. C 4. B 5. ignore
6. figure out 7. compatible 8. shut down 9. warning 10. failure
11. duplicate 12. accessing 13. display 14. search
15. deleted 16. allocated 17. C, delete 18. C, figured out
19. D, warning 20. C, compatible

Lesson 7 Office Technology: 1. B 2. D 3. B 4. C
5. is in charge of 6. durable 7. affordable 8. reduce
9. capacity 10. physical 11. initiates 12. stays on top of
13. recurring 14. provider 15. as needed 16. stock
17. C, physically 18. A, as needed 19. C, recurring
20. A, initiated

Lesson 8 Office Procedures: 1. B 2. A 3. C 4. D
5. appreciation 6. made of 7. reinforced 8. casually 9. code
10. out of 11. verbalize 12. practices 13. outdated
14. been exposed to 15. brought in 16. glimpse 17. C, casual
18. D, practices 19. D, warning 20. B, had been exposed to

Lesson 9 Electronics: 1. C 2. D 3. B 4. C 5. sharply
6. networks 7. facilitates 8. processing 9. disks 10. technical
11. storage 12. software 13. replacements 14. popular
15. revolutionized 16. skills 17. D, sharply 18. A, popular
19. B, revolutionized 20. D, storage

Lesson 10 Correspondence: 1. A 2. B 3. B 4. A
5. proofed 6. revision 7. beforehand 8. assemble 9. folding
10. courier 11. express 12. registered 13. layout
14. mention 15. complicated 16. petition 17. C, proofed
18. A, revised 19. C, complicated 20. D, folded

Word Review #2: 1. C 2. D 3. B 4. D 5. B 6. A 7. B 8. B
9. C 10. B 11. D, as needed 12. A, affordability 13. D, display
14. D, practices 15. B, proof 16. D, shut down 17. A, recurring,
reccurent 18. B, assembled 19. B, revolution 20. C, reduce

Lessons 11–15 Personnel
Lesson 11 Job Advertising and Recruiting: 1. C 2. A
3. D 4. B 5. time-consuming 6. match 7. recruit
8. accomplishments 9. bring together 10. abundant
11. candidates 12. qualifications 13. Coming up with
14. profile 15. commensurate 16. submit 17. B, recruiters
18. B, candidates 19. C, qualified 20. C, match

Lesson 12 Applying and Interviewing: 1. C 2. D 3. B
4. A 5. experts 6. confidence 7. weaknesses 8. constantly
9. follow up 10. backgrounds (or abilities) 11. abilities (or
backgrounds) 12. apply 13. called in 14. are ready for
15. present 16. hesitant 17. A, applicant's 18. B, be ready for
19. B, confident 20. D, constantly

Lesson 13 Hiring and Training: 1. A 2. D 3. C 4. B
5. conducted 6. rejected 7. successfully 8. generate
9. hires 10. training 11. update 12. keep up with 13. set up
14. mentor 15. look up to 16. on track 17. B, conducted
18. A, hire 19. D, updates 20. D, successful

Lesson 14 Salaries and Benefits: 1. C 2. B 3. A 4. C
5. negotiated 6. benefits 7. compensated 8. delicate 9. be
aware of 10. wage 11. flexibility 12. basis 13. raise
14. retirement 15. eligible 16. vested 17. D, flexible
18. A, vested 19. B, delicate 20. C, eligible

Lesson 15 Promotions, Pensions, and Awards: 1. C 2. A
3. C 4. C 5. recognition 6. loyalty 7. value 8. promoted
9. merit 10. achievers 11. looked to 12. dedicated
13. contributions 14. productive 15. obvious 16. look forward to 17. C, dedication 18. A, valuable 19. C, obvious
20. C, productive

Word Review #3: 1. A 2. A 3. B 4. C 5. D 6. C 7. B 8. B
9. D 10. A 11. D, successful 12. B, training 13. B, recognition
14. A, recruited 15. B, promotion 16. B, compensate
17. A, negotiating 18. D flexible 19. C, on track 20. B, set up

Lessons 16–20 Purchasing
Lesson 16 Shopping: 1. C 2. A 3. D 4. C 5. bear
6. behavior 7. mandatory 8. strictly 9. items 10. expand
11. exploring 12. comforting 13. merchandise 14. bargains
15. checkout 16. trend 17. B, behavior 18. A, bear
19. C, expand 20. B, items

Lesson 17 Ordering Supplies: 1. A 2. C 3. B 4. A
5. everyday 6. stationery 7. obtainable 8. diverse
9. maintaining 10. essential 11. prerequisite 12. smooth
13. functioning 14. enterprise 15. source 16. quality
17. A, maintaining 18. D, essential 19. D, diversity
20. A, smoothly

Lesson 18 Shipping: 1. A 2. C 3. A 4. C 5. integral
6. catalog 7. Shipping 8. minimize 9. accurate 10. carrier
11. inventory 12. sufficient 13. fulfill 14. on hand
15. remember 16. supplies 17. A, accurate 18. A, fulfill
19. D, minimize 20. A, remember

Lesson 19 Invoices: 1. C 2. D 3. A 4. A 5. efficient
6. order 7. compiled 8. Charges 9. customer 10. estimated
11. terms 12. imposed 13. discount 14. mistake 15. rectified
16. promptly 17. C, rectified 18. A, imposed 19. C, discount
20. A, efficient

Lesson 20 Inventory: 1. B 2. A 3. A 4. D 5. verifies 6. crucial
7. liability 8. running 9. subtracts 10. adjusted
11. automatically 12. scanning 13. reflect 14. tedious
15. discrepancies 16. disturbances 17. A, verify 18. B, running 19. C, subtracts 20. C, reflect

---

Word Review #4: 1. A 2. B 3. A 4. A 5. C 6. C 7. B 8. A
9. D 10. B 11. B, efficiently 12. A, bargain 13. B, essential
14. B, accuracy 15. D, discount 16. A, tedious 17. C, promptly
18. D, quality 19. B, strictly 20. D, disturbing

Lessons 21–25 Financing and Budgeting
Lesson 21 Banking: 1. A 2. B 3. C 4. B 5. transact
6. borrow 7. mortgages 8. cautious 9. down payment
10. dividends 11. restrict 12. take out 13. balance
14. deductions 15. accept 16. signature 17. B, accepted
18. B, restrictions 19. C, deducted, deductible 20. B, cautious

Lesson 22 Accounting: 1. C 2. A 3. B 4. D 5. accumulated
6. budget 7. clients 8. outstanding 9. profitable 10. audited
11. accounting 12. building up 13. turnover 14. reconcile
15. debt 16. assets 17. B, reconcile 18. A, accumulation
19. D, profits 20. C, budget

Lesson 23 Investment: 1. C 2. A 3. B 4. D 5. invest
6. resources 7. wise 8. portfolio 9. pull out 10. returns
11. committed 12. long term 13. fund 14. attitude
15. conservative (or aggressive) 16. aggressive (or conservative)
17. C, returns 18. B, commitment 19. A, aggressive
20. C, pull out

Lesson 24 Taxes: 1. D 2. B 3. A 4. A 5. prepares 6. deadline
7. fill out 8. filed 9. spouse 10. joint 11. refund 12. calculated
13. owe 14. gave up 15. withhold 16. penalized 17. C, file
18. C, file 19. B, withheld 20. D, refund

Lesson 25 Financial Statements: 1. C 2. B 3. A 4. D
5. level 6. target 7. forecasts 8. overall 9. projected
10. desired 11. yield 12. translate 13. realistic 14. perspective
15. detailed 16. typical 17. B, desired 18. A, projected
19. C, realistic 20. C, translated

Word Review #5. 1. A 2. B 3. D 4. B 5. C 6. C 7. D 8. A
9. D 10. D 11. B, accept 12. D, budget 13. C, conservative
14. C, detailed 15. A, caution 16. D, pulling out 17. B, return
18. C, yield 19. D, owing 20. A, filling out

Lessons 26–30 Management Issues
Lesson 26 Property and Departments: 1. C 2. B 3. A 4. C
5. disruptive 6. adjacent 7. lobby 8. inconsiderate
9. collaboration 10. hampered 11. move up 12. scrutinized
13. opting 14. conducive 15. concentrate 16. open to
17. B, scrutiny 18. C, collaboration 19. B, disruption
20. D, inconsiderate

Lesson 27 Board Meetings and Committees: 1. C 2. A 3. B
4. B 5. waste 6. agenda 7. matters 8. goals 9. lengthy
10. adhered to 11. brought up 12. priority 13. go ahead
14. periodically 15. progress 16. concluded 17. A, adhering to
18. D, progress 19. B, priority 20. A, matters

Lesson 28 Quality Control: 1. C 2. C 3. A 4. C 5. conform
6. defects 7. garment 8. inspect 9. throws out 10. enhance
11. repel 12. take back 13. brand 14. uniform 15. wrinkle
16. perceive 17. D, defects 18. A, inspector 19. B, enhanced
20. C, repelled

Lesson 29 Product Development: 1. A 2. B 3. C 4. A
5. anxious 6. decade 7. supervisor 8. responsible 9. logical
10. systematic 11. ascertain 12. solve 13. researched
14. examining 15. experiments 16. assume 17. D, solving
18. B, responsibilities 19. D, ascertain 20. A, examine

Lesson 30 Renting and Leasing: 1. D 2. B 3. C 4. B
5. apprehensive 6. lease 7. Occupancy 8. indicator
9. fluctuations 10. due to 11. condition 12. lock themselves into
13. get out of 14. circumstances 15. options 16. subject to
17. B, lease 18. C, apprehensive 19. B, fluctuations
20. B, get out of

Word Review #6: 1. C 2. A 3. C 4. A 5. C 6. D 7. D 8. C
9. B 10. D 11. C, disruption 12. A, adhere to 13. C, throwing out
14. A, circumstances 15. B, ascertaining 16. C, wastes
17. D, conclude 18. D, conform 19. B, moving up
20. C, uniformly

Lessons 31–35 Restaurants and Events
Lesson 31 Selecting a Restaurant: 1. D 2. D 3. C 4. A
5. secure 6. relies 7. guidance 8. suggestion 9. subjective
10. daring 11. appeal 12. majority 13. compromise 14. mix
15. familiar 16. arrive 17. C, suggest 18. D, subjectivity
19. B, mixes 20. D, compromise

Lesson 32 Eating Out: 1. A 2. C 3. D 4. C 5. random
6. patrons 7. predict 8. forget 9. remind 10. mix up
11. complete 12. judged 13. excite 14. basic 15. flavor
16. ingredients 17. C, mixed up 18. D, predicted 19. B, remind
20. B, flavorful

Lesson 33 Ordering Lunch: 1. C 2. A 3. B 4. C 5. falls to
6. burdensome 7. multiple 8. narrow 9. common 10. individual
11. settled 12. list 13. delivered 14. pick up 15. impress
16. elegant 17. C, impressed 18. C, multiple 19. D, common
20. D, delivered

Lesson 34 Cooking as a Career: 1. D 2. B 3. A 4. B 5. outlet
6. drawn 7. profession 8. demanding 9. influx 10. incorporate
11. methods 12. themes 13. accustomed 14. relinquish
15. culinary 16. apprenticeship 17. C, methods
18. B, profession 19. B, relinquish 20. C, incorporate

Lesson 35 Events: 1. C 2. A 3. B 4. B 5. coordinated
6. planning 7. site 8. stage 9. exact 10. dimensions
11. regulations 12. lead time 13. ideally 14. assist
15. proximity 16. general 17. A, assistance 18. B, ideal
19. D, exact 20. A, coordinate

Word Review #7: 1. C 2. D 3. B 4. A 5. D 6. C 7. C 8. C
9. D 10. B 11. C, daring 12. D, elegant 13. C, mix-up
14. D, patrons 15. C, exact 16. A, Accustomed to
17. D, compromising 18. B, arrival 19. C, forgotten
20. B, remind

Lessons 36–40   Travel
Lesson 36 General Travel: 1. C 2. A 3. A 4. D 5. agency
6. valid 7. itinerary 8. delayed 9. prohibited 10. embarkation
11. board 12. depart 13. beverage 14. blanket
15. announcements 16. claim 17. B, delayed
18. C, embarkation 19. A, valid 20. D, prohibited

Lesson 37 Airlines: 1. D 2. C 3. A 4. B 5. deal with
6. expensive 7. substantial 8. economical 9. destination
10. system 11. prospective 12. situation 13. excursion
14. equivalent 15. extending 16. indistinguishable
17. B, substantial 18. C, extend 19. B, distinguish
20. A, prospective

Lesson 38 Trains: 1. C 2. A 3. B 4. B 5. relatively 6. punctual
7. fares 8. directories 9. comprehensive 10. remote 11. operate
12. remainder 13. duration 14. deluxe 15. offset 16. entitle
17. A, punctual 18. C, remote 19. A, comprehensive
20. B, operates

Lesson 39 Hotels: 1. B 2. D 3. A 4. B 5. preclude 6. rates
7. reservations 8. advance 9. notify 10. confirm 11. quoted
12. service 13. expect 14. housekeeper 15. chains
16. check in 17. A, reservations 18. D, precluded 19. B, expect
20. D, notified

Lesson 40 Car Rental: 1. C 2. D 3. D 4. A 5. tempted
6. nervous 7. coincided 8. disappointment 9. busy
10. contacted 11. license 12. confused 13. intended
14. optional 15. tier 16. thrill 17. C, disappointed
18. D, nervous 19. A, confused 20. B, tempt

Word Review #8: 1. D 2. C 3. A 4. D 5. C 6. D 7. A 8. B
9. D 10. B 11. A, reserving 12. B, distinguish 13. B, validity
14. D, contact 15. A, economical 16. A, expectations
7. D, relatively 18. C, announcements 19. A, optional
20. D, delay

Lessons 41–45 Entertainment
Lesson 41 Movies: 1. A 2. C 3. A 4. B 5. continues
6. entertaining 7. dispersement 8. influence 9. descriptions
10. represent 11. successive 12. range 13. combines
14. released 15. attain 16. separate 17. B, combines
18. A, influence 19. C, continued/continues 20. D, representing

Lesson 42 Theater: 1. B 2. D 3. C 4. A 5. created
6. elements 7. performance 8. occurs 9. approach 10. action
11. experiences 12. dialogue 13. rehearsal 14. audience
15. reviews 16. sold out 17. A, creative 18. B, performance
19. C, occurs 20. D, reviews

Lesson 43 Music: 1. A 2. A 3. D 4. D 5. reason 6. available
7. category 8. taste 9. divided 10. broad 11. disparate
12. urge 13. instinctive 14. prefer 15. favorite 16. relax
17. D, available 18. B, divided 19. C, preference 20. B, relax

Lesson 44 Museums: 1. C 2. A 3. C 4. B 5. admire
6. spectrum 7. responded 8. expressing 9. significant
10. fashion 11. criticism 12. schedule 13. leisure 14. collected
15. specialize 16. acquire 17. C, express 18. B, acquired
19. D, collection 20. D, leisure

Lesson 45 Media: 1. C 2. B 3. B 4. A 5. subscribes
6. chooses 7. thoroughly 8. constitutes 9. disseminated
10. investigative 11. assignments 12. decisions 13. impact
14. links 15. constant 16. in-depth 17. A, decisive
18. D, constant 19. B, investigates 20. B, assigned

Word Review #9: 1. D 2. B 3. C 4. D 5. A 6. A 7. B 8. C
9. B 10. B 11. C, specialists 12. B, criticism 13. C, impact
14. D, preferences 15. C, investigative 16. A, reviews
17. C, leisure 18. D, response(s) 19. B, constant
20. B, constitutes

Lessons 46–50 Health
Lesson 46 Doctor's Office: 1. D 2. A 3. D 4. C 5. annually
6. effective 7. diagnosing 8. preventing 9. appointment
10. record 11. assessment 12. instruments 13. manage
14. recommend 15. refer 16. serious 17. C, assess
18. B, diagnosis 19. A, effective 20. B, recommends

Lesson 47 Dentist's Office: 1. D 2. B 3. C 4. A 5. aware
6. catch up 7. regularly 8. encourage 9. habit 10. position
11. irritates 12. illuminates 13. overview 14. evident
15. restores 16. distraction 17. B, encouraging 18. D, restore
19. B, distract 20. C, irritating

Lesson 48 Health Insurance: 1. C 2. A 3. B 4. B 5. concerns
6. personnel 7. policy 8. portion 9. salary 10. allow
11. suitable 12. emphasize 13. alternatives 14. regardless
15. aspect 16. incurs 17. B, emphasis 18. B, incurring
19. C, suitable 20. D, concerned

Lesson 49 Hospitals: 1. B 2. D 3. C 4. B 5. mission
6. pertinent 7. results 8. authorization 9. identification
10. admitting 11. procedures 12. usually 13. escort 14. statement
15. permitted 16. designated 17. C, admit 18. B, usual
19. C, designate 20. D, authorization

Lesson 50 Pharmacy: 1. B 2. D 3. A 4. C 5. consulting
6. control 7. samples 8. volunteers 9. limit 10. convenient
11. factors 12. sense 13. interactions 14. monitor
15. potential 16. detection 17. A, consulting 18. C, volunteered
19. B, convenient 20. C, interactions

Word Review #10: 1. D 2. A 3. D 4. A 5. C 6. D 7. A 8. B
9. A 10. D 11. A, convenient 12. C, effectively 13. A, manage
14. A, admitted 15. C, result 16. C, referring 17. D, aware
18. B, allow 19. A, volunteer 20. A, Distracted

Word Index

The number indicates the lesson in which the word is taught.

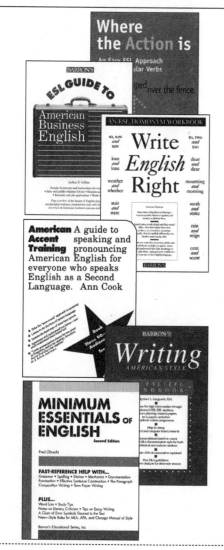

BARRON'S

Business Success Guides

For career-minded men and women, here are the facts, the tips, the wisdom, and the commonsense advice that will pave the way to success. A total to date of 32 short, pocket-size, entertaining and easy-to-read volumes advise on succeeding at all levels of management, marketing, and other important areas within the business and corporate world. They're written by the people who have been there, who currently hold top positions, who know the ropes—and know the facts *you* need to know!

Each book: Paperback, approximately 96 pages, priced individually

0-8120-9893-5: Conducting Better Job Interviews, 2nd Ed.—$6.95, Canada $8.95

0-7641-0403-9: Creative Problem Solving, 2nd Ed.—$6.95, Canada $8.95

0-7641-1410-7: Entrepreneurship 101—$7.95, Canada $11.50

0-7641-0684-8: Interview Strategies That Lead to Job Offers—$7.95, Canada $11.50

0-8120-9892-7: Make Presentations with Confidence, 2nd Ed.—$6.95, Canada $8.95

0-7641-0400-4: Maximizing Your Memory Power, 2nd Ed.—$6.95, Canada $8.95

0-8120-9898-6: Motivating People—$7.95, Canada $11.50

0-7641-1645-2: 100+ Tactics for Office Politics—$7.95, Canada $11.50

0-7641-1644-4: 100+ Winning Answers to the Toughest Interview Questions—$7.95, Canada $11.50

0-7641-0883-2: Performance Management—$6.95, Canada $9.50

0-8120-9823-4: Running a Meeting That Works, 2nd Ed.—$6.95, Canada $8.95

0-7641-0401-2: Speed Reading, 2nd Ed.—$7.95, Canada $11.50

0-7641-0071-8: Successful Assertiveness—$6.95, Canada $8.95

0-7641-0074-2: Successful Direct Mail—$6.95, Canada $8.95

0-7641-0072-6: Successful Leadership—$7.95, Canada $11.50

0-7641-0073-4: Successful Team Building—$7.95, Canada $11.50

0-7641-0060-2: Successfully Managing Change—$6.95, Canada $8.95

0-7641-0402-0: Time Management, 2nd Ed.—$7.95, Canada $11.50

0-7641-0305-9: Understanding the Virtual Organization—$7.95, Canada $11.50

0-8120-9894-3: Winning with Difficult People, 2nd Ed.—$7.95, Canada $11.50

0-8120-9824-2: Writing Effective Letters and Memos, 2nd Ed.—$6.95, Canada $8.95

Barron's Educational Series, Inc. • 250 Wireless Blvd., Hauppauge, NY 11788
Order toll-free: 1-800-645-3476 • Order by fax: 1-631-434-3217
Canadian orders: 1-800-247-7160 • Fax in Canada: 1-800-887-1594
Visit us at www.barronseduc.com

Books and packages may be purchased at your local bookstore or by mail directly from Barron's. Enclose check or money order for total amount, plus sales tax where applicable and 18% for postage and handling (minimum $5.95). All books advertised here are paperback editions.
Prices subject to change without notice.

(#73) R 1/02